WRITING CENTERS AND RACIAL JUSTICE

WRITING CENTERS AND RACIAL JUSTICE

A Guidebook for Critical Praxis

EDITED BY
TALISHA HALTWIWANGER MORRISON
AND DEIDRE ANNE EVANS GARRIOTT

UTAH STATE UNIVERSITY PRESS
Logan

Published by Utah State University Press
An imprint of University Press of Colorado
1580 North Logan Street, Suite 660
PMB 39883
Denver, Colorado 80203-1942

Printed in the United States of America

ASSOCIATION of UNIVERSITY PRESSES The University Press of Colorado is a proud member of the Association of University Presses.

The University Press of Colorado is a cooperative publishing enterprise supported, in part, by Adams State University, Colorado State University, Fort Lewis College, Metropolitan State University of Denver, University of Alaska Fairbanks, University of Colorado, University of Denver, University of Northern Colorado, University of Wyoming, Utah State University, and Western Colorado University.

∞ This paper meets the requirements of the ANSI/NISO Z39.48-1992 (Permanence of Paper).

ISBN: 978-1-64642-455-9 (hardcover)
ISBN: 978-1-64642-456-6 (paperback)
ISBN: 978-1-64642-457-3 (ebook)
https://doi.org/10.7330/9781646424573

Library of Congress Cataloging-in-Publication Data

Names: Morrison, Talisha Haltiwanger, editor. | Garriott, Deidre Anne Evans, editor.
Title: Writing centers and racial justice : a guidebook for critical praxis / edited by Talisha Haltiwanger Morrison and Deidre Anne Evans Garriott.
Identifiers: LCCN 2023014970 (print) | LCCN 2023014971 (ebook) | ISBN 9781646424559 (hardcover) | ISBN 9781646424566 (paperback) | ISBN 9781646424573 (ebook)
Subjects: LCSH: Writing centers—United States—Administration—Handbooks, manuals, etc. | Writing centers—Social aspects—United States. | English language—Rhetoric—Study and teaching (Higher)—Social aspects—United States. | Racism in higher education—United States. | Critical pedagogy—United States.
Classification: LCC PE1405.U6 W738 2023 (print) | LCC PE1405.U6 (ebook) | DDC 808/.0420711—dc23/eng/20230606
LC record available at https://lccn.loc.gov/2023014970
LC ebook record available at https://lccn.loc.gov/2023014971

Cover art: "M-Swirls," © Maria Echave. https://marialaurae13.wixsite.com/portfolio

CONTENTS

LIST OF FIGURES AND TABLES

FIGURES

TABLES

ACKNOWLEDGMENTS

We want to acknowledge that this collection is the result of not just our and the contributors' efforts but also of the support and encouragement of many others. We each have those who have supported us as individuals and jointly through the journey of this publication.

Talisha: First, I want to thank all the administrators, tutors, writers, and administrative support personnel I've worked with since I first began my writing center journey almost thirteen years ago. These writing centers, and the people who make them go, have shaped so much of how I have come to approach my own administration and scholarship.

In particular, I'd like to thank my former and forever mentor, Harry Denny, my former Director and dissertation Chair, and other WCAs I've had the pleasure to work with, including Ashton Foley-Schramm, Michele Eodice, Moira Ozias, Vicki Kennel, Tammy Conard-Salvo, and Matthew Capdevielle. Finally, I thank my husband, Joseph Morrison, my biggest supporter, and my son, Isaiah, my biggest source of joy.

Deidre: I want to thank the WCAs who mentored me, especially Carol Bledsoe and Kirsten Benson, and all the colleagues who helped me grow as a tutor and anti-racist practitioner. I am especially grateful to Lisa M. King, Malea Powell, Andrea Riley-Mukavetz, Christina Victoria Cedillo, Marilee Brooke-Gillies, and, of course, Talisha Haltiwanger Morrison. I also cannot thank enough my husband and best friend, Todd Garriott.

We: We both thank and acknowledge Isaac Wang, who served as an Associate Editor for this project and Lisa M. King, who both offered invaluable feedback to help shape this collection. Finally, a huge thanks to Maria Echave, undergraduate consultant at the University of Oklahoma Writing Center, who designed the cover art for this collection.

WRITING CENTERS AND RACIAL JUSTICE

INTRODUCTION

Talisha Haltiwanger Morrison and Deidre Anne Evans Garriott

Writing Centers and Racial Justice is a book born both of frustration and hope. In its pages, you will find contributors wrestling with some of the same questions and dilemmas writing center administrators have been discussing for decades. And to be honest, that is part of the point. The questions here are not new, but we hope that some of the answers will be. We have given this book the subtitle "a guidebook for critical praxis," and it is our intention that this collection will provide guidance for current and aspiring writing center administrators dedicated to (or just curious about) racial justice. While we won't claim that this book holds all the answers to our most challenging questions, we do feel that this collection provides some of the clear advice and recommendations that writing center administrators have asked for to help them make concrete changes.

INSPIRATIONS AND ORIENTATIONS

In their 2018 International Writing Centers Association (IWCA) keynote address, Kendra Mitchell and Robert Randolph Jr. (2019) questioned the progress we have made as a field by interrogating the conference theme, "The Citizen Center," asking, "Haven't we done this before? What have we done about it?" (23). Many writing center administrators (WCAs) walked away from Mitchell and Randolph's keynote seeking concrete examples of how to cultivate racially just centers. Administrators sought answers with increased urgency following the murders of George Floyd, Breonna Taylor, and other unarmed Black people in 2020. On WCenter, the professional LISTSERV for writing centers, as well as the Writing Center Directors and Writing Center Network Facebook pages and at annual meetings of the IWCA Anti-Racism Special Interest Group, we observed many administrators expressing a sense of frustration and inadequacy, wondering how to enact racial justice in and through the writing center. As we put this collection together, an additional motivating

https://doi.org/10.7330/9781646424573.c000

factor arose as more than twenty states across the nation restricted or introduced legislation that could restrict conversations about race in public education, and colleges and universities in conservative states also experienced increased pressure and surveillance from their local governments and news sources regarding conversations about race. The ongoing pandemic, along with the heightened racial and political tension, fueled our desire to provide actionable guidance to navigate this challenging climate.

Talisha

Prior to starting this collection, in the late spring and early summer of 2020, I originally had plans to continue working on a solo-authored book based on my dissertation, *Nooses and Balancing Acts* (Haltiwanger Morrison 2018). In this project, I spoke to Black writing tutors about their experiences with racism both in their writing centers and on their campuses. However, in the midst of the nationwide upheaval over the murder of George Floyd and at the beginning of a pandemic taking disproportionately the lives of Black and Brown Americans, it did not seem like the best time to ask Black students about their trauma. Further, I did not want to talk about it. I did not want to hear more stories of pain. What I was hearing, however, was people from both writing centers and Writing Studies more broadly taking up the conversation about racism and racial justice more vigorously. White people had awakened and wanted to do something. Everywhere people were asking, "What do we do?" My initial feelings about this awakening were annoyance and frustration. The bewilderment of white "allies" was painful, and the constant conversation about Black death and destruction was exhausting. I found myself withdrawing even further from the internet and social media, trying to escape. But, even as I withdrew, I kept thinking about that question, "What do we do?" I had served as co-leader of the IWCA anti-racism SIG from 2017 to 2019 and during that time also heard that question repeated, "What do we do?" or "How do we do this?" But also, I knew that there were people in the field, directing writing centers, who were doing meaningful racial justice work already.

I decided to put together a collection of current writing center administrators giving clear and practical advice about what steps they were actually taking to enact racial justice through their centers. As I thought more about the project, I began rereading scholarship and was struck by Kendra Mitchell and Robert Randolph Jr's powerful words from their 2018 IWCA keynote. In that address, Mitchell and Randolph question the field's reliance on decades-old scholarship by white administrators. They demand to know where the central texts are by scholars of color. They challenge the field to realize our circuitous nature of our conversations around race, racism, and racial justice in writing centers, noting that we've had these conversations before and arguing that we will continue to have them unless we make an intentional effort to do differently. My hope was that a collection such as this might be part of that intentional effort. If a major barrier to more directors taking up actionable racial justice in their centers was that they did not know where to start, then a guidebook with specific examples and recommendations would remove that barrier.

Deidre

During the spring and early summer of 2020, as I worked from home teaching and directing my university's Writing Center, I planned to focus on publishing my solo-work on public memory in the South. But the immediacy of COVID turned my attention away from sites of public memory—most of which were shut down, along with the physical archives—and toward webinars and literature about being an effective teacher in digital environments. In these lessons, I repeatedly encountered sentences or asides mentioning issues with accessibility that arose from systemic barriers. More bluntly, someone would warn us to "make sure your digital class is accessible because many people don't have the bandwidth for synchronous learning." *Which people?* I wondered, already knowing the answer, the words that so many white people are reluctant to utter. Black and African American people. But how should I improve accessibility, and how does the idea of accessibility change when I center racial justice?

George Floyd's death, his murder by cops, changed the discourse and the motivations of Writing Center Studies by demanding that writing center professionals center Black excellence and racial justice. In addition to emails sent to the Writing Studies community and new statements such as "This Ain't Another Statement! This is a DEMAND for Black Linguistic Justice!," our organizations provided workshops and webinars. In the writing and meetings, I observed more direct conversations among participants about the ways that writing centers are complicit in racism and institutional barriers that keep BIPOC, LGBT+, and women from accessing institutions in the same ways as cis-het white people. We moved away from euphemisms and spoke directly about race, racism, and Writing Studies. Most important, I saw WCAs asking,

"How do we make our centers more racially just?" I saw an opportunity for us to move beyond platitudes toward real actions.

Which is why I was excited when Talisha asked me to join her on this project. As both a white woman who wanted more help and who was already doing some anti-racist work in her profession, I wanted to contribute to resources that help spark more conversations about practice. This is especially important, I thought, for early career WCAs who needed a place to turn for ideas. As a white woman, I sought to work with Talisha and the contributors to create a place where writing center practitioners could learn from each other.

WHAT THIS BOOK DOES AND DOESN'T DO

Writing Centers and Racial Justice: A Guidebook for Critical Praxis responds to our field's ongoing quest for practical guidance for the racial justice work in which so many want to engage. Writing Center scholars have drawn increasing attention to the importance of racial justice in writing center work over the past several decades. Recent writing center scholarship centered on racial justice has explored the ways in which writing centers perpetuate linguistic injustice (Greenfield 2011; Young 2011; Gallagher et al. 2017; Alvarez 2019), served as primarily white spaces (Pimentel 2014; García 2017; Haltiwanger Morrison 2019), and continued a white-savior paradigm in higher education (Villanueva 2011; Greenfield 2011; Wilson 2011; Denny et al. 2019; Bond 2019). This body of scholarship has advanced the study of racial justice as a writing center concern and accelerated efforts to adopt anti-racist policies in writing centers. However, the field overall is still struggling to turn problematizing into meaningful change.

We feel strongly that this collection helps us turn toward that change. There does not currently exist any book that offers clear and actionable advice on how writing centers and their staff may take up racial or social justice work as part of everyday administrative practice. Two popular guidebooks for writing center administrators, *The Longman Guide to Writing Center Theory and Practice* (Barnett and Blumner 2007) and *The Writing Center Director's Resource Book* (Murphy and Stay 2006), offer collections of previously published scholarship on various writing center matters such as historical perspectives and tutoring practices. While some of the texts included in these collections speak to ethical matters in writing center administration, neither collection gives substantial attention to race or racial justice pedagogies. An emphasis on race can be found in more recent collections, such as *Writing Centers and the*

New Racism (Greenfield and Rowan 2011) and *Out in the Center* (Denny et al. 2019). While these collections have been valuable additions to the field, they do not offer the kind of grounded examples offered in our collection. We hope that the advice here, including the appendices accompanying several chapters, will help current administrators revise or implement racial justice practices in their own centers, campuses, and communities.

Difficult Decisions

As we were developing this collection, we found ourselves wrestling with several difficult editorial decisions. One of our first considerations for the collection was that we wanted to include as many scholars of color as possible. We developed a list of people whom we knew (or knew of) and believed could offer clear and accessible guidance on how to do racial justice work through the writing center. What we found, however, was that our initial list consisted overwhelmingly of writing center directors from predominantly and historically white (research) institutions (PHWI). We understand that writing centers exist at a variety of institution types, and these differences affect practical considerations such as the size and diversity of the writing center's staff, how the writing center engages with faculty, and budgetary constraints that shape programming, outreach, and other administrative matters. So, we shifted gears to intentionally recruit scholars and administrators from diverse institution types. We reached out to potential contributors from both public and private institutions, from PHWIs, and also from historically Black colleges and universities (HBCUs), Hispanic serving institutions (HSIs), Tribal colleges and universities (TCUs), and Asian-American and Native American Pacific Islander serving institutions (AANAPISIs). We reached out to scholars from four- and two-year institutions and from high school writing centers. We still wanted to include as many scholars of color as possible and found ourselves trying to balance racial diversity with institutional diversity, a process made more challenging by the lack of racial diversity in the field. Our efforts to attract scholars of color were also affected by the ongoing pandemic. Many of the writing center administrators we initially reached out to did not respond to our invitations. Others accepted and then withdrew their proposals as they prepared for and began their first full pandemic semester in fall of 2020. Eventually we decided to open the call for proposals outside of our initial list and solicit proposed chapters, knowing that there were others out there doing good work but whom we simply did not know or had overlooked.

The collection we've ended up with includes chapters from both invited and accepted contributors. The racial makeup of our contributors is not quite what we initially hoped for, but we feel proud to elevate the work of so many scholars of color and to include several pieces authored or coauthored by tutors. And we hope that the variety of institutional and writing center structures represented here will be useful to readers as they imagine how to adapt and enact similar efforts at their own centers.

The collection has other limitations as well. We were unable, for example, to include a contribution from a high school writing center or a community college. We regret that these institutions are not represented here and know that our collection would benefit from their inclusion. Another limitation is that the collection speaks most directly to centers that are staffed by peer undergraduate tutors. Although several of the centers discussed here also (or in one case only) employ graduate tutors, the peer undergraduate tutor model is most represented in these chapters. Readers who direct centers staffed by professional and/or faculty tutors may have to make additional considerations for how to apply the advice given here to their own contexts.

Additionally, contributors in this collection speak to different audiences within the larger writing centers' community. Some of the white contributors (including Deidre) speak directly to white audiences, in acknowledgment that most WCAs are white and approach racial justice from a different standpoint than BIPOC administrators. The collection offers a variety of frameworks and approaches. Some we would not personally use; others we have already begun adopting at our own centers. We intend the collection to speak to WCAs who differ in race and in other ways, such as geography, class, gender, institution and position type, and others. We hope that audiences from many backgrounds and contexts will find something useful within the book's chapters and that the suggestions here will spearhead new practices and progress toward increased racial and social justice in the field.

Finally, an intentional decision is what some readers may consider limited engagement with writing center theory. Many early drafts of chapters included lengthy literature reviews that situated their advice in existing scholarship. However, as editors, we wanted to maintain the essential purpose of the collection: to offer clear and actionable advice. Most current work on race and racism in Writing Center Studies is theoretical and/or narrative based. We find this work to be valuable and important. Indeed, readers will also find narrative and theory in this collection, particularly in the first section. However, they will also find clearly defined lessons and takeaways, actionable recommendations, and sample materials. While we expect praxis to grow out of and be linked to writing center scholarship, we were not interested in repeating the same conversations that can be found elsewhere. Others have done that and have done it well. Instead, we asked contributors to limit their reviews of existing scholarship and their arguments for particular theoretical frameworks and to offer as clear and uncluttered advice as they could. We hope that readers will appreciate the selectivity and concision and are able to use the work here alongside important theoretical scholarship.

PART OVERVIEW

We have divided the collection into five thematic parts: part I: "Countering Racism and Colonialism in Higher Education"; part II: "Recruitment, Hiring, and Retention"; part III: "Tutor Education and Professional Development"; part IV: "Engaging with Campus and Community"; and part V: "Holding Our Professional Organizations Accountable." Although the parts are separate, we consider the conversations within them as building upon one another through considerations of, for example, how well-developed tutor education enhances retention, or how faculty and community outreach offer additional professional development opportunities.

The first part, "Countering Racism and Colonialism in Higher Education," is the most theoretical of the collection and helps provide some framing for the remaining pieces. In Part I, contributors Jennifer Martin and Mark Latta confront the institutional structures that make anti-racist, decolonial pedagogies and labor difficult in higher education. Opening the collection with chapter 1, "Tutoring and Practice at a Tribal College," Jennifer Martin, an Indigenous peer tutor, examines the writing tutor's opportunities, challenges, and obligations to clients at Tribal Colleges and suggests a methodology for equipping writing centers and tutors to better meet the needs of Indigenous writers as allies rather than perpetrators of settler-colonialism. Following Martin, Latta, in "Another White Voice in the Room," chapter 2, identifies and critiques popular racial justice rhetoric of Writing Center Studies that have allowed white supremacist pedagogies to maintain strongholds in higher education and offers his own efforts as a white administrator to decenter whiteness and advance racial justice in the writing center.

Part II, "Recruitment, Hiring, and Retention," meanwhile, makes visible the realities and constraints of enacting racial justice in writing centers within higher education. In chapter 3, "Why Do White Tutors 'Love' Writing?," Rachel Herzl-Betz uses quantitative research methods to study the variables that motivate undergraduate peer tutors to apply to work at a writing center. The chapter not only offers Herzl-Betz's findings but also details how she applied the data to improve her own recruitment and hiring procedures at Nevada State College, an HSI in Las Vegas, and how others might generalize the findings to improve their own recruitment and hiring.

Jamie P. Bondar, Kristina Aikens, and Devon Deery, in "Toward Anti-racist Writing Center Hiring and Retention Practices," chapter 4, extend Herzl-Betz's investigation by analyzing administrative policies and practices around hiring, recruitment, and retention. They explain their efforts as white WCAs to dismantle white racial frames (Feagin 2013) and offer strategies to handle tutors' reports of bias and harassment and promote retention.

Part III, "Tutor Education and Professional Development," provides readers guidance into racial justice in tutor education. In chapter 5, "Beyond the Tutor Training Seminar," Zandra L. Jordan, writing from a womanist position, outlines both her tutor-training seminar and ongoing professional development for cultivating a tutoring staff equipped to engage race(ism) and promote racial justice. Extending Jordan's examination of tutor education, Lindsay A. Sabatino asserts in "Addressing Racial Justice through Re-imagining Practicum to Promote Dialogue on Campus," chapter 6, that centralizing racial justice in tutor education empowers tutors to become agents of change inside and out of the writing center. Similarly, Rachael Shapiro and Celeste Del Russo, in "Working toward Racial Justice in the Writing Center," chapter 7, offer strategies for a translingualism approach to tutor training to promote racial and linguistic justice in the writing center. Next, Lisa Eastmond Bell, in "Disrupting Systems," chapter 8, offers recommendations for how writing center practitioners can better understand power, increase access to services, and use data to build more racially and socially just online tutoring services. Talisha Haltiwanger Morrison closes the part with chapter 9, "Tutors Matter Too," by arguing that WCAs must think carefully and proactively about how to support peer tutors, particularly those of color, as they engage in anti-racist tutoring work.

Part IV, "Engaging with Campus and Community," considers various ways that WCAs and tutors can expand the center's work and reach when they make racial justice central to their practices. In chapter 10, "Anti-Blackness Professional Development to Pro-Blackness Actions," peer tutor Brianna Johnson and administrators Rebecca Johnson and Nicole I.

Caswell describe their center's nine-month process of researching, drafting, and revising a letter to faculty calling for a commitment to racial linguistic justice on their campus, and they offer readers advice on how to engage faculty in conversations on anti-Blackness. Deidre Anne Evans Garriott, in "Leveraging Faculty Pedagogical Development to Center Racial Justice," chapter 11, offers readers examples of and guidance in using their position as WCAs to engage non-writing instructors in anti-racist pedagogies and practices to extend the anti-racist work of writing centers beyond its walls. In chapter 12, "Community Is the Center," Nicole Emmelhainz, along with peer tutors Graciela Greger and Amanda Ballou, reflect on Emmelhainz's tutor education course and the tutors' individual research into the need for a community writing center in Newport News, Virginia. The part concludes with chapter 13, Kamille Bostick's "Writing Revolution." Drawing on her experience directing the center at her HBCU, Bostick argues that writing centers should pursue social justice and civil rights engagement by working closely with student writers to produce public texts and reflects on the transformative power for the center and writers when that work becomes a priority for WCAs.

Finally, the chapters in part V, "Holding our Professional Organizations Accountable," expand readers' view by turning our attention to our professional organizations, specifically the International Writing Centers Association (IWCA) and the Southeastern Writing Center Association (SWCA). LaKela Atkinson, in "Practicing What We Preach," chapter 14, reflects on her experiences as the HBCU representative on the SWCA board and argues that organizational boards can center anti-racist practices by being more innovative when creating and filling board positions. In "Remaking IWCA," chapter 15, Genie Nicole Giaimo, Nicole I. Caswell, Marilee Brooks-Gillies, Elise Dixon, and Wonderful Faison frame their experiences advocating for IWCA to change its structures and goals to better center racial justice as its core principle. The collection ends with an afterword by Kendra L. Mitchell, whose work helped inspire this project.

CONCLUSION

The collection offers detailed examples of the anti-racist and racial justice work current writing center directors and tutors are doing and explanations of how this work might translate to readers' own contexts. Several contributors have also provided appendices, such as sample recruitment materials, tutor training activities, and course syllabi. We do not expect the chapters here to provide a definitive "how to" for racially just writing center work. Rather, we seek to spearhead conversations about concrete practices with examples, advice, and lessons learned about the challenges of this work. We hope that you, as current or aspiring directors, will take the guidance here and use it to begin implementing change in your own centers and institutions.

REFERENCES

Alvarez, Nancy. 2019. "On Letting Brown Bodies Speak (and Write)." In *Out in the Center: Public Controversies and Private Struggles*, edited by Harry Denny, Robert Mundy, Liliana M. Naydan, Richard Sévère, and Anna Sicari, 83–89. Louisville: University Press of Colorado.

Barnett, Robert W., and Jacob S. Blumner. 2007. *The Longman Guide to Writing Center Theory and Practice.* New York: Longman.

Bond, Candis. "2019. I Need Help on Many Things Please." *Writing Center Journal* 37, no. 2: 191–194. https://www.jstor.org/stable/26922021.

Denny, Harry, Robert Mundy, Liliana M. Naydan, Richard Sévère, and Anna Sicari, eds. 2019. *Out in the Center: Public Controversies and Private Struggles.* Louisville: University Press of Colorado.

Gallagher, Mary, Katherine Morris, Adam Binkley, and Baneza Rivera. 2017. "A Union of Voices: Building a Multilingual Positive Community through a Multilingual Writing Mentors Program." *Peer Review* 1, no. 2. https://thepeerreview-iwca.org/issues/braver-spaces/gallagher/.

García, Romeo. 2017. "Unmaking Gringo-Centers." *Writing Center Journal* 36, no. 1: 29–60. https://www.jstor.org/stable/44252637.

Greenfield, Laura. 2011. "The 'Standard English' Fairy Tale: A Rhetorical Analysis of Racist Pedagogies and Commonplace Assumptions about Language Diversity." In *Writing Centers and the New Racism*, edited by Laura Greenfield and Karen Rowan, 33–60. Logan: Utah State University Press.

Greenfield, Laura, and Karen Rowan, eds. 2011. *Writing Centers and the New Racism: A Call for Sustainable Dialogue and Change.* Logan: Utah State University Press.

Haltiwanger Morrison, Talisha. 2018. *Nooses and Balancing Acts: Reflections and Advice on Racism and Antiracism from Black Writing Tutors at Predominantly White Institutions.* PhD diss., Purdue University.

Haltiwanger Morrison, Talisha. 2019. "Being Seen and Not Seen: A Black Female Body in the Writing Center." In *Out in the Center: Public Controversies and Private Struggles*, edited by Harry Denny, Robert Mundy, Liliana M. Naydan, Richard Sévère, and Anna Sicari, 21–27. Boulder: University Press of Colorado.

Mitchell, Kendra L, and Robert E. Randolph. 2019. "A Page from Our Book: Social Justice Lessons from the HBCU Writing Center." *Writing Center Journal* 37, no. 2: 21–40.

Murphy, Christina, and Byron Stay, eds. 2006. *The Writing Center Director's Resource Book.* New York: Routledge.

Pimentel, Octavio. 2014. "Learning to Write in Writing Centers: The Racial Experiences of Two Mexican Students." *English in Texas: A Journal of the Texas Council of Teachers of English Language Arts* 44, no. 2: 34–39.

Wilson, Nancy Effinger. 2012. "Stocking the Bodega: Towards a New Writing Center Paradigm." *Praxis: A Writing Center Journal* 10, no. 1: 1–9. http://hdl.handle.net/2152/62149.

Young, Vershawn Ashanti. 2011. "Should Writers Use They Own English?" In *Writing Centers and the New Racism*, edited by Laura Greenfield and Karen Rowan, 71–72. Logan: Utah State University Press.

PART I

Countering Racism and Colonialism in Higher Education

1
TUTORING AND PRACTICE AT A TRIBAL COLLEGE

Jennifer Martin

I write this chapter as an Ani-Yun'wi'ya ᏣᎳᎩ (Cherokee, Tsalgi) citizen and scholar. I have chosen to write in an informal narrative style, not only because this tends to be more engaging for the average reader but because it makes knowledge more accessible and relevant for those with whom I work. Throughout this chapter, I employ unconventional uses of capitalization as examples of the ways Indigenous Peoples can use english. Unless it is at the beginning of a sentence, english will not be capitalized. I wish to make a point that Native writers can denounce the colonizing power english has over our lives by giving it a little less power in the written form.

I have introduced myself to better articulate my perspective and to make my work more accessible. Ultimately, I can only speak for myself, but I have insights into the shared experiences of many Indigenous students and educators that may be helpful for those working with Indigenous students in a writing center.

As this chapter pertains specifically to the ways Indigenous students and tutors within a Tribal college writing center engage with colonial rhetorical practices, I will do my best to lead by example and illustrate Indigenous Worldviews. Having some background information on the importance of Indigenous Worldviews in writing is paramount.

Indigenous researchers and theorists Gregory Cajete (Tewa) (2016), Linda Tuhiwai Smith (Ngāti Awa and Ngāti Porou iwi) (2012), and Shawn Wilson (Opaskwayak Cree) (2008) define Indigenous research methodology. These scholars argue the importance of establishing research, writing, and educational pedagogies within Indigenous communities based upon "Relationality" as characterized by Wilson, who describes Indigenous Relationality as encompassing an understanding of one's responsibility to a holistic system of interacting players, including one's lands, families, ancestors, future generations, plants, other animals,

https://doi.org/10.7330/9781646424573.c001

spirits, knowledges, and so on. Indigenous Relational Accountability is being accountable to the relations one has. Choices, actions, and ideas have consequences, and no one individual functions independently but remains intricately connected to their environment. Relationality functions within a collectivist cultural framework and decries hierarchy and radical individualism.

Ideally, Indigenous education systems should work via cooperative action instead of academic competition. Indigenous research writing includes personal or family narratives, interviews with elders and community members, sharing traditional stories, and any other methods that allow the Indigenous student to express themselves, their cultural reality, and the information they wish to convey.

Writing centers can have a positive effect by affirming Indigenous worldviews and research methods and editing papers or giving suggestions according to those values rather than typical conventions alone. Dismissing Indigenous methodologies and writing as "informal" or "unprofessional" is problematic. An ideal writing center would have administrators and tutors who are knowledgeable and competent in the worldviews of the populations they serve and the methodologies and priorities those students have.

Tutoring and writing centers on college campuses play important roles in student success and support, but in a Tribal community they double as places for cultural and community interactions. Tutors may be required to go far beyond their actual job description to meet the demonstrable needs of students. Tutors become counselors, advocates, teachers, and friends to the students with whom they engage. As tutors, we can meet needs and address fears with students that would otherwise go unheard. The hierarchical divide between student and tutor, especially in a Native community, is far less pronounced than in mainstream academic settings.

Above all, it must always be within our minds that english is not our language. English has been a tool of oppression within our communities for hundreds of years. It has divided us. It has stripped us of our culture and subsumed our identities. I remind students that english is a colonial tool that we have adapted to our own aims. English teaching should never take higher precedence over teaching our own languages. With this fact established, however, english is the language of communication between Tribes. It is also our mode of communication with mainstream society. We can use english and engage in political resistance. Still, we must never accept the idea that english deserves preeminence or is anything more than a tool to further our aims of political, educational, spiritual, and cultural liberation.

Working at a Tribal college comes with a unique set of challenges and responsibilities. The mere existence of Tribal colleges is a political act, and they did not come about until the 1970s. Native students attend Tribal colleges because, as communities, we value the right to educate ourselves and our children in an environment where our unique values, cultures, and priorities are paramount. The United States has long stripped us of that right through centuries of genocide and colonialism. Angela Cavender Wilson (Wahpetunwan Dakota) (2004) states that

> this flagrant dedication to Indigenous goals is openly political because it defies those who have been defining our existence for us and who have attempted to make us believe we are incapable of self-determination. This means that our first obligation as Native scholars engaged in this kind of work is not to the academy but to our Nations. (74)

Every action we take as tutors and mentors to aid our community members' success is one step closer to liberation our own terms. There are many discussions in Indigenous education about decolonizing or Indigenizing the academy. As tutors, especially writing and english tutors, there are academic conventions and practices that we must confront and discontinue as part of our own practice and decolonization process. I do not use the word "decolonize" lightly as some do. In line with the original definition, I firmly believe that true decolonization is a thorough and political process where the colonizer ultimately gives up power and returns the land to the Indigenous Peoples. Every educator is ultimately responsible for engaging in their decolonization process as well as the political one to help Indigenous students succeed.

TRIBAL COLLEGES AND WRITING CENTERS

Tribal colleges seek to alleviate many of the problems caused by colonial education, but we bring our trauma with us. Some may survive these systems with the help of their family or community, but support rarely comes from within the institution. Joshua Mihesuah (Comanche) (2004) believes that one would be hard-pressed to say that Indigenous Peoples can thrive in a western institution without assimilating. Daniel Heath Justice (Ani-Yun'wi'ya) reminds us that despite the realities present in universities, we still have a right to be there. "We belong to this land; we're not guests of the Invaders, to be given access at their whim. The knowledge of Native peoples is the voice of turtle island that speaks closest to all of humanity. This is our inheritance" (Justice 2004, 102).

All colleges and universities in North America operate upon our lands. Justice (2004) questions if mainstream institutions can Indigenize as they are built upon colonial models. However, since universities are the places that organize ideas and create meaning for the culture at large, it is our responsibility to fight that system actively. We belong anywhere with the power to dictate our reality.

An Indigenized or a decolonized institution does not merely offer us a seat at the table; it burns the table and gives us the whole building. As Taiaiake Alfred (Kanien'Kehaka) (2004) states, colonialism is not over until our spaces are indeed ours. This includes the actual returning of the lands mainstream universities reside upon. Colonialism is more than a historical era or theories of economic and political statuses of Nations; "it is a total existence, a way of thinking about oneself and others always in terms of domination and submission that has come to form the very foundation of our individual and collective lives" (89). North America is the heart of the new colonial empire. Though it seeks to force us into submission, we are uniquely positioned to defy the production of imperial ideology and halt its spread by living upon this continent.

Although chartered by Tribal Nations and consisting of predominately Native students, Tribal Colleges and Universities (TCUs) mostly employ non-Native educators. Indigenous tutors become essential advocates when problems arise in the classroom as we mediate cultural misunderstandings between students and teachers. Brian Compton, Cheryl Crazy Bull (Wacinyanpi Win, Sicangu Lakota), and Ted Williams (2016), who worked at Northwest Indian College (NWIC), discuss how students who choose to attend an Indigenous-run institution such as a TCU still face many of the same hurdles as they might encounter at a mainstream institution. In the academic year 2013–2014, "American Indians or Alaska Natives made up 19% of full-time faculty and 24% of part-time faculty" (69). The non-Native staff often possess no prior knowledge or experience interacting with Indigenous students before starting their position. Tribal colleges must actively fight to decolonize their own methodologies and practice; simply being a Tribal college is not enough.

However, the ideals and dreams of the Tribal college movement are very much alive, and many dedicated individuals continually strive to improve and further Indigenize our places of learning. Every tutor has their own method of overcoming these obstacles. As a tutor at a small center, I can speak only to what I have learned and practiced the last five years as a tutor. I have no position of power within my institution, but I still actively fight racism and exclusion on campus. Academic support and tutoring centers provide the nuts and bolts of student services. Anyone can theorize about student retention, but the tutor and the underpaid staff worker help the students pass their courses, connect them with career services, and inform them where they can find free food and showers.

Northwest Indian College is a small, Tribally operated college within the Lummi Nation with satellite campuses throughout Washington and Idaho. We operate a small Math and Writing Center on the Lummi campus, consisting of a supervisor, several volunteers, and half a dozen tutors. Most of the tutors employed at the center are Tribal Citizens, though neither of the two supervisors I have had was Native. Unfortunately, formal training in culturally appropriate methodologies has not been provided for tutors. Therefore, the reader may find themself disappointed by the lack of concrete examples of an institutional writing center praxis.[1] I have built my practices around lessons and training that I sought out individually through books and discussions.

Whether in english or our Native languages, writing can be an act of resistance and hope, but there is no hope in unthinkingly regurgitating what we are told: "Through education, Northwest Indian College promotes Indigenous self-determination and knowledge" (Northwest Indian College 2017). Tribal colleges exist to build self-determined Nations and individuals. This goes beyond simply having students read and write about what white teachers feel would be relevant or exciting to Native students. Part of my practice is to remind struggling students that english is merely a tool and not a meter stick of their intelligence. Their ability to write a five-paragraph essay is not a symbol of their worth. When a student is willing, I will tell them about the differences between oral and written cultures. I will also share my own experiences as a student and the tools I use to overcome educational trauma. I ask them to tell me what they are good at and interested in, and why they have gone back to school.

Although this chapter is predominately about what I do as an individual, there are some practices that would benefit non-Natives working with Indigenous students. They are simple but not easy. Firstly, listen deeply and seek to understand that the Indigenous experience in this country is both a complicated and violent one. One must learn the history of genocide on this continent and how it has continued to shape our daily realities as Peoples. Second, one must become trauma informed. We often think of this methodology for human services, but

1. A formal word that means "practice."

institutions, especially those focused on english writing, must understand how trauma affects the experiences and reactions of Native students. Understanding educational trauma also helps a tutor or educator better navigate the specifics of editing or making suggestions for a student who may be deeply insecure.

It is common for students to react defensively and become emotional and irrational if they feel they are being criticized. Even when the criticism is constructive, trauma can cause a student to shield against it, and their fight-or-flight response becomes activated. Learning how to navigate these responses is essential. The only thing I have found to be effective is trust-building through reciprocal relationships. If a student feels that they are engaging with an equal, even a friend, then they are more likely to accept suggestions. Due to consistently having their view of the world silenced in other areas of their life, Native students find writing to be a vulnerable act. Yet, if a relationship has developed, trust can overcome much of that fear.

Building reciprocal relationships falls outside of what western institutions typically consider to be appropriate boundaries. However, when working with Indigenous students, it is essential to understand that our cultural boundaries and priorities are different. Sharing where one comes from, and about family, interests, and background helps to build these necessary and reciprocal relationships. A level of vulnerability is required.

There are three main issues that, as a tutor, I encounter regularly. These are the assumed superiority of english and western academic practices, overcoming the mental and emotional barriers created by previous educational experiences, and overcoming students' genuine lack of essential resources for their daily lives.

THE ASSUMED SUPERIORITY OF ENGLISH AND WESTERN ACADEMIC PRACTICES

Writing in english for american Indians has never been a neutral process. Teaching english to an Indigenous population carries the legacies of colonialism and oppression. Suppose a teacher is unaware of this or the implications and privileges they hold as an instructor in a colonial language. In that case, they are likely to continue engaging in colonial practices and methodologies. Mainstream english teaching has little to no place in Native communities. Although we had complex knowledge attainment and recording systems, very few Indigenous communities in North or South America had written languages. This does not in any way mean that we are incapable of writing and reading with the same skill and attention as others, simply that our priorities and way of viewing knowledge and what is authoritative have historically differed.

Our oral languages have been actively quieted and suppressed. Most of our languages are critically endangered, and many are extinct. The industrialized world gives ultimate power to both the pen and the sword. The adoption of writing drastically changed our cultures. The systems of writing that exist for Indigenous languages, except for my own language, Cherokee, were predominately created by non-Native linguists using symbology from other languages. Most of the emphasis was on translating the Bible into Native languages to further the colonial effort.

Native Children were taken far from their families, and their traditional hair and clothing were destroyed. They held a pencil for the first time as they copied out line after line of biblical passages. Their hands were whacked when they made a mistake; they could not speak their own language until they forgot how to speak. They were raped, they ran away, and they died. The remains of 215 children were recently found buried near the former Kamloops Residential School in British Columbia, Canada (Peters 2021).[2] Colonizers built graveyards rather than playgrounds for Tribal students. When this is the history of english language teaching, writing, reading, and formal education for Indigenous communities, no simple praxis can alleviate the historical pain or inspire students to academic success.

English worldviews do not historically recognize the personhood of nonhuman entities. As a result, Native communities have begun to throw off capitalization conventions. In my experience, we capitalize the words that seem essential to our communities or us. Likewise, we do not capitalize things that do not seem important to us. Intentionally choosing not to capitalize words such as god, the united states of america, the british empire, and the white house are in themselves political statements. This can be a liberating use of forced colonial language. Robin Wall Kimmerer (Citizen Potawatomi) (2015), in her popular book *Braiding Sweetgrass: Indigenous Wisdom, Scientific Knowledge and the Teachings of Plants*, uses capitalization to recognize the personhood of nonhuman entities such as Deer, Plants, Blackberries, and Mountains. More important, we capitalize and use the linguistically correct names for our Nations. Many Indigenous languages do not use capitalization at all in their written forms.

2. The number of dead Native children found buried at residential schools has continued to swell to over 6,000. This number is only expected to increase as schools in the so-called united states are searched.

One invaluable tool and resource I use continually when editing and writing is *Elements of Indigenous Style: A Guide for Writing by and about Indigenous Peoples* by Gregory Younging (Opaskwayak Cree) (2018). He discusses the many racist ways even well-meaning people write about Indigenous Peoples, and he also argues for developing an Indigenous style that respects our cultural priorities. As Indigenous People, we have been researched and written about but do not see ourselves correctly represented. I encourage the use of his work to my students. I follow his guidelines when editing papers, what words should be avoided when referring to Indigenous Peoples, suggestions for capitalization, and other conventions. A few examples of what Younging covers in his style guide are lists of words and phrases that should not be used to describe Indigenous Peoples.

Younging is an editor, publisher, and writer. I follow his guidelines when editing papers, avoiding certain words when referring to Indigenous Peoples, and adhering to his suggestions for capitalization and other conventions. He includes words and phrases to avoid when discussing Indigenous Peoples, resources for editors to better understand Indigenous perspectives, advice for collaboration with Native writers, and other imperative information for those in writing education and publication. His book is essential for non-Native editors to assist Native writers appropriately.

PAST EDUCATIONAL TRAUMA

Tribal students are exposed to racist or ignorant teaching material and methods from an early age. Only some students, and only recently, have had access to schools run by their own Nations. These schools have their own problems and still tend to be staffed by non-Native teachers, but they are steps toward sovereignty and Tribal control. Many Native students learn to believe in their own inferiority from the minute they enter a mainstream academic setting.[3] By the time they reach a Tribal college, they have often passed through primary education with insufficient reading and writing skills in English or their Indigenous language.

When I was a younger student, I sought academic perfection to ward off my own feelings of inferiority and stupidity. However, like many

3. I would consider any institution that focuses on preparing a student's level of marketability for the capitalist workforce, and that is based upon white colonial institutional values and that perpetuates Americanisms (myths relating to the founding and reality of white settlement), to be a mainstream institution even if it serves minority populations.

students, I came to a point where I could no longer compete, and I flunked out of a private university. After dropping out, I felt an extreme sense of failure and shame. My ticket to having value and being intelligent and competent were, in my mind, gone. It was only through returning to a Tribal college and having the investment of my teachers and Native peers that I came to accept my own worth and intelligence apart from my grade point average.

Most of the students I teach are middle-aged adults returning to college after years of working or caregiving. Often a student has not attended school since the eighth grade. Many attended boarding schools. I worked with a seventy-year-old man who needed assistance learning computer skills. Laid off his job of thirty years because he could not type reports, it was evident that he had been a victim of ageism and racism. "I guess I am just a dumb Indian," he would say. He was a Vietnam veteran and told me many stories about his life. "All my friends are dead. Most of them killed themselves or drank themselves to death." He would become emotional and put his hand next to mine. Since he was thirteen, he had not attended school, and his previous typing experience was on a 1930s typewriter. I, in turn, told him about my grandfather's experience in the shipyards, about Oklahoma and Cherokee country. This was not a time for institutional professionalism. This was community and reciprocal relationship in action. I never learned if he returned to work, but he did tell me he had a good time working with me. For me, that was the greatest affirmation of my work that I could receive.

Students often enter the tutoring center feeling insecure. Still, I have learned that reminding people and permitting them to be proud of their nonacademic learning and accomplishments translates to better confidence. Listening and asking meaningful questions that require students to think for themselves and tailoring my teaching to their interests lead to better engagement. Treating students with respect, believing they have something unique to teach me (and to offer their community), and encouraging them to ask questions allow us to build a relationship. It is only through relationships that people can reach their full potential. Of course, there is no universal practice applicable to all students, not even to all Native students. A big problem within academia is believing there is only one way to do things, which is why Indigenous students face discrimination and exclusion in the first place. Typically, this is the "white way," but it can also devolve into whatever cult-like methodology a group or university espouses.

I have gone through the rigors of rigid academic writing, receiving reports back from teachers where the pages bled red. Teachers underlined my original Native ideas as naïve or illogical. I learned english grammar, and I could write a five-paragraph narrative essay in thirty minutes, but I could not think critically. I did not have confidence in my own ideas. That confidence came from having a teacher and mentor who believed in me and did not pass me through because they thought I could not write correctly. Instead, they gave me extra assistance. They taught me how to think critically, yet not through their framework but my own. When I thought I was taking advanced science courses, I was learning how to write about the ethics of science and the ideologies and contradictions between western and Indigenous thought. The more I learned to communicate, and the more culturally aware and competent I became, the more hindered I felt in using the english language. As the english language is the only language I speak fluently, my relationship with it has become an uncomfortable compromise. My practice is to help students find their own compromise between a colonial language and their own identities—a compromise that creates our own conventions and abides by our own cultural values.

When It Comes to Writing

When Patrick Robert Reid Stewart (Nisga'a) (2015) submitted his doctoral dissertation to the University of British Columbia, Vancouver, he intentionally used unconventional english, including unusual spacing meant to imitate oral pauses and lowercase letters, as well as his own language throughout. He faced tremendous opposition despite showing in his abstract and various other portions of his dissertation the ability to competently write in standard english. Below is an excerpt. I have done my best to retain his style and spacing, but it may not be exact.

> writing this dissertation reinforced my thinking it reinforced my confidence it reinforced my culture by reinforcing my writing as spoken word part of an oral tradition that has existed since time immemorial this writing style requires particular deliberation it is not random it is democratic it is not hierarchical as you have no doubt noticed there is little adherence to punctuation [xii]. . . . in my defense my style of writing is not laziness or lack of knowledge of proper usage of the english language it is a form of grammatical resistance as a deconstructionist in the manner of many writers especially american poet e e cummings he graduated with a master degree in english from harvard university and they called him experimental and innovative not words likely to be used to describe an Indigenous writer who breaks all the rules of writing [the behavioural ethics board at the university of british columbia suggested that i hire an editor as it appeared that i did not know the english language] times though they are changing. [xvi]

A writing center can support a student on the front lines of confronting racism in writing. When students seek to define themselves outside of a western academic construct of writing conventions, a writing center can support them or go along with institutional control. When I was learning to write, I internalized the mantra "learn the rules; then you can break them." I have since learned that the rules were never meant to be broken by Indigenous Peoples. Those rules have often become prisons that use language to chip away at an Indigenous person's sense of self and identity, write off their ideas, and write about them as abstract concepts and not human beings.

However, Natives have been writing for themselves for hundreds of years and developing various ways to express themselves inside and outside classical writing styles. Malea Powell (Shaawanwaki, Miami) (2002) calls this early breadth of writing by Indigenous Peoples survivance writing. Even though we have learned how to express ourselves and resist in the relatively new (to us) medium of writing and english, we continue to learn how to adapt this tool of oppression for our own aims and use it in conjunction with our ways of being and communicating rather than as an all-consuming replacement.

Scott Richard Lyons (Anishinaabe/Mdewakanton Dakota) (2000) states that what Natives do not want from writing is "stereotypes, cultural appropriation, exclusion, ignorance, irrelevance, rhetorical imperialism" (462). Indigenous Peoples, and more specifically in the case of writing centers, students

> want sovereignty, and in the context of the colonized scene of writing, rhetorical sovereignty. As the inherent right and ability of peoples to determine their own communicative needs and desires in the pursuit of self-determinization, rhetorical sovereignty requires above all the presence of an Indian voice, speaking or writing. (462)

Lyons goes on to discuss the importance that this voice uses Native Language. Haunani-Kay Trask (Pi'ilani/Kahakumakaliua) (1999) wrote passionately about the need for Indigenous languages to be used anywhere Indigenous People go. If one's Indigeneity is to be present in the academic writing center, school, or institution, then language comes too. Through thinking in and using our Native languages, we bear opposing worldviews to the dominant ideology (Trask 1999). Vine Deloria Jr. (Hunkpapa Lakota) (2004) argues that as Indigenous scholars, we must write back against anti-Indianisms in the academy, and I would argue that this would not only be in what we write but how we write—writing in, using, and promoting our Indigenous languages as

Indigenous Peoples is one of the surest methods of dismantling rhetorical imperialism in the academy and in our lives.

Tutors and teachers working within a writing center must learn how to support the creativity and uniqueness of expression present among Indigenous students by actively engaging with Indigenous communities and reframing their ideas of academic writing success to include Indigenous languages and unconventional uses of english. I hope to see writing centers in and outside of TCUs supporting unconventional uses of english by Indigenous students and the use of our languages. It is common for Indigenous students to introduce themselves in their Native language then continue in english. However, some may desire to use their language throughout all their writing. If centers are committed to equity, then the original voices of this land must be allowed to speak. It is by using our Indigenous languages that we decolonize our minds. Roxana Quispe Collantes (Quechua) was the first to write and present her doctoral thesis in her Native language of Quechua at Lima's San Marcos University in Peru, the oldest university in the Americas (Robinson 2020). Conventional academic writing has thus far excluded Indigenous languages.

As a tutor and Indigenous scholar working with Native students, it is my responsibility to help Native students find their voice yet never dictate the rules they must follow. We must learn to communicate effectively in english. However, to enforce standardized english as the rule of law in Native communities while not considering the colonial parameters of such rules of law is to continue colonizing through conventions.

Many Indigenous scholars acknowledge that english is a poor tool for communicating Indigenous ideas. Nevertheless, many of us are isolated from our mother tongues through the horrors and abuses of assimilation. However, we still try to express our souls to each other and non-Native communities through english. Our ideas are stripped down in english and made less than they are, yet their essence still cries out to be understood. We still cry out to be understood.

OVERCOMING STUDENTS' LACK OF ESSENTIAL RESOURCES FOR THEIR DAILY LIVES

While in college, I researched the different resources available in our local area that students could use and printed out posters and flyers for the tutoring center. These included places where people could take free showers, receive free meals, obtain school supplies, or pursue career services. Informing students about other campus services, especially disability services, occupational rehabilitation, and Tribal rental assistance, became a priority. I used many of these resources while I was a student, and having access to them increased my comfort and ability to stay in college.

The brain uses 20 percent of the body's total calories, and studying requires intense concentration (Heid 2018). There is debate as to what percentage of college students experience food insecurity. Studies done on the topic are not always reliable at gauging what it means to have food insecurity (much less access to high-quality food). As a tutoring center, we tried to alleviate acute discomfort for students who entered the center. We purchased snacks and ready-made meals and kept them above the microwave or in the fridge when possible. We provided free coffee and tea. Students knew they could find something to eat. Meal and resource insecurity is a problem for Indigenous students, and no one can be realistically expected to succeed in academia when their belly hurts.

Women and people who menstruate would ask if we had tampons or pads in the tutoring center on more than one occasion. I had to say no the first few times, but I tried to make sure there were feminine hygiene products in the bathroom after that. At NWIC, women make up the higher percentage of students. Many of these women are mothers and cannot afford childcare. They knew that they could bring their children if they came to the tutoring center. I changed many diapers and held or played with many children while their parents took exams. Treating these mothers as integral parts of our college community rather than a burden allowed me to create many lasting friendships and be an auntie to a good number of tiny humans.

Many Tribal students struggle to meet basic needs. Food, hygiene products, school supplies, jump drives, a warm place to sit when homeless are things many take for granted when they have never had the need. Several of my friends were homeless while in school. Creating equitable access for students requires meeting those needs wherever possible. Although feeding, clothing, and sheltering may not be in the description of a writing center or be a long-term possibility, the responsibility remains to do something while working towards a long-term solution. Confronting true poverty and trying to help feel like putting a Band-Aid on a gaping wound.

Natives entering the academy are aware of the poverty and suicide rates in their communities. Most enter with dreams of using any gained skills to empower themselves and their Peoples. For a higher education experience to aid in those goals, it must support the recovery of traditional knowledge. Outsiders have theorized how to solve our problems for far too long, trying everything except what we need—the return of our lands and revival of our languages and traditions. From these things, our identities and existence as Indigenous Peoples stem.

Verna Kirkness (Cree) and Ray Barnhardt (1991) say it best when they describe the methods and practices that work for Indigenous students: "The four R's—respect, relevance, reciprocity, responsibility" (1). Educators and administrators must genuinely respect students. Students must feel that what they are learning is relevant to them, their Nations, and their goals. They must be allowed to engage in reciprocal relationships with peers and faculty rather than hierarchal ones. There must be a sense of responsibility on behalf of an institution to change its colonial structure. If there is one thing we hate, it is complicated bureaucracy. Only when these four requirements are met can Native students achieve success without selling their souls.

Many institutions and businesses have adopted social justice lingo regarding decolonization while continuing their power positions. They create multicultural and diversity programs and form special committees devoted to retaining or attracting minority students. These same institutions sponsor centers designed to teach students the skills to be successful in an industrialized world but rarely consider that it is the colonial structure of competitive, capitalist, and racist institutions that must change. If we are to have any lasting impact on combating racism in this country, we cannot allow our writing centers to play this game. As an educator, I refuse to ask my students to change their identities to provide a brown face that is more comfortable for status quo institutional bigwigs and donors. I push the institution to change in whatever way I can.

Eve Tuck (Unangax̂) and K. Wayne Yang (2012) criticize this common stance by reminding those in mainstream institutions "what is unsettling about decolonization. Decolonization brings about the repatriation of Indigenous land and life; it is not a metaphor for other things we want to do to improve our societies and schools. . . . Decolonization is not a metaphor" (1). If writing centers truly wish to decolonize, they must make our goals their own.

As a tutor, I continually push my fellow students to seek their own cultural ways and delve into that wisdom. I also remind them repeatedly that every personal success, every essay they write, and every skill they perfect is a step toward their own sovereignty. We are strong people, and tutors can daily remind their fellow students that we are more than resilient—we are smart, capable, and competent, and we can learn.

There are some specific practices that I employ as a tutor that may be helpful for readers, although they are somewhat subjective:

- Consistent self-reflection and acceptance of critique
- Research into the overarching problems our communities face and what resources are available in the local communities
- Developing a greater knowledge of historical colonial educational practices that must be avoided and discontinued
- A conscious returning to a cultural ideology of humble and compassionate instruction
- Personal acts of decolonization such as learning my Indigenous language, involvement with community processes, and investing in the lives of youth
- Providing food, hygiene products, and school supplies in the tutoring center
- Decorating our small space with relevant Native artwork, lights, and plants

In the age of COVID-19, many of these methods can be harder to put into practice via distance learning, but I find my job deeply vital as I am sometimes one of the few listening ears someone has encountered in their recent isolation.

Recovering pride and confidence in ourselves as students, scholars, and writers is a statement of nationalism, of politics. There is nothing apolitical about being Indigenous and having the audacity to be alive on this continent. Taiaiake Alfred (Kanien'Kehaka) (2004) proclaims that these universities are where we wage war. Our experiences in universities are examples of our experiences in the wider world. Writing centers can have a positive role and be an ally in that war if they so choose by understanding that english is not our language, by engaging in culturally informed editing, and providing for the basic needs of Tribal student.

REFERENCES

Alfred, Taiaiake. 2004. "Warrior Scholarship: Seeing the University as a Ground of Contention." In *Indigenizing the Academy: Transforming Scholarship and Empowering Communities*, edited by Devon Abbott Mihesuah and Angela Cavender Wilson, 88–99. Lincoln: University of Nebraska Press.

Cajete, Gregory. 2016. *Native Science: Natural Laws of Interdependence.* N.p.: Clear Light Publishers.

Compton, Brian, Cheryl Crazy Bull, and Ted Williams. 2016. "Relationality and Student Engagement: Connecting Teaching and Learning at a Tribal College." *Tribal College and University Research Journal* 1, no. 1: 65–80.

Deloria, Vine, Jr. 2004. "Marginal and Submarginal." In *Indigenizing the Academy: Transforming Scholarship and Empowering Communities*, edited by Devon Abbott Mihesuah and Angela Cavender Wilson, 16–30. Lincoln: University of Nebraska Press.

Heid, Markham. 2018. "Does Thinking Burn Calories? Here's What the Science Says." *Time Magazine*, September 19. https://time.com/5400025/does-thinking-burn-calories/.

Justice, Daniel Heath. 2004. "Seeing (and Reading) Red: Indian Outlaws in the Ivory Tower." In *Indigenizing the Academy: Transforming Scholarship and Empowering Communities*, edited by Devon Abbott Mihesuah and Angela Cavender Wilson, 100–123. Lincoln: University of Nebraska.

Kimmerer, Robin Wall. 2015. *Braiding Sweetgrass: Indigenous Wisdom, Scientific Knowledge and the Teachings of Plants*. N.p.: Milkweed Editions.

Kirkness, Verna J., and Ray Barnhardt. 1991. "First Nations and Higher Education: The Four R's—Respect, Relevance, Reciprocity, Responsibility." *Journal of American Indian Education* 30, no. 3: 1–15. http://www.jstor.org/stable/24397980.

Lyons, Scott Richard. 2000. "Rhetorical Sovereignty: What Do American Indians Want from Writing?" *College Composition and Communication* 51, no. 3: 447–468. https://doi.org/10.2307/358744.

Mihesuah, Joshua K. 2004. "Graduating Indigenous Students by Confronting the Academic Environment." In *Indigenizing the Academy: Transforming Scholarship and Empowering Communities*, edited by Devon Abbott Mihesuah and Angela Cavender Wilson, 191–199. Lincoln: University of Nebraska.

Northwest Indian College. 2017. 2017–2019 Catalog. N.p.: Northwest Indian College.

Peters, James. 2021. "First Nation in Kamloops, B.C., Confirms Bodies of 215 Children Buried at Former Residential School Site." *Global News*, May 27. https://globalnews.ca/news/7900737/bc-first-nation-childrens-bodies-kamloops-residential-school-site/.

Powell, Malea. 2002. "Rhetorics of Survivance: How American Indians Use Writing." *College Composition and Communication* 53, no. 3: 396–434. https://doi.org/10.2307/1512132.

Robinson, Leanna. 2020. "PhD Student Makes History as First to Defend Thesis in Quechua." *Language Magazine*. https://www.languagemagazine.com/2020/02/24/phd-student-makes-history-as-first-to-defend-thesis-in-quechua/.

Stewart, Patrick Robert Reid. 2015. "Indigenous Architecture through Indigenous Knowledge: Dim sagalts'apkw nisim' [Together we will build a village]." *UBC Theses and Dissertations*. PhD diss. https://open.library.ubc.ca/soa/cIRcle/collections/ubctheses/24/items/1.0167274.

Trask, Haunani-Kay. 1999. *From a Native Daughter: Colonialism and Sovereignty in Hawaii*. Honolulu: University of Hawai'i Press.

Tuck, Eve, and K. Wayne Yang. 2012. "Decolonization Is Not a Metaphor." *Decolonization: Indigeneity, Education and Society* 1, no. 1: 1–40.

Tuhiwai Smith, Linda. 2012. *Decolonizing Methodologies: Research and Indigenous Peoples*. 2nd ed. London, UK: Zed.

Wilson, Angela Cavender. 2004. "Reclaiming Our Humanity: Decolonization and the Recovery of Indigenous Knowledge." In *Indigenizing the Academy: Transforming Scholarship and Empowering Communities*, edited by Devon Abbott Mihesuah and Angela Cavender Wilson, 69–84. Lincoln: University of Nebraska Press.

Wilson, Shawn. 2008. *Research Is Ceremony: Indigenous Research Methods*. N.p.: Fernwood Publishing.

Younging, Gregory. 2018. *Elements of Indigenous Style: A Guide for Writing by and about Indigenous Peoples*. N.p.: Brush Education Inc.

2

ANOTHER WHITE VOICE IN THE ROOM

On the Limitations of Good Intentions, the Seeming Durability of White Supremacy, and Our Complicit Terrain of Settler Colonialism

Mark Latta

HIGHER ED, MYTHOLOGIES OF EQUALITY, AND MAGICAL THINKING

> *The fundamental problem is not that some are excluded from the hegemonic centers of the academy but that the university (as a specific institutional site) and academy (as a shifting material network) themselves cannot be disentangled from the long historical apparatuses of genocidal and protogenocidal social organization.—Dylan Rodríguez (2012, 812)*

What is it that we expect of higher education? What do we hope to accomplish through our writing centers? These questions seem unsettled, particularly when we speak of education as a tool for generating social change and realizing a vision of equality. Is higher ed—an institution founded upon stolen land and constructed through slave labor for the central purpose of providing professional classes (Wilder 2013) that could accelerate settler-colonial "logic of elimination" (P. Wolfe 2006, 388)—capable of anti-racist practices? As Sandy Grande writes, "Historically, the university functioned as the institutional nexus for the capitalist and religious missions of the settler state, mirroring its histories of dispossession, enslavement, forced assimilation and integration" (2018, 48). Given this history, what remains possible to accomplish through higher education?

To add to the challenge of grappling with difficult questions and uncomfortable histories (or maybe because of them), there is also a sense that a heavy dose of *magical thinking* often accompanies work in higher ed and writing centers. Magical thinking, a concept popularized by Joan Didion (2007), refers to the belief that if one simply wishes hard

https://doi.org/10.7330/9781646424573.c002

enough, gives up one's sense of self or something of value, or behaves in the right way and follows the "correct" steps an unavoidable outcome may be prevented.

The "grand narrative" (McKinney 2013) of writing centers is one that often tells the story of promise and possibility of transformation not only through higher ed but also through literacy development and support. Revealing how our own engagement in magical thinking might prevent us from appreciating the limitations of higher education and writing centers prevents us from truly and fully working beyond these limitations (or recognizing their permanence and perhaps adopting different approaches). The appeal of the grand narrative is self-evident, but does this mythology move us closer to achieving genuine equality and dismantling structural conditions of oppression? Are these goals capable of being achieved through writing centers or higher education? Are they achievable at all?

I propose that two of the most significant mythologies that define our current moment of magical thinking are the commonly paired beliefs that (1) equality is an inevitable, albeit challenging to obtain, outcome, and (2) decolonization can be achieved through incremental changes with minimal sacrifice or discomfort.

This chapter is an invitation to consider other structural causes for why so much more work remains and why efforts to dismantle and challenge oppression seem only to achieve limited and short-term success. I argue that this remains true because we labor in a system designed to mask the centrality and ubiquity of white supremacy and settler colonialism in part by rewarding those who participate within it. This masking feature makes it all too easy to locate ourselves (here, a reminder I am writing primarily to a white audience) outside of settler colonialism and white supremacy rather than recognizing we are situated within these structures.

Additionally, this masking allows us to believe that racial and colonial oppression is an aberration rather than a central feature of our current system. For many of us (white writing center administrators [WCAs]), these masks are difficult—perhaps impossible?—to remove partly because of our own need to survive in a system that rewards us through the unearned privileges of whiteness, and partly because many of us mistakenly believe surface-level anti-oppressive and decolonizing maneuvers will bring about fundamental change to a system rooted in anti-Blackness, anti-Indigeneity, and white supremacy. We have discounted the durability of settler colonialism and white supremacy partly because we have overlooked our places within them, and our roles in maintaining them, and embraced a mythology of equality.

What do we expect from and believe possible to be achieved through higher education and our writing centers, particularly when it comes to anti-racist and anti-oppressive goals? This question seems relevant on multiple levels. First, when viewed through the lens of the stated aims of anti-racist work and the commitment of many in the profession toward anti-racist practices, the inherent tensions between these aims and the settler-colonial origins and the centrality of whiteness in higher education need to be more fully surfaced. Otherwise, we risk reducing anti-racist and anti-oppressive work to the good intentions and magical thinking feedback loop. Second, data suggest writing centers are, on average, some of the whitest spaces in an already predominately white terrain (Valles, Babcock, and Keaton Jackson 2017). What should we do with this knowledge?

This chapter is part of a nascent, yet growing body of literature focused on generating pathways of racial reconciliation that centers this labor on those who reap the rewards of whiteness. By offering an autobiographical sketch of one ongoing approach to confronting and challenging white supremacy, this chapter invites others to begin their learning journey of unsettling and resisting the allure of being another white voice in a room of white voices. As it does this, this work also asks us to pull back the veneer of magical thinking about anti-racism and decolonization through reflexivity, critical self-examination, and commitment to "unhook from whiteness" (Hayes and Hartlep 2013).

Using critical autoethnographic inquiry, this chapter hopes to contribute to a growing body of literature focused on generating pathways of racial reconciliation and recognizing how this reconciliation and whiteness are part of the more extensive settler-colonial terrain. To accomplish this goal, I use snippets of my own experiences to call attention to how our structural conditions mask the ways many of us benefit from whiteness while also centering the labor of removing these masks on those who reap their rewards.

MEANS OF UNSETTLING: TRACING THE CONTOURS OF WHITENESS AND SETTLER COLONIALISM THROUGH AUTOBIOGRAPHICAL SKETCHES AND UNDERSTANDINGS OF MATERIALISM

In addition to taking up the theoretical strands known collectively as critical race theory (CRT) and settler colonialism, this research also emerges from the posthuman traditions and the epistemic/ontological groupings that have distinct yet complementary names, including new materialism, feminist materialism, and the post-post (or, "posties") (Barad 2008; Lather 2017). Posthuman understandings share some commonalities. First is the desire not to reject critical theory but to build upon its aspirations of a socially just world. Posthumanism attempts to make good on the promises of critical theory and humanism. Still, it recognizes that "the theoretical and philosophical frameworks that humanism uses to try and make good on those commitments is actually self-defeating" (Wolfe 2012, n.p.). Posthumanism contends that the Cartesian notion of man, a center of humanist understanding, has narrowly defined who and what counts as human. This narrow concept of human is at the heart of social structures that have operated with a premise that not everyone or everything counts as much as those viewed as more fully human (Ferrando 2017).

I orient analysis through a posthuman lens via a feminist materialism framework (Barad 2008) primarily to generate explanatory power related to material conditions and the possibility of decolonizing outcomes. I recognize posthuman understandings and feminist materialism are often associated with embodied knowledge. While I acknowledge my own embodied knowledge as a white settler male is intertwined with patriarchy and settler colonialism, I find the standpoint of feminist materialism useful in revealing patriarchal entanglements and building from them to generate openings of explorations for other entanglements with white supremacy and settler futurity.

This work utilizes critical autoethnography (Diversi and Moreira 2009) to explore how whiteness and settler colonialism are deeply embedded structurally and within personal and subjective experiences. As the author, a white male WCA, I contend with whiteness and settler colonialism and the tensions of possessing an identity centered on these concepts and reaping their unearned rewards while also professing a commitment to dismantling these constructs and disentangling myself from them. While I can recognize I am wrapped up in various degrees with whiteness and settler colonialism, knowing the extent to which this entanglement forms the substantive nature of my identity is a work in progress. Critical autoethnography is helpful as a tool to fully reveal this entanglement.

This research is not concerned with mapping endpoints, identifying conclusions, or establishing credibility through objective empiricism. Instead, this is an attempt to reveal a *becoming* through "the intersection of theory and story" (Fitzpatrick 2018, 43) and to contribute to the futurity—the "ways that groups imagine and produce knowledge about futures" (Goodyear-Ka'opua 2018, 86)—of possible as-yet-unrealized moments in which anti-racist intentions and outcomes more closely align within a terrain constructed for making these outcomes the norm rather than the exception. In acknowledging the *being-of-and-not-of-ness* as a work in progress, this autobiography surfaces implications and tensions of doing the work of anti-racism while also recognizing I am bound up in and likely contributing to the reasons the work of anti-racism remains necessary.

What follows are two stories that center my experiences as a white WCA engaged in anti-racist practices. These stories convey the as-yet failed attempts of developing a site defined by anti-racism and equality within the broader terrain of higher education and how these attempts have motivated me to return to deepen my unsettlings through continued interrogation of critical race theory and settler colonial theory. This writing is presented as a braided essay (Fertig 2011), a counterstory of the entanglements between racism, settler colonialism, and good intentions that reveals itself through mosaic snippets, each contributing more than they could individually when placed next to one another.

". . . it's just that you seem racist against white people"

A colleague requested an informal sit-down in her office to discuss what she referred to in an email, "a potentially delicate subject, but probably just a misunderstanding." After exchanging polite niceties, my colleague informed me that one of her advisees, a student in my first-year seminar course, had approached her and accused me of directing racism toward white people. "Obviously," she said while gesturing to me and my white skin, "this seems a little odd."

"Well, that is interesting," I replied. "Did this student offer any explanation?"

"Only that she found a recent class discussion very uncomfortable." When I pressed for details about why the discussion was so disquieting, she seemed to get flustered and said, "Well, that it's just that you seem racist against white people. She's considering dropping the course, and I offered to reach out to you and speak off the record."

I knew to which class discussion she was referring. The theme of my first-year seminar course was urban issues, and the course covered a broad range of topics that nearby community residents had indicated they wanted more of our students to understand: redlining; the development of the interstate; food apartheid (as opposed to food deserts); gentrification; and the relationship between education, poverty, and the criminal justice system. The university where I teach and direct the

Writing Center is a predominately white institution (PWI) in an urban environment. Like many urban PWIs, the neighborhoods in which we are located are predominately Black. When discussing the material conditions of these neighborhoods, it is impossible to fully account for these conditions without also accounting for the racist structures that produced them. Therefore, race and socioeconomic status quickly become central and recurring topics of discussion within the class. It is difficult to engage in meaningful or critical conversations about these systemic issues without discussing our own racial identities and racialized understandings.

During one class, I shared my racial autobiography and my path toward developing a critical consciousness. During this conversation, I noted my upbringing in a profoundly racist and patriarchal family and community and how these beliefs and worldviews shaped my understanding of the world. "But the views of my immediate and extended family didn't emerge from nowhere," I told my class. "Rather, these understandings were carried across generations and cultivated over hundreds of years. We may not have enslaved anyone, but my family still benefited from a society founded on the legal enslavement of Africans and the genocide of Indigenous peoples. I believe it's important to spend time understanding how I've also benefitted from white supremacy—and come to terms with how white supremacy has shaped my own identity—even though I reject those beliefs."

This testimony was the basis for the student's accusation of my being racist against whites. Although this instance was disconnected from my role as a Writing Center Director, I surface it here to highlight the degree to which whiteness can drive narratives of racism in higher education spaces. In another instance, within our peer tutoring course, a student—white, female—continued to raise objections about the mention of African American English vernacular and confided that the acknowledgment of nonacademic Englishes and expressive legitimacy felt like an attack on her family because of her parents' insistence she learn "proper English."

The hints and allegations that critical and anti-racist approaches to teaching are themselves racist function as a backlash against perceived attacks against an identity entangled in unexamined whiteness (Matias 2016) and are animated by a white fragility (DiAngelo 2018). Indeed, the belief of reverse racism is difficult to take seriously when there is no structural power oppressing whites, and the concept has been largely debunked as a myth motivated by the constant recentering of whiteness (Newkirk II 2017). Although I find these explanations to be valid, they also fall short of achieving the goal of cultivating a critical curiosity, one that hopefully leads to an anti-racist stance and a willingness to question the normativity of settler colonialism. If my response to racism and settler colonialism, while accurately represented through scholarship, drives people away, what have I accomplished?

From the perspective of examining material outcomes, introducing concepts of anti-racism, anti-white supremacy, and anti-settler colonialism have led to some students doubling down on how their identities and worldviews center the opposite of these concepts. If the goal is to diminish white supremacy vis-à-vis raising awareness of its prevalence, why does it sometimes feel like I am doing the opposite?

It may be easy to think of those who retreat into the shadows of white discomfort as racist and to write them off as such. But doing this focuses attention on the individual and ignores the more extensive system in which they operate. Racial identities provide an affect, an emotional response (Zembylas 2018), and "the feeling of having a feeling" (Rutherford 2016, 286). One reason for the durability of whiteness is that we live in a system in which whiteness provides so much to those who can participate effectively within it and take it on as an identity marker. Economic, cultural, political, and social benefits, yes. But whiteness also provides an emotional benefit, and this emotional dimension of whiteness is underexplored. We live in a system that manifests a wide range of rewards through whiteness, but our responses rarely consider these rewards and focus instead on individual moral failures.

Although I was able to have what I felt were productive conversations with the student who accused me of being racist against whites, our relationship was, at best, chilly. She did not drop the course. While her performance in the class met most of the expectations, she rarely engaged in conversation outside of small groups or questions directed to her. While she ultimately passed the class, doubts remained about her ability to apply the course information in understanding that "inevitable" urban "problems" are, to the contrary, a structure doing what it was designed to do.

The Only White Ears in the Room

I had been invited to attend Talk it Out Tuesday, an ongoing, informational open-dialogue hosted by the campus Unity Center. During Talk it Out Tuesday, students are invited to share whatever is on their minds in a brave space. While the Unity Center is open to all students, the center is populated predominately by Black, Latinx, Asian, and LGBTQ+ students.

During this particular Talk it Out Tuesday, I was the only white person in the group. I wondered why this might have been and highlighted the importance of receiving an invitation to enter this space. Darren,[1] the Unity Center's Black male Director, welcomed and introduced me to the rest of the students gathered in the space. I knew most of the students gathered here, either from a previous class or through the Writing Center. Darren mentioned that I am "well known in the community" and motioned his arms toward an undefined yet mutually understood geographic location beyond the campus boundaries. "The community" refers to the neighborhoods surrounding campus, a predominately Black area, and his mention of my relationship with the community was interpreted by me as a solidification of the invitation to join in the discussion. Still, I double-checked with the gathered students, ensuring they were comfortable with my presence, and they indicated they were.

As I listened to the conversation unfold, I marveled at how at ease these students were with one another. Their comfort with each other was self-evident, and while Darren reminded everyone that there were no such things as entirely safe spaces, all the students gathered there behaved and positioned their bodies in ways that conveyed a sense of safety and deep trust with one another. What also struck me was seeing the majority-minority group of students gathered here in the Unity Center, a chorus of Black and Brown faces. In nearly every other area on campus, these same faces would be disproportionately underrepresented among their white peers.

Sitting in the Unity Center that day, I realized I was witnessing Black excellence (Muhammad 2020) and the embodied joy that comes from cultivating identity rather than suppressing it. Collectively, these students were guiding their education by centering their own "funds of knowledge" (Moll et al. 1992): their home and community literacies. As they did this, they worked to upend and resist the "damage centered" (Tuck 2009) pedagogies, which commonly route Black and Brown students through a remedial and dehumanizing gamut of curriculum and orientation activities under the guise of preparing them for academic success.

Although the conversational topics were heavy and of urgent importance, there was also an undercurrent of happiness and appreciation. I saw before me the gratitude and desire to make and remake a space according to their needs, identities, and sense of community. The Unity Center was a space created in the image and according to those who

1. Pseudonym.

needed the space to feel free to be themselves. It was a space centered on understanding and joy. Of course, the Unity Center is no panacea, and the entrenchment of white supremacy and settler colonialism runs too deep to be fully disentangled merely by setting aside a token area of campus for non-majoritized students. But, watching and being in the company of the students in the Unity Center that day provided a glimpse, even a faint one, of what it might look like to create a space and practice for joyful learning that existed beyond the shadows of anti-Blackness.

In comparison, our Writing Center was a predominately white space amid a predominately white institution. Despite numerous targeted recruitment initiatives, an equity audit action plan, and numerous collaborations with our university groups representing Black, Latinx, Asian students, our center's staff remains predominately white (although non-white representation among our staff is slightly higher than the overall university demographics). However, sitting in the Unity Center that day, being invited to participate in the conversation, allowed me to think about the ways our center had performed the typical diversity, equity, and inclusion maneuvers. Despite these efforts, it became clear I had failed to consider something vitally important: the ways we were (or were not) fostering joy—Black, Latinx, Asian, LGBTQ+, and Indigenous joy.

This invited experience in the Unity Center encouraged me to explore how we might position our center to generate and foster Black joy (Johnson 2015). Conversations with several Black and Latinx students confirmed that while the equity efforts of the Writing Center and key personnel were known and appreciated, the space and process of initiating a peer tutoring session still felt inaccessible. Another way of understanding this is that writing centers, as typically white spaces cast in the larger structure of typically white institutions of higher education, were effective at generating conditions that fostered white joy but were ineffective at producing joy in non-white students or able to account for its importance.

The structure of our educational system produces some students who have been cultivated to excel in a space uniquely centered on the support of literacy and type of English, which more closely resembles their own home and school literacy. At the same time, those who have been routed through a majority-minority educational track find their educational experiences have positioned them adversely and more likely to fail when navigating higher education spaces. However, altering conditions of our educational spaces so that they account for and bring about joy as a culturally responsive approach to learning and development has been shown to cultivate achievement and involvement (Muhammad 2020) among students who have not been immersed in the "culture of power" (Delpit 1988) of whiteness. My center, unknowingly effective at producing an outcome of joy for those who benefit from and intuitively understand systems built around whiteness, had failed to consider the ways we might intentionally begin to instead produce outcomes of joy for Black, Brown, and Indigenous students.

CONCLUSION: A LOVING CRITIQUE

These narrative braids begin to reveal how the dominant social structures guiding social ordering, higher education, and, by extension, the writing centers located within these structures generate conditions that work to prevent anti-racist and decolonizing maneuvers from achieving their stated aims despite the best of intentions. As a structure of social ordering, whiteness remains durable and resistant to change. Although the literature surrounding critical race theory clarifies that structural racism is a central feature of American society, many faculty and administrative professionals have failed to fully attend to the persistent entanglement of American society with structural racism, opting instead to believe incremental reforms will somehow produce wholesale structural change.

These stories also highlight struggles—failures perhaps—but each has begun to reveal an opportunity for deeper understanding and a return to the central theories and insights that animate my work. The scholarship of social change and of writing centers that attempts to embrace a mission of remaking the world does not often like to discuss failures or hold up examples of things gone wrong, anti-racist motivations that generate racist realities, or attempts to decolonize that only reify the centrality of settler visions. However, through a lens of materialism and posthumanism, "failures" are not an individual's moral failing. Instead, they are opportunities to begin to realize the limitations of the broader structures we operate within. Through these perspectives and an exploration of individual actions situated within structures, I feel better equipped to resist the appeal of magical thinking and avoid settling for the empty promise of good intentions.

This chapter is not meant as a criticism of individuals, many of whom operate in various states of precarity and within the intersections of multiple forms of oppression and positioned identities. Instead, it is an attempt to share a "loving critique" (Paris 2012) I have to provide for myself and to tell the partial, incomplete, and as-yet-not-fully realized story of what moved me to this space. This story reminds that each of us operates within a structure designed not only to prevent us from achieving our humanizing aims but also to invisiblize the ways we are undermined both by structural constraints and our own magical thinking.

Although I have presented these experiences through the subjective lens of myself, I did not enter these narratives or travel through them alone. I had theory to guide me. Specifically, I relied upon the Black feminist and Indigenous traditions of understanding theory as a potentially liberatory practice[2]—a turn made admittedly because I was "desperate, wanting to comprehend—to grasp what was happening around and within me" (hooks 1991, 59). Additionally, I wanted to understand how I was contributing to and benefiting from what I was attempting to comprehend. I desired to trouble my relationship with what had presented itself as normal, so naturally I turned to understandings that made moves to denormalize my understanding of the status quo and helped me make sense of my growing discomfort.

There is a danger to anti-racist and decolonizing work that is primarily performed by white folks and those who have little embodied knowledge about oppression. There are many examples of anti-racist movements that while starting with intentions to decenter whiteness end up recentering whiteness and overlooking (or refusing to see) the CRT roots which inspired their origins. As Black voices and perspectives find themselves overwhelmed and crowded out by white voices, anti-racism devolves to cater to and protect white needs. Allyship becomes less about serving as an ally and more about maintaining an identity through an allyship narrative. Meanwhile, anti-Blackness continues, bolstered and accelerated by those who claim to challenge it.

To prevent the recentering of white and settler futures, we must turn to the theories and perspectives that center non-white and non-settler futures. How might one go about locating these theoretical tools and incorporating these ways of seeing? In my case, I listened. There are rich traditions that trouble the white, Eurocentric notions of organizing the world according to settler-colonial, neoliberal, and capitalistic logics. But do we want to find them? And if we find them, do we want to listen? And if we listen, do we dare act? If we are to ever achieve equitable, nonoppressive futures, we will need structures that generate these conditions. If we are to ever have these structures, we will first need to develop the tools to identify and root out the current structures that prevent the conditions and futures we desire.

2. I do not claim these as identities or their resulting perspectives and wisdoms as my own. Rather, I use these theoretical frames as lenses through which to see and understand my orientation with the world.

REFERENCES

Barad, Karen. 2008. "Posthumanist Performativity: Toward an Understanding of How Matter Comes to Matter." In *Material Feminisms,* edited by Stacy Alaimo and Susan Hekman, 120–156. Bloomington: Indiana University Press.

Delpit, Lisa. 1988. "The Silenced Dialogue: Power and Pedagogy in Educating Other People's Children." *Harvard Educational Review* 58, no. 3: 280–298.

DiAngelo, Robin. 2018. *White Fragility: Why It's So Hard for White People to Talk about Racism.* Boston: Beacon Press.

Didion, Joan. 2007. *The Year of Magical Thinking.* New York: Knopf Doubleday Publishing Group.

Diversi, Marcelo, and Claudio Moreira. 2009. *Betweener Talk: Decolonizing Knowledge Production, Pedagogy and Praxis.* Walnut Creek, CA: Left Coast Press.

Fertig, Carol. 2011. "The Mosaic, Segmented, or Braided Essay." *On Writing.* http://bycarolfertig.blogspot.com/2011/11/mosaic-segmented-or-braided-essay.html.

Ferrando, Francesca. 2017. *What Does "Posthuman" Mean?* YouTube, December 7. https://www.youtube.com/watch?v=zi6APyooW9A&t=282s.

Fitzpatrick, Esther. 2018. "A Story of Becoming: Entanglement, Settler Ghosts, and Postcolonial Counterstories." *Cultural Studies—Critical Methodologies* 18, no. 1: 43–51. https://doi.org/10.1177/1532708617728954.

Goodyear-Ka'opua, Noelani. 2018. "Indigenous Oceanic Futures: Challenging Settler Colonialisms and Militarization." In *Indigenous and Decolonizing Studies in Education,* edited by Linda Tuhiwai Smith, Eve Tuck, and K. Wayne Yang, 82–102. New York: Routledge.

Grande, Sandy. 2018. "Refusing the University." In *Toward What Justice? Describing Diverse Dreams of Justice in Education,* edited by Eve Tuck and K. Wayne Yang, 47–65. New York: Routledge.

Hayes, Cleveland, and Nicholas D. Hartlep. 2013. *Unhooking from Whiteness: The Key to Dismantling Racism in the United States.* Boston: Sense.

hooks, bell. 1994. "Theory as Liberatory Practice." In *Teaching to Transgress: Education as the Practice of Freedom,* edited by bell hooks, 59–75. New York: Routledge.

Johnson, Javon. 2015. "Black Joy in the Time of Ferguson." *QED: A Journal in GLBTQ Worldmaking* 2, no. 2: 177–183.

Lather, Patti. 2017. *(Post)critical Methodologies: The Science Possible after the Critiques.* New York, Routledge.

Matias, Cheryl. 2016. " 'Why Do You Make Me Hate Myself?': Re-teaching Whiteness, Abuse, and Love in Urban Teacher Education." *Teaching Education* 27, no. 2: 194–211.

McKinney, Jackie Grutsch. 2013. *Peripheral Visions for Writing Centers.* Boulder: University Press of Colorado.

Moll, Luis, Cathy Amanti, Deborah Neff, and Norma Gonzalez. 1992. "Funds of Knowledge for Teaching: Using a Qualitative Approach to Connect Homes and Communities." *Theory Into Practice* 31, no. 2: 132–140.

Muhammad, Gholdy. 2020. *Cultivating Genius: An Equity Framework for Culturally and Historically Responsive Literacy.* New York: Scholastic.

Newkirk, Vann R., II. 2017. "The Myth of Reverse Racism." *Atlantic,* August 5. https://www.theatlantic.com/education/archive/2017/08/myth-of-reverse-racism/535689/.

Paris, Django. 2012. "Culturally Sustaining Pedagogy: A Needed Change in Stance, Terminology, and Practice." *Educational Researcher* 41, no. 3: 93–97.

Rodríguez, D. 2012. "Racial/Colonial Genocide and the 'Neoliberal Academy': In Excess of a Problematic." *American Quarterly* 64, no. 4: 809–813.

Rutherford, D. 2016. "Affect Theory and the Empirical." *Annual Review of Anthropology* 45, no. 1: 285–300.

Tuck, Eve. 2009. "Suspending Damage: A Letter to Communities." *Harvard Educational Review* 79, no. 3: 409–428.
Valles, Sarah Banschbach, Rebecca Day Babock, and Karen Keaton Jackson. 2017. "Writing Center Administrators and Diversity: A Survey." *Peer Review* 1, no. 1: n.p.
Wilder, Craig Steven. 2013. *Ebony and Ivy: Race, Slavery, and Troubled History of America's Universities.* London: Bloomsbury Press.
Wolfe, Cary. 2012. *Cary Wolfe on Posthumanism and Animal Studies.* YouTube, July 12. https://www.youtube.com/watch?v=5NN427KBZlI.
Wolfe, Patrick. 2006. "Settler Colonialism and the Elimination of the Native." *Journal of Genocide Research* 8, no. 4: 387–409.
Zembylas, Michalinos. 2018. "Affect, Race, and White Discomfort in Schooling: Decolonial Strategies for 'Pedagogies of Discomfort.'" *Ethics and Education* 13, no. 1: 86–104.

PART II

Recruitment, Hiring, and Retention

3

WHY DO WHITE TUTORS "LOVE" WRITING?

Recruitment and What Brings Us to the Center

Rachel Herzl-Betz

This particular recruitment journey began when I joined the Nevada State College (NSC) Writing Center in 2017. As of spring 2020, Nevada State was a Hispanic-serving institution (HSI) that served just over 7,000 students, 37 percent of whom identified as Hispanic and 46 percent of whom identified as first-generation college students. As a new colleague, I was pleased to see that our student workers reflected the full diversity of the campus community. Most of our tutors were multilingual, first-generation students of color, and that representation translated directly into strengths in research and praxis. As I began taking part in our writing center's recruitment process, our existing strengths multiplied as current writing specialists shaped our institutional culture and inspired others to apply.[1] At the same time, I wondered what had allowed historically marginalized students to feel welcome in the first place.

I wanted to understand what made potential tutors at NSC's Writing Center and in centers at other institutions comfortable applying for employment. While writing center scholars have become increasingly invested in anti-racist recruitment, little research exists on the choices that make a difference for potential employees. At the same time, the field has demonstrated a growing interest in empirical research, as a valuable resource alongside counterstory, theory, and personal reflection (Driscoll and Perdue 2012; Simpkins and Schwartz 2015; Martinez 2016). For this collection, I discuss two hypotheses about how racial self-identification impacts applicants' choice to apply for writing center employment:

1. The candidates' reasons for applying would correlate with how they self-identify.

1. The Nevada State Writing Center refers to undergraduate employees as "writing specialists." This chapter will use "specialists" in local references and "tutors" in cross-institutional contexts.

https://doi.org/10.7330/9781646424573.c003

2. Distinct elements of writing center culture and practice would make minoritized and majoritized respondents feel welcome as potential employees.

In this chapter, I trace the prior research that led to both hypotheses, the methods for both parts of the study, the results relevant for anti-racist recruitment, and the implications of those results for writing centers seeking change.

RECRUITMENT IN WRITING CENTER AND HUMAN RESOURCES RESEARCH

Calls for anti-racist recruitment in writing center leadership and tutorial staff have grown more common in recent scholarship. These calls often appear in the final pages of inclusion-centric research, where anti-racist recruitment isn't part of the author's argument, so much as it is one means of effecting change. Arguments often emphasize how hiring can lead to measurable change and is, at the same time, only one part of a much larger ecosystem.

Arguments that mention, but do not center on, recruitment can be divided into two categories based on where hiring falls in the transformative processes. There are those that frame recruitment as the first of many steps toward institutional change (Valentine and Torres 2011), while others frame recruitment as a latter step that ought to come after internal reflection, revision, and anti-racist change (Camarillo 2019). These arguments share common understanding that anti-racist recruitment is worth the necessary labor. Practitioners have talked about diversity in tutor recruitment since the mid-1990s (Kilborn 1995), but the field lacks concrete data on how to actually make it happen.

In conversation, practitioners often suggest three strategies to increase the racial diversity of their applicant pools, particularly in cross-institutional conversations: (1) tutor pay, (2) outreach to identity-based organizations on campus, and (3) diversity and inclusion statements. This isn't to say that these strategies have been solely employed for recruitment. For example, a center may decide to create an inclusion statement for several reasons, of which increased racial equity in recruitment is only one. However, as logical as all three strategies may seem, they rarely appear in published scholarship because the verification isn't there.

At the same time, the broader field of research into hiring and recruitment has established two known parameters with equal relevance in writing center contexts: (1) ethnoracial hiring discrimination is real,[2] and (2) employers don't do a good job of anticipating what will make minoritized applicants feel welcome as potential employees. The first of the two parameters may feel too obvious to mention, but it's important to acknowledge that we know a great deal about the nature of racism in recruitment work that has yet to be included in writing center conversations.

Despite extensive knowledge about employer bias, little is known about how communities react to company representation (Breaugh, Macan, and Grambow 2008), and that knowledge gap is particularly apparent in relation to racially marginalized applicants. The presence of employees of color in printed materials, inclusive policies on company websites, targeted outreach, and other advertising choices intended to signal inclusion consistently motivates anti-racist white applicants but have little impact for racially and ethnically marginalized candidates (Casper, Wayne, and Manigold 2013). Notably, Goldberg and Allen (2008) find that "the presence or absence of voluntary diversity statements appeared to have little effect" for racially marginalized applicants, a fact that they find particularly surprising (229). To explain these discrepancies, scholars point to the ways that racial and ethnic status serves as "an imperfect proxy for individuals' value for diversity." (Avery et al. 2013, 185) In other words, employers expect racially marginalized candidates to appreciate diversity signaling. Instead, signaling inspires white applicants who claim to value inclusion (Avery et al. 2013).

Writing center and human resources (HR) practitioners share an expressed desire for anti-racist recruitment practices, but much of the work still looks like good intentions. I hope this project can address one small part of that gap by testing for its two main hypotheses, which are (1) that application motivations will correlate with identities and (2) that minoritized and majoritized applicants will respond to different invitations into writing center spaces. Finally, in response to the existing research, I'd add a third, implied hypothesis, that empirical recruitment data are a useful complement to nonempirical knowledge.

Methods

To answer my two hypotheses, I gathered survey data from current writing center employees who had been hired as undergraduate tutors.[3]

2. For relevant scholarship on the ways that race intersects with hiring practices, see Reskin, McBrier, and Kmec (1999); Watson, Appiah, and Thornton (2011); and Ndobo et al. (2018).

3. Ethical approval for this study was obtained from the Nevada State College Institutional Review Board (Protocol #1806-0250).

The first stage of analysis used Statistical Product and Service Solution (SPSS) (IBM) Statistics to measure correlation between applicants' stated reasons for applying to work in a writing center and their self-identified race, gender, sexuality, linguistic background, family educational background, and ability. The second stage of analysis turned toward the factors that made applicants feel that someone with their racial identity would be welcome as an employee.

Data Collection and Analysis

I distributed a thirty-six-question survey in February 2020 to potential respondents,[4] through LISTSERVS for the International Writing Centers Association (IWCA) and regional affiliates, and through posts on Twitter and writing-center-related Facebook groups. In each case, I invited leaders to share the survey with their current employees. By the end of the survey period, the study included responses from 216 current writing center employees, all of whom were either current undergraduates or were originally hired as undergraduates. To protect anonymity, participants were not given the opportunity to identify their institution.

Participants moved through seven sections of questions about the motivations that led them to this work, each of which centered on a single identity category. These identities included race/ethnicity, sexuality/gender, disability, family educational background, and linguistic background. The first statistical analysis focuses on the relationship between question 5—"What do you recall as the most important reasons why you applied to be a writing center employee?"—and each participant's self-identification. Since the answers to question were qualitative, I used exploratory thematic coding to separate the responses into nine themes, each of which included between two and five unique codes. I also coded each participant for their identification with marginalization in seven categories. For the full list of themes and codes, see appendix 3.A. This round of analysis aimed to identify statistical correlations between identity categories and the nine motivations. Since all given categories were nominal, I ran the Chi-square test for all permutations of the two variables. The second stage of analysis coded responses from question 4, which asked which factors made applicants feel that someone with their racial identity would be welcome as a writing center employee. For the full list of themes and codes for both stages of analysis, see appendix 3.A.

4. For the full text of the survey, see appendix b.

Results

Stage-One Results

Of the fifty-six tests run in SPSS, four resulted in a statistically significant correlation and three resulted in a near-significant correlation. This section outlines both the significant and near-significant results. Six of the nine themes didn't reach significance for the included identity categories. Those themes were "help," "skill," "apply," "community," "job," and "other." Motivations categorized as "other" included a desire to improve their writing centers, the idea that the job sounded appealing (or "fun"), and those who responded that they didn't know.

The "I want to learn/gain skills in" theme exhibited a statistical correlation with two identity categories: (1) participants with a historically marginalized gender or sexuality (SG1), X^2 $(1, N = 173) = 7.045$, $p = 0.008$ (2) and first-generation participants (1G), X^2 $(1, N = 1\ 73) = 4.172$, $p = 0.041$. The Pearson Chi-square p-value also approached significance for participants with a historically marginalized race/ethnicity (R), X^2 $(1, N = 173) = 3.380$, $p = 0.066$. This means that those participants were more likely to identify a desire to learn something or gain a specific skill (such as tutoring or writing) as a primary reason for applying to work in a writing center.

In the "I care about/I love" category, the Chi-Square test indicated significance for participants with a historically marginalized race/ethnicity (R), X^2 $(1, N = 173) = 4.976$, $p = 0.026$. It also approached significance for first-generation participants (1G), X^2 $(1, N = 173) = 3.559$, $p = 0.059$. These participants were less likely to identify their love or affection for writing or tutoring as a primary reason for applying to work in a writing center. Conversely, this result indicates that white participants are more likely to identify affection as a reason to apply.

In the "professor recommendation" category, the Chi-square test indicated significance for multilingual participants (M), X^2 $(1, N = 173) = 3.871$, $p = 0.049$. It also approached significance for disabled, neurodivergent, or mentally ill participants (D), X^2 $(1, N = 173) = 3.355$, $p = 0.067$. These participants were all more likely to identify a professor's recommendation or encouragement as a primary reason for applying to work in a writing center.

Stage-Two Results and Limitations

Eighty-nine respondents provided specific reasons for why they felt welcome applying, given their racial and ethnic background. Of those respondents, thirty-five self-identified as having a historically marginalized race

Table 3.1. Reasons for welcome: participants of color

Responses from participants of color		
Code	Raw number of responses	Percentage of total
Representation	17	47%
Language	7	19%
General acceptance	8	22%
Policies	2	6%
Never considered it	2	6%
Total	36	100%

Table 3.2. Reasons for welcome: white participants

Responses from white participants		
Code	Raw number of responses	Percentage of total
Representation	12	21%
Language	1	2%
General acceptance	10	18%
Policies	2	3%
Never considered it	11	20%
Never had to consider it	20	36%
Total	56	100%

or ethnicity and fifty-four self-identified as having a historically majoritized race or ethnicity. Tables 3.1 and 3.2 show the coded responses.

Combining the final two codes for white applicants arrives at the full number who had not considered race as a factor in their own application process until they took part in this survey. Fifty-seven percent of white applicants didn't consider whether race would shape their reception as a potential tutor (compared with 5 percent for applicants of color), and 37 percent retroactively identified whiteness as the reason why race hadn't been a consideration.

This study presented three limitations that may have impacted the results: the self-reported nature of participants' identities and motivations, our dependence on long-term recall, and the survey's limited list of identity categories. Without a consistent source of demographic data, respondents' understanding of their own identities may not align across institutions. The survey also didn't include definitions for key terms, so the respondents may have used their own understandings to define marginalization. This means that the study may measure how participants perceive their identities but not how those identities track across academic contexts. It, likewise, can measure how the participants represent and remember their reasons for applying but cannot rely on the accuracy of their representations. Finally, future variations on this study should give participants the opportunity to consider their class positionality and citizenship status, since respondents mentioned both as significant omissions.

MAKING SENSE OF THE RESULTS

For both parts of the analysis, the results differed from my expectations and from the disciplinary conversation around "diverse" recruitment in writing centers. However, they stuck closely to scholarship on racism in writing center praxis.

The statistical correlation between white applicants and an expressed "love" of writing and tutoring connects with the ways white grammars are positioned as academic norms. When writing excellence means being good at white mainstream English, white students are positioned to be editors, mentors, and scholars in the high school classroom (Abdullah-Matta 2019; Baker-Bell 2020). This isn't to say that writing center employees of color don't express a deep affection for language, writing, and the work of student support. Instead, the study results suggest that their affection has been reshaped by systemic white supremacy and linguistic racism. The expected linguistic supremacy of white mainstream English doesn't allow students of color to love their own language(s), let alone their existence in school (Condon, Green, and Faison 2019). To quote Neisha-Anne Green (2016), "Being at war with one's self is not ideal."

The most compelling connection between the first- and second-stage results lies in respondents' relationships to language. Twenty percent of applicants of color identified their centers' relationship to language as the element that made them feel welcome as potential tutors, compared to 1 percent of white applicants. Responses from racially marginalized applicants included the following considerations of language practices in the training and application processes:

- "The course that I took prior to being hired addressed inclusivity and the importance of code-switching and its impact on students of color."
- "The position description stated that bilingual people were welcome."
- "The application encouraged us to write about experiences with learning English."

Respondents of color also reflected on language in sessions and casual center interactions. The discrepancy between the relevance marginalized and majoritized respondents gave to language use suggests that applicants of color are (1) more likely to see linguistic norms as a proxy for anti-racist practices or (2) more aware of using language as a signifier of center culture. Both majoritized and minoritized applicants likely notice whether a center's linguistic framework connects with their own, but as members of the dominant culture, white students may be less likely to connect writing and race. If, as the statistical analysis suggests, applicants of color experience a more nuanced affection for writing, seeing that complexity in academic institutions could be a powerful motivator. It makes sense, then, that those applicants would feel welcome in centers that signal enthusiasm for a more nuanced understanding of language.

A wide range of applicants were also aware of racial representation in their own centers. Applicants typically called attention to other tutors or leaders in their centers. For example, one respondent explained, "My boss is an Asian / Asian American, which is the first thing that immediately gave me comfort." Others simply said that they felt welcome because "other Latinx tutors [were] working" or because "people looked like me." Respondents didn't mention representation when asked about why they applied, which suggests that presence might signal whether a candidate *could* apply without becoming a motivator in its own right. Those who cited staff members as a sign of welcome typically recalled seeing tutors at work. References to recruitment materials, websites, or other performative contexts were limited. Perhaps surprisingly, no one mentioned visits to social groups dedicated to diversity. Instead, a small number recalled when current tutors were members of those groups (rather than strategic visitors). This gap suggests an awareness of how white-led organizations deploy tokenized diversity and use the markers of inclusion in the recruitment process. The spaces where existing diversity mattered was in the work itself; that's where potential applicants were more likely to see a snapshot of what their working lives might look like, rather than how it had been framed.

What of the gap between white applicants (57 percent) and applicants of color (5 percent) who either hadn't considered race in the application process until they took this survey or who believed the question wasn't relevant in their context? It's important to note that many white tutors were deeply aware of systemic racism. They knew about their own white privilege and, often in the same breath, spoke about how they wished their centers weren't so white. For example, one applicant explained that they hadn't considered race because "reverse racism does not exist," going on to say, "but I do wish we had more POC as consultants." Others echo this writer's awareness of white privilege while ending with a kind of apology. As one writer explained, "[the] vast majority of staff are white . . . unfortunately!" Their responses suggest that education about systemic racism will not, in and of itself, diversify a center. Knowing the ways that racism functions in each system and changing that system to decenter whiteness are at least two different steps.

These results also connect directly to the recruitment research outside of writing centers that suggests recruiters do not know what will be appealing, welcoming, or genuine for marginalized applicants. In fact, recruitment choices designed to welcome applicants of color actually welcomed diversity-minded white applicants (Avery et al. 2013). Center leaders who are engaged in cross-institutional conversations tend to care about representation and incorrectly assume that internal training about racism will transform recruitment on its own. These results should not diminish the value of teaching white tutors about systemic racism. However, these results suggest that racial awareness in tutor training will not transform the recruitment process without conscious, targeted effort. In other words, knowing the problem isn't enough.

PUTTING THE RESULTS TO WORK

Here I offer two frameworks for understanding these results in practice. First, I outline how our writing center used the results to shape recruitment. This section offers one possible model for how the results can move from cross-institutional data to site-specific practice. Second, I offer three generalized takeaways that may help centers in the application process. Both sections arise as much from existing anti-racist writing center scholarship as from the results of this specific study. This section uses the results as a lens through which to reinterpret existing conversations about race, recruitment, and programmatic change.

One Center Turns Data into Practice

In our center, the recruitment revision process broke down into four iterative steps. This is a process of change that continues as I write this chapter. I hope that when I reflect on this work in five or ten years, we will have gone much further than these early choices.

Internal Reflection

The process began as a conversation with our team of undergraduate Writing specialists and with our two-person leadership team. I invited our team to silently reflect on the reasons they had been motivated to join our writing center, introduced the study results, and then created spaces for the group to share their impressions. The reflection process began in a Google Doc, moved to small groups, and then finally came back for a full-group conversation (appendix 3.C). Although I didn't directly ask for their reasons (to maintain the study's anonymity), several participants expressed surprise that tutors with similar identities shared their motivations. For example, several queer specialists expressed a connection with "the desire to learn" as a motivation, while specialists of color related to an ambivalent or complicated relationship with academic writing. These conversations echoed those that we'd had about linguistic diversity and growth mindset in writing center work, but this was our first time connecting those conversations to the recruitment process.

We began our conversation in abstract terms and then shifted to talking about the ways those motivations manifested in recruitment images and rhetoric. Together, we reviewed example recruitment fliers from other centers and discussed how their rhetorical choices created an implied applicant community. In one example, the specialists drew attention to the call for applicants who "love to write" and want to "develop leadership skills." When combined with the dark color scheme and serious font, they identified the implied audience as confident, normative students and classroom leaders, who've mastered standardized academic English. Several felt that they wouldn't have felt welcome as applicants for that program, despite having been successful specialists for a year or more. They simply didn't feel that these writing center leaders had students like them in mind.

External-Facing Assessment

Analyzing how other centers presented their values provided a framework for doing the same work with our own materials. We analyzed our fliers, emails, and other advertising contexts for our own rhetorical choices, and then the results of the study provided context for how those choices may have resonated for the larger campus community.

For example, we found that up until very recently our advertisements had called for applicants who "love writing" and hadn't explicitly welcomed multiple languages or forms of English. Even in our most recent materials, engagement with linguistic diversity and anti-racist language practices was often indirect. We used coy terms to signal welcome rather than risking direct engagement with faculty, staff members, and other campus leaders who might oppose translanguaging or codemeshing in their classes. In an email to faculty from the spring 2020 recruitment process, for example, we welcomed applicants who had experience writing for "diverse audiences, contexts, and genres," but we never actually mentioned anti-racism. We likely hoped to clue in the engaged instructors without drawing ire, but that choice doesn't tell anti-racist applicants of color that we will have their back. Instead, it told applicants that our center would prioritize conflict avoidance over direct change.

Internal Assessment and Change

Before we implemented any changes, it was important that we audited our center's training practices to make sure our current recruitment language accurately reflected our center's culture and values. In our case, we found that our training and internal conversations about anti-Black linguistic racism was consistently more direct than our recruitment rhetoric would suggest. We had incorporated readings, activities, speakers, and research about codemeshing and linguistic diversity into every aspect of our training process, so we had to focus on making our external rhetoric as strong as our internal practice.

However, we discovered the reverse in relation to queer communities in our center. Our ads emphasized the "desire to learn" as a reason to apply, and the study suggested that choice would appeal to queer tutors. I also teach a course on Queer Literature, so LGBTQ+ applicants could reasonably expect to find a supportive work environment. The large percentage of our employees who identify as LGBTQ+ seems to support that finding, but we found a demonstrable lack of internal engagement with queer theory in training. Therefore, the mismatch between internal and external rhetoric needed to be addressed before we could continue using that recruitment language. In response to this gap, we chose to add in two workshops about queer theory in writing center work: one focused on specialist research and the other focused on an external scholar. We also made sure that half of the speakers in our series for that fall were practitioners and researchers whose work intersects with queer theory. We also made note of the fact that queer-focused work had been allowed to lapse, so we wouldn't find ourselves once again relying on veteran specialists or institutional memory.

External Change

Once we had completed the first round of internal reflection, external assessment, and internal change, we focused on implementing changes in our public-facing rhetoric. The specialists agreed that they wanted to maintain the following priorities:

1. Welcome those who are excited to learn
2. Invite applicants with a complicated or fraught relationship with academic writing
3. Make our commitments to anti-racism and linguistic diversity more explicit

We used these priorities to guide our revisions to student and faculty emails about recruitment, which featured a direct call for "multilingual specialists and students who write in multiple forms of English" and for applicants with a "desire to learn about anti-racist and accessible student support." It also specifically invited applicants who felt more confident encouraging other writers than they did in their own drafts. We hoped that call would inspire applicants who enjoyed playing with language but who hadn't been treated as exemplars of white mainstream English. For more text from the email, see appendix 3.C. Finally, we used our email text to guide fliers, presentations, and social media posts.

GENERALIZING THE DATA

Once we began making changes to the public face of the recruitment process, we could also start thinking about the larger takeaways that could inform future iterations of the revision process. The following section outlines three of those lessons that may help other centers (and our future leaders) find their own revision paths.

Disrupt Your Lore

Before engaging with your full community in any decision process, take the time to reflect on the lore you and other leaders in your context have internalized about equitable recruitment. Even more than the statistically significant correlations in the study, it's important to note which correlations didn't emerge. Before I saw the results of the study, I would have bet that pay rates and ease of access to campus employment would emerge as reasons why historically marginalized students applied to work in writing centers. I also expected respondents to talk about recruitment visits to identity-based campus organizations or the results of careful training. In a conference presentation, I even offered a bet about what my study would find:

> Writing Center lore suggests that directors . . . should focus on a combination of practice and direct outreach. For example, a tutor's sensitive handling of my paper about representation in YA literature combined with recruitment outreach to a Queer Student Union might suggest to me, as a bisexual writer, that I'll be welcome as a potential tutor. That seems like reasonable advice, and I doubt my study will overturn the basics of that recommendation.

To a large extent, I lost that bet.

The treatment of marginalized student visitors did matter to potential applicants. Interest group presentations, on the other hand, didn't show up at all. A small number of respondents mentioned clubs and organizations but only to note that current writing center employees were also active members. No one mentioned being persuaded by a recruitment visit to a multicultural student club or a Black student union.

In retrospect, my expectations had been set by years of casual conversations with mostly white colleagues at conferences, meetings, and panels. Time and again, leaders responded to calls for center diversity with their "outreach plans" and with campaigns to raise student worker wages. The data suggest that these options are still worthwhile; after all, everyone appreciates fair wages and knowing when their centers are hiring. They also suggest that these moves are not uniquely valuable for historically marginalized applicants. Most of all, they call for collective reflection. Why did our majority-white community of leaders assume those correlations? Why did we assume they were so obvious as to not require evidence?

Be Honest about Your Audience(s)

Evaluate existing recruitment content for its primary audience and purpose. All advertisements will serve multiple campus stakeholders. A single ad may speak to potential tutors, but it may also perform a writing center's identity for faculty members, staff members, and administrative staff members who make choices about that center's future. It's important for any program to be aware of their specific audiences, the messaging that their centers have chosen, and how those messages have been prioritized thus far. I want to emphasize the choice inherent in all three of those recruitment variables because so many directors regard their current audiences, messages, and priorities as institutionally mandated facts. In other words, we often treat the campus audiences we address as existing obstacles rather than as rhetorical choices.

For example, when I joined NSC, I assumed that my recruitment ads needed to speak to faculty members who might be nervous about recommending our services. More experienced leaders elsewhere implied that recruitment materials had to show that our staff would be qualified to serve the entire campus. However, my choice to draw on the language of prestige probably alienated students who weren't already treated as writing experts or classroom leaders. In fact, when I showed my current tutors one of those previous advertisements that focused on expertise, they were visibly uncomfortable. If we had used those kinds of recruitment materials, one explained, they wouldn't have applied.

Being honest about recruitment means acknowledging our choices and recognizing the impact of shifting rhetorical priorities. Changes can jeopardize existing campus relationships and sources of financial support. In some cases, they can jeopardize a leader's employment or a center's ongoing existence. Some instructors might not recommend our services because they no longer recognize our expertise. The risks are real, but to make anti-racist choices, we have to honestly acknowledge the choices we're making right now. Too often we tell ourselves that we've been forced to do harm, and don't address the ways we've chosen to cause harm rather than face it ourselves.

Don't Get Ahead of Yourself

It's tempting to skip directly from recognition of gaps to revising recruitment materials. However, I hope this research won't be used as a quick fix. After all, students are smart. They know empty rhetoric when they see it, and if every other part of a center is still driven by unchanged motivations, they will know exactly what's up. More important, students who apply because they see themselves and their motivations in this new advertisement might find themselves in a center that isn't really driven by those shared goals. Instead, they may find themselves isolated in a sea of tutors who are doing the work for very different reasons.

Changing recruitment materials without addressing the culture that created those original choices curbs retention and, more significant, leads to further harm. When centers hire marginalized tutors without doing the work to create anti-racist spaces and structures, tutors are merely made complicit in racist labor (García 2017; Camarillo 2019). Hiring practices in a vacuum won't prevent isolation, hostility, or fear of misperception, nor will they ensure that tutors feel comfortable translanguaging or codemeshing in professional spaces (Abdullah-Matta 2019; Haltiwanger Morrison 2019; Sévère 2019). In the absence of explicit, ongoing anti-racist work, writing center leaders must assume the presence of white supremacy in their team's experience because even the most proactive centers exist within larger academic structures that are designed for white success.

This isn't to say that recruitment labor should be dismissed as futile in the face of racial injustice. Instead, I hope it inspires majoritized leaders to aim for both ambition and care. I hope they see just, evidence-based recruitment as one part of an ambitious anti-racist project and resist the urge to present anti-racist recruitment as a self-contained goal. The most actively inclusive recruitment process is ultimately pointless if the center in question isn't doing the work to complicate how white tutors think about writing and create more opportunities for students of color to love their words.

APPENDIX 3.A

Reason coding for application motivation in stage 1 analysis:

100-HELP—These applicants applied because they wanted to help others with a specific skill or within a specific context:

Write—1
Learn—2
Improve—3
feel like they belong—4
think differently about writing—5
They helped me—6

200-CARE/LOVE—These applicants applied because they care about, love, or enjoy a specific aspect of writing center work:

Writing—7
Tutoring—8

300-GOOD AT/Skill/I could do X well: These applicants applied because they perceived themselves as being skilled in a specific aspect of writing center work:

Writing—9
Tutoring—10
the job—11

400-LEARN—These applicants applied because they wanted to learn about or gain skills in a specific aspect of writing center work:

Writing—12
Tutoring—13
Teaching—14

500-APPLY—These applicants applied because they explicitly wanted to use their writing center experiences to gain other employment after college:

apply my degree—15
For my cv/resume—16

600-COMMUNITY—These applicants applied because of feelings about the center as a community or because of an existing connection with current student workers:

Love the center community—17
wanted a community—18
Encouraged by others to apply (current employee or other peer)—19

700-RECOMMENDATION—HELP—These applicants applied because they were encouraged by a specific person who saw their potential:

Professor/teacher/Director recommendation—20
Peer recommendation—21

800-JOB—These applicants applied for reasons that were less specific to the work, including the pay, the location, the convenience, or the timing when they needed employment:

Money—22
needed a job—23
Convenient jobs—24
on-campus job—25

900-OTHER—These applicants applied for reasons that didn't fit within the other existing themes:

Wanted to improve the center—26
Writing center presentation or other advertisement—27

Reason coding for sense of welcome in second stage analysis:

Representation: These students felt welcome because they saw others with a similar racial or ethnic background doing writing center work.

Language: These students felt welcome because of some aspect of how language was used or represented in the center.

General acceptance: These students felt welcome because of their overall sense of invitation and openness in the center.

Policies: These students felt welcome because of some aspect of center policies.

Never considered it: These students felt welcome because they never considered the possibility that they wouldn't be seen as a valid applicant.

Never had to consider it (only for white applicants): These students felt welcome because they never considered that their whiteness wouldn't be seen as valid.

APPENDIX 3.B

Survey questions and response options

1. How long have you worked in a writing center?

   a. 5+ years
   b. 4 years
   c. 3 years
   d. 2 years
   e. 1 year
   f. less than 1 year

2. Roughly how many undergraduate employees currently work in your writing center?

   a. 100+
   b. 75–99
   c. 50–74

d. 25–49
e. 10–24
f. 0–9

3. How would you describe the environment where your college or university is located?
   a. Rural
   b. Urban
   c. Suburban
   d. Other
4. How does your community tend to travel to campus?
   a. Most commute to campus
   b. Most live on (or very close to) campus
   c. Equally divided between commuters and on-campus students
   d. Other
5. What do you recall as the most important reasons why you applied to be a writing center employee?

The next section will feature questions about five specific identity categories. You will see the questions in a random order. You may or may not have previously considered how these identities relate to writing center work. Please answer to the best of your ability.

1. Do you identify with a racial identity that is politically or culturally marginalized?
   a. Yes
   b. No
   c. Not sure
2. How would you define that racial identity?
3. Before you were hired, did anything about the Writing Center, the Writing Center culture, or the recruitment process suggest that your racial identity would be welcome in an employee?
   a. Yes
   b. No
   c. Not sure
4. If you answered "yes" or "not sure," what you do recall? If you answered "no," why did you still choose to apply?

These questions repeat, in randomized order, with the same questions as they relate to sexuality and gender, disability, multilingual background, and first-generation experience.

1. Do you identify with a marginalized background that has not yet been mentioned in this study? That might include documentation status, religion, age, or the experience of economic instability.
    a. Yes
    b. No
    c. Not sure
2. If you answered "yes" or "not sure," how do you identify? [space for written response]
3. Before you were hired, did anything about the Writing Center, the Writing Center culture, or the recruitment process suggest that these identities would be welcome in an employee?
    a. Yes
    b. No
    c. Not sure
4. If you answered "yes" or "not sure," what you do recall? If you answered "no," why did you still choose to apply?
5. Are there any identities that should have been included in this survey? Why?
6. Are there any identities that shouldn't have been included in this survey? Why?
7. Is there anything else we should know about how your writing center made you feel welcome (or unwelcome) as a possible employee?

APPENDIX 3.C

Reflection questions for group discussion

1. Why do you think someone would want to work in a writing center?
2. What might make someone feel welcome applying to work in our writing center?
3. Where do you see connections between the study and our campus?
4. The study demonstrated a link between motivations, a sense of welcome, and historically minoritized communities. Based on our ads, who likely feels welcome applying to work in our center? Why?
5. Who might feel less welcome applying to work in our center? Why?
6. Why do you hope someone would want to work in our writing center? What motivations would you like to see?
7. What could we do in our training, praxis, and culture to emphasize those motivations?
8. What could we do in our new recruitment materials to emphasize those motivations?

Text from recruitment email to faculty, staff, and students

We hire students from any major. We also hire multilingual specialists and students who write in multiple forms of English. Most of all, you don't have to see yourself as a perfect writer. In fact, our strongest specialists are often more confident supporting others than they are navigating their own drafts. We provide extensive training and mentorship, so you just need to be excited to learn.

Here are a few more qualities we value in potential tutors:

- Enthusiasm for helping writers (and colleagues) succeed
- Experience writing for different audiences, contexts, and genres
- Willingness to collaborate and seek solutions to difficult problems
- Empathy for the difficult work of academic writing
- Desire to learn about anti-racist and accessible student support

REFERENCES

Abdullah-Matta, Allia. 2019. "Bodies in Space: His, Hers, and My Race." In *Out in the Center: Public Controversies and Private Struggles*, edited by Harry Denny, Robert Mundy, Liliana M. Naydan, Richard Sévère, and Anna Sicari, 51–65. Louisville: University Press of Colorado.

Avery, Derek R., Sabrina D. Volpone, Robert W. Stewart, Aleksandra Luksyte, Morela Hernandez, Patrick F. McKay, and Michelle R. Hebl. 2013. "Examining the Draw of Diversity: How Diversity Climate Perceptions Affect Job-Pursuit Intentions." *Human Resource Management* 52, no. 2: 175–194.

Baker-Bell, April. 2020. *Linguistic Justice: Black Language, Literacy, Identity, and Pedagogy.* Abingdon, UK: Routledge.

Breaugh, James A., Therese H. Macan, and Dana M. Grambow. 2008. "Employee Recruitment: Current Knowledge and Directions for Future Research." In *International Review of Industrial and Organizational Psychology*, edited by Gerald P. Hodgkinson and J. Kevin Ford 23:45–82. https://doi.org/10.1002/9780470773277.ch2.

Camarillo, Eric C. 2019. "Dismantling Neutrality: Cultivating Antiracist Writing Center Ecologies." *Praxis: A Writing Center Journal* 16, no. 2. https://doi.org/10.26153/tsw/2673.

Casper, Wendy J., Julie H. Wayne, and Jennifer G. Manigold. 2013. "Who Will We Recruit? Targeting Deep and Surface Level Diversity with Human Resource Policy Advertising." *Human Resource Management* 52, no. 3: 311–332.

Condon, Frankie, Neisha-Anne Green, and Wonderful Faison. 2019. "Writing Center Research and Critical Race Theory." In *Theories and Methods of Writing Center Studies: A Practical Guide*, edited by Jo Mackiewicz and Rebecca Day Babcock, 30–39. Abingdon, UK: Routledge.

Driscoll, Dana Lynn, and Sherry Wynn Perdue. 2012. "Theory, Lore, and More: An Analysis of RAD Research in *The Writing Center Journal*, 1980–2009." *Writing Center Journal* 32, no. 2: 11–39. http://www.jstor.org/stable/43442391.

García, Romeo. 2017. "Unmaking Gringo-Centers." *Writing Center Journal* 36, no. 1: 29–60. https://www.jstor.org/stable/44252637.

Goldberg, Caren B., and David G. Allen. 2008. "Black and White and Read All Over: Race Differences in Reactions to Recruitment Websites." *Human Resource Management* 47, no. 2: 217–236. https://doi.org/10.1002/hrm.20209.

Green, Neisha-Anne. 2016. "The Re-education of Neisha-Anne S Green: A Close Look at the Damaging Effects of 'a Standard Approach,' the Benefits of Code-Meshing, and the Role Allies Play in this Work." *Praxis: A Writing Center Journal* 14, no. 1. http://www.praxisuwc.com/green-141.

Green, Neisha-Anne. 2018. "Moving beyond Alright." *Writing Center Journal* 37, no. 1: 15–34. https://www.jstor.org/stable/e26537358.

Haltiwanger Morrison, Talisha. 2019. "Being Seen and Not Seen: A Black Female Body in the Writing Center." In *Out in the Center: Public Controversies and Private Struggles*, edited by Harry Denny, Robert Mundy, Liliana M. Naydan, Richard Sévère, and Anna Sicari, 21–27. Louisville: University Press of Colorado.

Kilborn, Judith. 1995. "Cultural Diversity in the Writing Center: Defining Ourselves and Our Challenges." *Writing Lab Newsletter* 19, no. 1: 7–10.

Martinez, Aja. 2016. "Alejandra Writes a Book: A Critical Race Counterstory about Writing, Identity, and Being Chicanx in the Academy." *Praxis: A Writing Center Journal* 14, no. 1. http://www.praxisuwc.com/martinez-141.

Ndobo, André, Alice Faure, Jeanne Boisselier, and Stella Giannaki. 2018. "The Ethno-racial Segmentation Jobs: The Impacts of the Occupational Stereotypes on Hiring Decisions." *Journal of Social Psychology* 158, no. 6: 663–679. https://doi.org/10.1080/00224545.2017.1389685.

Reskin, Barbara F., Debra B. McBrier, and Julie A. Kmec. 1999. "The Determinants and Consequences of Workplace Sex and Race Composition." *Annual Review of Sociology* 25: 335–361. https://doi.org/10.1146/annurev.soc.25.1.335.

Sévère, Richard. 2019. "Black Male Bodies in the Center." In *Out in the Center: Public Controversies and Private Struggles*, edited by Harry Denny, Robert Mundy, Liliana M. Naydan, Richard Sévère, and Anna Sicari, 43–50. Louisville: University Press of Colorado.

Simpkins, Neil, and Virginia Schwarz. 2015. "Queering RAD Research in Writing Center Studies." *Another Word—from the Writing Center at the University of Wisconsin Madison* (blog). November 9. https://dept.writing.wisc.edu/blog/queering-rad-research-in-writing-center-studies/.

Valentine, Kathryn, and Mónica F. Torres. 2011. "Diversity as Topography: The Benefits and Challenges of Cross Racial Interaction in the Writing Center." In *Writing Centers and the New Racism: A Call for Sustainable Dialogue and Change*, edited by Laura Greenfield and Karen Rowan, 192–210. Denver: University Press of Colorado. https://doi.org/10.2307/j.ctt4cgk6s.

Watson, Stevie, Osei Appiah, and Corliss G. Thornton. 2011. "The Effect of Name on Pre-interview Impressions and Occupational Stereotypes: The Case of Black Sales Job Applicants." *Journal of Applied Social Psychology* 41, no. 10: 2405–2420.

4

TOWARD ANTI-RACIST WRITING CENTER HIRING AND RETENTION PRACTICES

Jamie P. Bondar, Kristina Aikens, and Devon Deery

While much important research has been done in the writing center (WC) community on linguistic racism, anti-racist tutoring pedagogy, and bias in tutoring practices, little work has been done on anti-racist WC administrative practices that address issues *outside of the tutoring session.* This chapter intends to address this gap, specifically focusing on anti-racist WC hiring and retention practices.

The writers of this chapter are white, and as such see ourselves as answering Robin DiAngelo's (2018) call for white people to talk to other white people about the myriad ways they may knowingly or unknowingly participate in racist systems and practices. In various ways, we have been interrogating the administrative practices of our centers to examine how they may be complicit in white supremacist ideology. We do not presume to instruct people of color about racism when they experience it every day in many tangible ways. Instead, this chapter will call for other white WC directors to use their institutional power, which is all too often used to marginalize BIPOC, to dismantle practices of subtle racial oppression, and to avoid being the "whiting center" (Weaver 2006; Garcia 2017). The three of us work at different historically white colleges or universities (HWCUs)[1] in the New England area, Jamie and Kristina at midsized, private universities and Devon at a small, private Catholic college. While all our institutions are HWCUs, their differences allow us to address variations in how we have analyzed and changed our policies.

In this chapter, we will analyze administrative policies and practices that have been influenced by what Joe Feagin (2013) calls the "white racial frame," which obscures from view or naturalizes practices that

1. We follow Bonilla-Silva's (2012) critique of labeling historically black colleges and universities (HBCUs) as such, while thinking of HWCUs as simply just (default) colleges and universities.

https://doi.org/10.7330/9781646424573.c004

enact oppression of people of color. As white WC directors, we must interrogate the ways our white racial frame, which perpetuates ideologies of meritocracy and individualism (DiAngelo 2018), shapes our WC administrative practices—both what we see and what we do not see. Since the three of us work at HWCUs, if we simply replicate our traditional processes, we will likely replicate inequitable, white-centered practices (Posselt et al. 2020). In fact, racial hegemony depends on well-intentioned, uninterrogated complicity (Bonilla-Silva 2012).

Given that uncritical repetition of inherited practices results in complicit reproduction of white-centered power structures, we echo Özlem Sensoy and Robin DiAngelo's (2017) argument that "interrupting status quo procedures is a critical entry point for challenging the reproduction of inequity" (564). Further, we affirm Ibram X. Kendi's (2019) indictment of using our own view of ourselves as "not racist" as a safety blanket of protection against racist actions. Too often we use our view of ourselves as "not racist" to preclude anti-racist interrogation of our practices, but in doing so, we necessarily miss seeing our own complicity in racist systems. As Sensoy and DiAngelo (2017) suggest, the three of us have begun to interrogate the ways in which we are complicit in practices that reproduce a white-centered existing order.

In this chapter we will examine the evolution of our practices of tutor recruitment, hiring, and retention in an effort to provide both theoretical frameworks and practical examples of how we have changed our procedures to emphasize collaboration, nonhierarchical structures, and linguistic and racial diversity over "white frame values" such as meritocracy, hierarchy, individualism, supposed objectivity, homogeneity, and even efficiency.

Since the workflow of managing our WCs coincides with academic-year calendars, we structure our thinking about hiring and retention practices according to a semi-temporal breakdown of the major stages in the cycle of each academic year. Specifically, we have identified the following stages, which will also structure this chapter: tutor recruitment, hiring processes, training and evaluation, and retention—all occurring alongside regular review and reinterrogation of these processes through an anti-racist lens. We call this a "semi-temporal" breakdown because for us, recruitment and hiring occur at designated times of the year, while training, evaluation, and retention are ongoing. Further, while we created these categories to structure this chapter, we caution against thinking of each category in isolation because each category influences the others.

Since racism permeates all aspects of our society, anti-racist practice is always reiterative. As Kendi (2019) notes, "The only way to undo racism is to *consistently* identify and describe it—and then dismantle it" (9, emphasis ours). Thus, central to our argument is the notion that reinterrogating our hiring and retention practices is necessary for each academic-year cycle. This first requires explicit identification and codification of those practices, so they may be reevaluated through an anti-racist lens before each point in the cycle begins anew. Thus, we have found that much of our anti-racist work is "pre-work," the work we must do to set up the mechanisms to facilitate the anti-racist critique of our own processes.

RECRUITMENT

The three of us have discovered that it is critical not only to have representation among tutoring and administrative staff but also to recruit and select tutors through a transparently anti-racist process. While setting an anti-racist vision is a critical component of creating an inclusive writing center environment, which is important for anti-racist recruitment, Asao Inoue (2016), Frankie Condon (2007), and others discuss the process of writing anti-racist mission statements, so this chapter will not focus on them. Instead, we will focus here on the need to ensure that the tutors hired embody anti-racist attitudes and approaches that will create an inclusive culture where tutors and students from all backgrounds and experiences can learn and grow. To recruit and hire a tutoring staff that is both racially diverse and willing to uphold the anti-racist mission of our WCs, we are in various stages of doing the following: crafting job descriptions and application materials that reflect the anti-racist aspects of our missions, conveying those values when marketing positions, examining and expanding modes of outreach, and identifying and addressing potential barriers to applications.

One of the greatest of those barriers is what Isabel Wilkerson (2020) calls "occupational hierarchy"—the racist presupposition that some groups of people are naturally better suited for certain types of jobs than others. Racist presuppositions stemming from occupational hierarchy can affect the hiring decisions WCAs make, the nominations our faculty colleagues send us, and the campus roles that BIPOC students see as viable potential jobs. To encourage students of color to envision themselves working as writing tutors, they should literally see themselves in our WCs both as tutors and as tutees. Anti-racist hiring decisions from previous cycles create a positive feedback loop by encouraging more diverse applicant pools in future cycles.

Nominations and Advertising Positions

Many faculty simply nominate those students they see as the strongest writers in their courses, and if those faculty espouse racist notions of what constitutes good writing (i.e., adhering to the conventions of Dominant English, linear rhetorical style, lack of code meshing, etc.), then it's likely they will recommend white monolingual students. Because of this, we reduced the weight of faculty nominations and recommendations in the overall recruitment and hiring process, and we no longer view all faculty input equally.[2]

The three of us no longer require applicants to be nominated for the position. However, identifying anti-racist faculty allies and inviting nominations from them have assisted us in recruitment. If a faculty member consistently sends us the names of monolingual white students, then we already have some indication that this faculty member's notions of writing tutor qualifications may not align with our centers' anti-racist philosophies. By contrast, when we receive nominations of BIPOC or multilingual students, we know to pay special attention to the nominations coming from those faculty members in the future. We began setting up spreadsheets to record all faculty nominations, including demographic and linguistic information of the nominees. (We use only self-reported information from the students themselves, acquired from our universities' student information systems.)[3] After a few hiring cycles and with some spreadsheet magic, we expect to be able to see trends among faculty nominations. Due to the influence of occupational hierarchy, many students, especially those from marginalized groups, may not see themselves as potential writing tutors and benefit from the confidence boost that comes from a faculty nomination. When faculty nominate BIPOC students, we make the faculty aware of these obstacles and the importance of their nomination in helping applicants see themselves in a position of knowledge authority. We find that communicating this to faculty members leads them to nominate more BIPOC students in the future. Further, we invite nominations from campus partners such as identity-based centers, bridge programs, and other advisors of students from underrepresented groups. Current tutors are often

2. We use the term "nomination" to refer to the process in which faculty suggest students they believe would make good writing tutors. We use "recommendation" to refer to the more formal written faculty endorsement included in the candidate's application.
3. While we're focusing here on racial demographics, we also recommend tracking other self-reported aspects of nominees' identities such as gender, first generation status, etc.

excellent nominators, as they know firsthand our anti-racist approach in the center.

Finally, nominations should not be the only form of advertising the position. We (and our tutors) have historically visited student organizations and programs that serve BIPOC students to announce positions and clarify our stance on linguistic justice. However, in response to Rachel Herzl-Betz's research in chapter 3 in this volume, which found that such visits were not a motivating factor for BIPOC students to apply for writing tutor positions, we plan to shift more toward asking tutors who are already part of these groups to notify their peers of WC opportunities, which Herzl-Betz suggests had some impact on her survey respondents. Ultimately, we want to cast as wide a net as possible by posting the job on campus student employment websites such as Handshake and through work-study listings, which increases access and raises our profiles as campus employers.

Job Descriptions

Psychologists Danielle Gaucher, Justin Friesen, and Aaron C. Kay (2011) have shown that gender bias in job advertisements discourages female applicants from applying to certain jobs. While they remind us to watch out for implicit bias in the words we *include* in our job descriptions or job posts, Sensoy and DiAngelo (2017) draw our attention to the implications of what we *exclude*, and how that might indicate adherence to a status quo (563). If we do not reference our anti-racist and linguistically inclusive approach to writing consultation, potential applicants will justifiably assume we have a status quo approach to writing like so many other departments on campus—privileging Dominant (i.e., white) English and Eurocentric rhetorical traditions. Thus, we have reviewed our job descriptions not only to attempt to eliminate subtle racist coding,[4] but also to look for omissions that could allow the job description to be read as tacitly supporting an oppressive status quo.

Therefore, we state explicitly whom we seek as applicants and why, as well as clearly stating our anti-racist values in job descriptions. For example, the job description for Kristina's WC now states: "We strongly encourage applications from students who identify as Black, Indigenous, Latinx, Asian, multiracial, or POC, as well as from students who are bilingual/multilingual or who identify as a person with a disability." This same job description also states—"Our approach is informed by feminist and anti-racist pedagogies, and our community values diversity in all forms, especially when related to identities such as race, gender,

4. For equity-minded versus "deficit" language, see Liera and Ching (2020, 124).

disability, nationality, and language that have historically been marginalized by language-based oppressions"—and includes as one of the job requirements that applicants must "be willing to learn more about and commit to an anti-racist praxis." This way, the job application simultaneously promotes an anti-racist vision of the WC, connects recruitment of BIPOC students to the history of linguistic injustice we seek to address, and sets clear expectations that future tutors must learn about and uphold anti-racist approaches.

HIRING PROCEDURES

Application Materials

The application itself must convey the values promised in initial outreach efforts. While each of our applications differ in some aspects, the three of us have started carefully reconsidering each component of the application itself. We will address some of the most common WC application materials in order to interrogate general assumptions while leaving open possibilities for new approaches.

Writing samples have commonly been used to evaluate students' strengths in crafting an argument and knowledge of citation styles, as well as their adherence to Dominant English conventions. Now, the three of us use the sample more broadly to get a sense of the student as an engaged writer. Rather than evaluating an applicant's ability to follow dominant conventions of writing and grammar, we are trying to learn more about the candidate, to see what they consider to be their best writing. We find it illuminating to ask applicants to contextualize their choice, their process in writing it, and what they revised or would change with more time, to prompt reflection on process, revision, and growth. Students might display their levels of information literacy, ability to critically engage with dominant ideologies, or commitment to anti-racist ideals in their choice of writing sample. We are wary of applicants whose writing sample uncritically presents oppressive ideologies or uses biased language. Mainly, we are looking for students who are effective communicators in academic discourse, but our interpretation of effective communication has evolved far beyond qualifying a thesis statement and building an argument. The writing sample provides a better understanding of not only who the potential tutor is as a writer but who they are as a person, and even how well they might uphold our anti-racist approaches.

In addition to, or perhaps even instead of, an academic essay, we give students the option of submitting a text of any genre or medium that demonstrates rhetorical skill. Kristina's center asks for an extended analogy comparing a writing tutor to anything else of their choice, to get a sense of their creativity, humor, and sense of the role. In an effort to address Vershawn Ashanti Young's (2021) call to place more emphasis on orality, Jamie's center has invited students to answer application questions in videos or audio recordings. At Jamie and Devon's centers, the initial application includes reflective questions asking students why they want to be writing tutors, what they struggled with while adjusting to college, and when they learned from a challenge. With these questions, potential tutors consider their background and motivations separately from grades and praise from professors.

Like writing samples, the cumulative GPA requirement has long been a standard piece of the application. We assumed that a minimum 3.0 GPA demonstrates the student has maintained good academic standing and can, therefore, manage their own academic workload in addition to their tutoring. However, the three of us have begun viewing the cumulative GPA as a potential barrier, particularly for students who may have started college with fewer resources than their privileged peers, have family or personal demands, or who have experienced bias. Therefore, rather than requiring a baseline GPA, we focus mainly on whether the applicant is in good standing as determined by the university (a bar that determines whether they can remain enrolled) and look for evidence of overcoming academic adversity, such as comments in our application questions or upward-moving trends on transcripts. The three of us are also considering inviting students to comment on their transcripts as part of the application process.

Finally, we have each reconsidered the role faculty recommendations play in an applicant's portfolio. While we value the perspectives faculty can offer on how students interact with others in class or during peer review sessions, faculty letters often reveal misunderstandings about our mission or the role of writing tutors. To remedy this, Jamie and Kristina created simple forms requesting the specific information we seek rather than having recommenders submit freeform letters. This practice helps us communicate the characteristics we value in potential writing tutors and solicit faculty feedback only in those areas—which is also less arduous than writing a formal recommendation.

Interviewing

Unconscious bias is most likely to intrude during the interview stage of the hiring process. Therefore, we took concrete steps to control for our own unconscious and institutional racism in interviewing contexts. Many employers rely on a "gut reaction" interview style and decision-making process in which they assume they will intuitively know which candidates are suitable for the role. However, the three of us realized we cannot trust our gut reactions because our guts have been trained by a racist society (DiAngelo 2018). Thus, we replaced the arrogant assumption that we will "just know" whom to hire with a humility-based, explicit process that attempts to control for our own assumptions.

For example, Jamie's center has standardized its interview questions. In its former "gut reaction" interview style, Jamie's center used long lists of interview questions from which interviewers would select questions as they seemed to fit the flow of the interview. Thus, each interview contained its own hodgepodge combination of questions, so interviewers could not guarantee candidates would have an equal opportunity to answer each question. Jamie realized this approach was highly susceptible to bias and racism. What determined which questions would be asked of which candidates? Were interviewers asking tougher questions of candidates who did not appear to fit the racist conception of a "traditional" writing tutor? Were interviewers asking fewer questions of some candidates and letting them speak at greater length than others? Jamie realized he had to standardize interview questions and ask the same questions of every candidate to ensure that socially conditioned racism could not influence the impromptu selection. Further, standardizing interview questions allows us to reinterrogate them in each cycle. If we don't know what specific questions we will ask in any given interview, how could we review those questions through an anti-racist lens? A compiled list of interview questions from our own hiring processes is located in appendix A of this chapter.

The three of us have also reinterrogated how we react to candidate interviews through an anti-racist lens. For example, Sensoy and DiAngelo (2017) note that "friendly" personal mannerisms are often simply white cultural norms. They argue that because the mannerisms of white candidates more accurately match the (white) cultural expectation of white interviewers, they will seem to be a better fit than candidates who do not manifest them. When interviewers record their responses to interviews, Sensoy and DiAngelo advise recording descriptive observations ("He didn't smile") rather than evaluative observations ("He's not a team player"). We can interrogate our reactions to descriptive observations ("Why am I reacting negatively to the fact that he didn't smile?"), whereas interrogating an evaluative observation simply leads to presumptive speculation. When reviewing interview notes days or weeks after the fact, would any of us be able to accurately recall what observations led us to think the candidate is not a team player?

Another way to reduce individual bias in the interview process is to involve multiple interviewers, especially by developing a diverse interview team. Involving tutors in the interview process is also an effective way to control for interview bias. That said, before the interviews begin, the three of us made a stronger effort to ensure that all interviewers understand and agree to the WC's anti-racist goals and values, including linguistic justice and recruiting a diverse group of tutors. We explicitly train interviewers on avoiding bias in the process and on recording observations using the methods just discussed.

Of course, even with formalized interview questions that have been interrogated through an anti-racist lens, we still could find ourselves making decisions based on a gut reaction, which is closely aligned with what critics of higher education hiring processes call "fit." Damani K. White-Lewis (2020) suggests that "fit" is a "covert channel of racial bias," which conceals the "idiosyncratic preferences" of decision makers (834). As one way to combat this idea of fit, White-Lewis recommends greater use of rubrics and standard criteria. He suggests that such standardization allows search committees to make explicit the applicant characteristics they value; further, creating and calibrating rubrics allow decision makers "to explicitly state and defend their own leanings, expose their biases" (852). Before beginning the interview process, our interview teams explicitly define what we are looking for in candidates and craft rubrics around those areas. We use survey software to build rubrics and record responses. White-Lewis (2020) and Sensoy and DiAngelo (2017) both suggest that departments evaluate how candidates would further their mission or equity goals, including commitments to social justice. Thus, since there are anti-racist planks in our mission statements, learning outcomes, and/or job descriptions, the three of us include criteria that evaluate the extent to which any given candidate aids in achieving our anti-racist goals.

TRAINING, EVALUATION, AND RETENTION

Creating an atmosphere that retains BIPOC tutors is an ongoing, iterative process involving different levels of administration. Fundamentally, the three of us want to create an environment that affirms the experiences and concerns of BIPOC tutors, recognizes how their experiences might be different from those of white students, centers those experiences, and encourages tutors to come forward with concerns without requiring them to expose themselves unfairly. Creating an anti-racist culture in the WC requires more than just trying to be a good person; it requires intentional words and actions as well as the willingness to learn and be corrected. Tutor education and training programs are crucial to creating such an environment, but due to the abundance of literature focusing on the topic, we will not focus extensively on it here; rather, we want to consider how the three of us have attempted to infuse anti-racist values and theories into everyday practices that affect employed tutors.

The three of us strive to consistently remind tutors of the roles they play in fighting oppression and resisting what Laura Greenfield (2019) identifies as liberal values that privilege alleged "neutrality" and "multiple truths" over moral and ethical decision-making (48). Greenfield warns against "simply facilitat[ing] the strengthening of whatever ideological agendas" students bring to a session (47). In a recent interview at Kristina's WC, a graduate student applicant asked: Are tutors expected to help a student write a stronger argument, no matter what the argument is? Kristina assured this applicant that, in fact, tutors in her center *are expected* to resist oppressive ideas.

The three of us strive to ensure that tutors know they will be supported, not criticized, for addressing oppressive language and ideas in student papers. This empowerment, however, requires different strategies and awareness; white and BIPOC tutors face very different challenges in terms of dealing with students who consciously or unconsciously present oppressive writing. On the one hand, white tutors need to understand and accept their responsibilities in addressing oppressive language. When white tutors fail to recognize bias or choose to avoid addressing it, they are protecting white solidarity (DiAngelo 2018). The discomfort they may feel in initiating such discussions are related to their lack of experience, so we provide them with examples and role-plays that allow them to practice their skills while instilling a sense of responsibility for taking up the burden of addressing oppressive language and ideas, especially when working with other white students. On the other hand, BIPOC tutors sometimes ask how to handle the emotional weight of regularly confronting racist ideas or biased language that attacks their identities. The three of us strive both publicly and in private conversations to make sure that BIPOC tutors know we trust them to decide when they need, for their own self-preservation, to remove themselves from a tutoring situation, even as we provide tools for conducting difficult conversations (Greenfield 2019, 49).

In contrast to white tutors' possible inexperience addressing bias, BIPOC tutors might feel exhausted by the constant demands on them, particularly at HWCUs, to explain critical race theories and the histories of oppressed populations. Further, white students might unfairly seek informal education from BIPOC tutors. For example, a Black tutor at Kristina's center once explained that over the years, she worked with what seemed like an unusually high number of white students writing papers about the history of slavery. She felt that these white students were purposely booking appointments with her as an "expert" based on her racial identity rather than her research interests. At the tutor's suggestion, Kristina replaced individual tutor photos on the website with a group photo and individual bios so that it would be harder for white students to exploit Black tutors in this way.

The three of us strive to create space in staff meetings for BIPOC tutors to describe microaggressions and explicit displays of racism from students and other tutors. Several years ago, in a staff meeting at Kristina's WC, a white tutor who was an international student mentioned that white American students often questioned her credentials or feedback because she spoke with a non-American accent. Another international tutor, who was from China, echoed this sentiment. Then, two female Black American tutors expressed that they both had their credentials questioned on a regular basis by white students. For a moment in the staff meeting, there was a pause. What is the right response to hearing about such experiences, when one is stricken with the knowledge that tutors will experience discrimination based on their identities from students they intended to support?

The first step the three of us now take when we hear these experiences is to validate them, swiftly and publicly, rather than worrying about the "right response" or, worse, reacting with disbelief or shock. Gaslighting, downplaying bad experiences, or explaining "good intentions" are common mistakes made by administrators when confronted with the experiences of BIPOC tutors. White fragility manifests itself when white people deny or downplay racist interactions, turn the blame around on the person who experienced racism, or act personally attacked (DiAngelo 2018). The three of us strive to suppress such impulses and instead respond with validation. After all, we know racism exists, so thinking racism would never occur in WC interactions is to believe in a fantasy of the WC as a safe space existing outside of real-world experiences.

Since the initial example we have described, Kristina's training includes informing tutors that BIPOC tutors are likely to experience such microaggressions during their sessions, which calls attention to the problem rather than pretending it doesn't exist. This opens the door for BIPOC tutors to express their concerns and for white tutors and administrators to address their own privilege and explore ways to support BIPOC tutors who experience such microaggressions. We also supply suggested scripts for tutors to use when their credentials are questioned. Our policies about student-tutor interactions specifically state that discrimination will not be tolerated. Devon's center instituted a tutor incident report form that allows tutors to report discriminatory incidents for immediate follow-up, and all three of us respond to private reports of discrimination by centering the experiences of BIPOC students. Responding individually to a pervasive systemic problem is not the only or best solution, but it is an initial, concrete action we can take as administrators to stop harmful behavior and help BIPOC tutors and students feel supported, thus promoting retention of BIPOC tutors.

Tutors might also hear information from BIPOC or multilingual students about being treated unfairly by their professors based on their identities. The three of us train tutors in what institutional processes exist—both in our WCs and in the university at large—for reporting bias, so they can assist students in reporting inappropriate behavior from professors. For less clear situations, such as assignments that put BIPOC students at a disadvantage, we clarify with tutors that we trust them to help students find ways to complete assignments while reducing harm to themselves, and that they can bring complaints to us as administrators who can find processes for providing feedback on assignments without putting students at risk.

The three of us actively seek ways to engage and retain BIPOC tutors through leadership roles, such as roles that involve tutor mentorship, program development, logistical organization, recruitment efforts, and other projects. Further, BIPOC students too often are ironically either ignored in diversity, equity, justice, and inclusion (DEJI) efforts or only provided DEJI-related leadership roles—often uncompensated. While we must recognize that they may already be committed elsewhere, BIPOC tutors should always be invited to participate in work that is explicitly focused on DEJI efforts; however, it is vital that they are compensated for their participation, that their recommendations are taken seriously and implemented, and that they are recruited for other opportunities. Diversity, equity, justice, and inclusion work is worthy of compensation, and so is encouraging BIPOC tutors to lead on their own terms and explore their personal interests.

The three of us also consider the environments we create through our physical spaces. Unspoken racial grammar can shape perceptions of our WCs as white simply because of their association with the broader institution and its often uninterrogated cues toward whiteness (Bonilla-Silva 2012). For example, dress codes, whether for tutors or for students, are notorious for attempting to control the bodies of Black students, Muslim students, women, and many other groups with non-western or non-white forms of dress; therefore, our three centers eschew dress codes or statements about "professional" dress or behavior, which reify patriarchal, white supremacist notions of conformity. Wonderful Faison and Anna Treviño (2017) observe that the very aesthetics of the WC can send messages about who "belongs" in the WC. We three are currently examining how we might be promoting western, raced, classed, or gendered ideologies through the use of furniture, appliances, images, and other physical elements in our physical WC. Although administrators are often expected to use objects we inherit rather than choose, we should instead make conscious substitutions and additions to create a physical space that avoids promoting negative messages simply out of a lack of intention.

We have also needed to consider what will happen if a member of our community violates our stated anti-racist principles—will there be consequences, discussion? How will we hold ourselves and each other accountable while also maintaining a welcoming, call-in culture? This means holding white tutors and administrators accountable for their actions and words if, as Faison and Treviño (2017) discuss, we overhear white tutors questioning the experiences or skills of BIPOC tutors or disparaging students who make WC appointments. If a BIPOC tutor reports such an incident, we must treat it the same way we would treat any report of biased language or behavior; in other words, it can't be about protecting white tutors or about "public relations" but rather a true commitment to creating an inclusive environment. This has led to some uncomfortable conversations, but the three of us commit to and engage in them just as we expect tutors to.

Finally, to close the cycle that structures this chapter, retention feeds back into the reinterrogation of all other policies. While we solicit feedback from all tutors on our staff, the feedback of BIPOC tutors is often the most informative in improving our anti-racist practices. After all, as Alexandria Lockett (2019), a former writing tutor who is Black and queer, notes, "the perspectives of racially marginalized tutors are overwhelmingly absent from WC scholarship" (2). The three of us try to provide multiple opportunities for honest conversations about which decisions and actions are, or are not, achieving our anti-racist goals. We employ written surveys and mandatory check-in meetings at regular intervals, requiring all tutors to reflect on their experiences and communicate problems to us. We believe that reflecting, checking in, and soliciting feedback individually and in groups, anonymously and publicly, promotes a positive environment, as long as concerns are addressed in a thoughtful and timely manner.

CONCLUSION

Writing this chapter has been a continuing act of anti-racist metacognition for us as we not only reflected on changes we have already made but also reinterrogated and revised our practices as we wrote. In doing so, we were enacting our argument while we were discovering it. In this process, we have learned from each other and discovered areas where further revision of our processes is still needed. Recognizing that anti-racist work is always ongoing, we see this chapter as a beginning to a much longer conversation, rather than a definitive guide on how to staff an anti-racist WC.

Admittedly, thinking about how we do our work in addition to actually doing it creates more work. We realize our suggestions will put further strain on already overworked WC administrators. Codifying administrating practices, interrogating them through an anti-racist lens, executing those practices, and then reevaluating them before doing it all over again is indeed hard work. However, resistance to these extra steps follows the logic of racism that Kendi (2019) outlines. He argues that it is not hatred or overt aggression but self-interest that creates unjust policies and the racist explanations that uphold those policies. While Kendi has government policies in mind, we can say the same for academic administrative processes. Often, the self-interest that creates an unjust policy in a university setting is the desire not to increase our own workload. (Hopefully) no WC administrator deliberately sets out to create racist policies; rather, we often create policies out of convenience or pragmatism and then justify those policies with (often unknowingly) racist explanations such as "BIPOC students just aren't interested in becoming writing tutors" or "Our GPA requirements are the same for all students regardless of race." As Rasha Diab et al. (2013) remind us, we must view anti-racist work not as "in addition to other responsibilities" but rather as "integral to all our responsibilities" (10). Instead of perpetuating inaction, we encourage readers to look for other areas of work that could be reduced to make time for anti-racist work. If doing so reveals resource gaps in our centers, perhaps senior leaders at our universities who outwardly champion diversity will find an opportunity to fund their stated priorities.

APPENDIX 4.A

The following is a categorized compilation of questions that we have used in writing tutor interviews. Feel free to use any of these questions in your own interviews if you find them useful. As per our argument in the chapter, whatever questions you use, we recommend that you have a concrete list of questions that interviewers will use in every interview—a list that you can then reinterrogate through an anti-racist lens before each hiring cycle. We are not claiming that these are the best anti-racist writing tutor interview questions; we are ourselves reinterrogating these questions on an ongoing basis.

Introductory Questions

- Tell us about yourself. What made you want to apply to be a writing tutor?
- What pronouns would you like us to use when referring to you?
- What skills do you hope to develop and/or what additional opportunities are you hoping to access through this role?
- What key skills have allowed you to be a successful student?

Leadership

- (SET UP) Leadership can take on many forms and many people have different leadership styles. (STATEMENT) Tell us about a time where you took on a leadership role either formally or informally.
- What experience have you had in a service role? (This could be in a customer service-oriented job, volunteer work, etc.)

Addressing Challenges

- Tell us about a time when you encountered an obstacle in your academic life—how did you work through this difficulty?
- What challenges might you face in meeting your time commitment to this role? How will you address these challenges?

Tutoring Demeanor

- What do you think are the qualities of a strong tutor?
- Talk a little bit about a situation when you needed to be adaptable.
- Talk a little bit about what it means to you to learn differently.

- Tell us about a time that you were trying to explain a topic or idea to someone else and they were having a hard time understanding. What did you do to help them learn?
- A student comes to a tutoring session and appears to be overwhelmed and frustrated. How might you start this session?
- (SET UP) We have a very diverse student body with students from around the world and students of many different ethnic and racial backgrounds who have many different home languages, and we want all of them to feel welcome in the writing center. (QUESTION) With this in mind, what does inclusion mean to you?
- We value diversity. Can you tell us, what does diversity mean to you?
- How would you define an inclusive environment? How would you contribute to creating one?
- How do you set boundaries/realistic expectations?

Writing-Specific Questions

- How would you go about working with students who are very self-conscious about writing/very low esteem?
- What do you consider "good writing"? In other words, what constitutes "good writing" to you?
- Why should a student see a writing tutor? Have you ever used writing tutoring here at the writing center or elsewhere? What was your experience?
- A student who self-identifies as multilingual says they are self-conscious about their grammar, and they want to focus on grammar in the session because they have been criticized by their professor about it before. As you begin to discuss the paper, you realize the argument of the paper could be stronger, or the student has missed an important aspect of the prompt. What would your priorities be for the session and how would you work with this student?
- A student is writing a research paper and brings in a draft with a lot of long block quotes for a discipline that prefers paraphrasing. When you ask about this, the student says, "the writer says it so much better than I ever could" and says they don't feel they can put it well in their own words. How might you help the student feel more confident about paraphrasing?
- A student brings in an advanced physics paper (or math/chem./bio paper, depending on the interviewee's major). You have no idea what the technical issues are in this paper, and you feel a little inadequate. What might you do?
- Please describe your process of doing research for an academic essay.

REFERENCES

Bonilla-Silva, Eduardo. 2012. "The Invisible Weight of Whiteness: The Racial Grammar of Everyday Life in Contemporary America." *Ethnic and Racial Studies* 35, no. 2: 173–194.

Condon, Frankie. 2007. "Beyond the Known: Writing Centers and the Work of Anti-racism." *Writing Center Journal* 27, no. 2: 19–38.

Diab, Rasha, Thomas Ferrel, Beth Godbey, and Neil Simpkins. 2013. "Making Commitments to Racial Justice Actionable." *Across the Disciplines: A Journal of Language, Learning and Academic Writing* 10, no. 3. https://doi.org/10.37514/ATD-J.2013.13.3.10.

DiAngelo, Robin. 2018. *White Fragility: Why It's So Hard for White People to Talk about Racism.* Boston: Beacon Press.

Faison, Wonderful, and Anna Treviño. 2017. "Race, Retention, Language, and Literacy: The Hidden Curriculum of the Writing Center." *Peer Review* 1, no 2. http://thepeer review-iwca.org/issues/braver-spaces/race-retention-language-and-literacy-the-hidden -curriculum-of-the-writing-center/.

Feagin, Joe. 2013. *The White Racial Frame: Centuries of Racial Framing and Counter-framing.* New York: Taylor and Francis Group.

Garcia, Romeo. 2017. "Unmaking Gringo-Centers." *Writing Center Journal* 36, no. 1:29–60.

Gaucher, Danielle, Justin Friesen, and Aaron C. Kay. 2011. "Evidence That Gendered Wording in Job Advertisements Exists and Sustains Gender Inequality." *Journal of Personality and Social Psychology* 101, no. 1: 109–128.

Greenfield, Laura. 2019. *Radical Writing Center Praxis: A Paradigm for Ethical Political Engagement.* Logan: Utah State University Press.

Inoue, Asao B. 2016. "Afterword: Narratives That Determine Writers and Social Justice Writing Center Work." *Praxis: A Writing Center Journal* 14, no 1: http://www.praxisuwc .com/inoue-141.

Kendi, Ibram X. 2019. *How to be an Antiracist.* New York: One World.

Liera, Roman, and Cheryl Ching. 2020. "Reconceptualizing 'Merit' and 'Fit': An Equity-Minded Approach to Hiring," In *Higher Education Administration for Social Justice and Equity: Critical Perspectives for Leadership,* edited by Adrianna Kezar and Julie Posselt, 111–131. New York: Taylor and Francis.

Lockett, Alexandria. 2019. "Why I Call it the Academic Ghetto: A Critical Examination of Race, Place, and Writing Centers." *Praxis: A Writing Center Journal* 16, no. 2: 20–33. http://www.praxisuwc.com/162-lockett.

Posselt, Julie, et al. 2020. "Evaluation and Decision Making in Higher Education." In *Higher Education: Handbook of Theory and Research,* edited by Laura W. Perna, 453–515. New York: Springer.

Sensoy, Özlem, and Robin DiAngelo. 2017. " 'We Are All for Diversity, but . . .': How Faculty Hiring Committees Reproduce Whiteness and Suggestions for How They Can Change." *Harvard Educational Review* 87, no. 4: 557–580.

Weaver, Margaret. 2006. "A Call for Racial Diversity in the Writing Center." In *The Writing Center Director's Resource Book,* edited by Christina Murphy and Byron Stay, 79–91. Mahwah, NJ: Lawrence Erlbaum Associates.

White-Lewis, Damani K. 2020. "The Facade of Fit in Faculty Search Processes." *Journal of Higher Education* 91, no. 6: 833—857.

Wilkerson, Isabel. 2020. *Caste: The Origins of Our Discontents.* New York: Random House.

Young, Vershawn Ashanti. 2021. " 'This Ain't Yesterday's Literacy: Teaching Reading, Writing, Speaking, and Listening Post-George Floyd." Keynote at "Racism in the Margins." University of Connecticut, online, February 26.

PART III

Tutor Education and Professional Development

5

BEYOND THE TUTOR TRAINING SEMINAR

A Womanist Approach to Ongoing Education for Racially Just Writing Tutoring

Zandra L. Jordan

National outcry over anti-Black violence erupted during the global COVID-19 pandemic. As the virus disproportionately ravaged communities of color, and as essential workers, also disproportionately Black and Brown, risked their lives to ensure that vital services remained open, the world learned about a new spate of heinous murders. Three white men hunted Ahmaud Arbery, a Black male jogger and aspiring electrician, and one fired the fatal shot that took his life. White plainclothes officers killed Breonna Taylor, a Black female emergency medical technician, when they burst into her home under cover of night and shot her eight times. A white officer asphyxiated George Floyd, a Black father of five, by kneeling on his neck and ignoring his pleas to breathe. These instances of anti-Black violence evoked painful recollections of the state-sanctioned police murders of Sandra Bland, Eric Garner, Atatiana Jefferson, Tamir Rice, and many others.[1]

With moratoriums on social gatherings, public entertainment, and travel, as well as frequent news cycles keeping us up to date on rising COVID death tolls, we could not look away. If we were not among the thousands of multiracial protesters marching through city streets and demanding justice, we were watching the televised coverage and becoming increasingly aware of the intersecting coronavirus and racial violence pandemics. Outrage mounted as anti-Black police violence continued alongside a surge in anti-Asian hate crimes incited by Trump's xenophobic rhetoric. A rash of violent and deadly public assaults, including the

1. While Blacks are killed by police at disproportionately higher rates than whites and other people of color (Foster-Frau 2021), anti-Brown police violence is also dire and should not be overlooked or "undercounted" (Chavez 2021). All BIPOC people are at significantly greater risk of fatal encounters with police than whites (Belli 2020).

https://doi.org/10.7330/9781646424573.c005

murder of six Asian women in Atlanta, made leaving home a frightening prospect for Asian, Asian American, and Pacific Islanders.

These events precipitated a critical moment for anti-racist pedagogy in the academy. Writing programs and academic departments have been curating resources, decolonizing syllabi, and developing or recommitting to anti-racism statements (e.g., wclistserv on "social justice statements"). Academic institutions, professional organizations, and scholarly journals have been featuring anti-racist praxis in their agendas (e.g., Towson University's 2021 Anti-racist Pedagogy Symposium, the 2021 Writing Program Administrators [WPA] Symposium on Black Lives Matter, and the *Peer Review* issue 4.2: "Researching and Restoring Justice"). Writing and language scholars continue to challenge white supremacy in their publications and professional affiliations (e.g., Inoue 2021; Baker-Bell 2020; Lockett et al. 2021) and are doing so at a time when the academy seems more inclined to listen. Colleges and universities have been hiring DEI officers and expressing commitment to programmatic changes impacting student education, like departmentalization of Stanford's African and African American Studies Program after fifty years of critical contributions to teaching, scholarship, and university culture.

But as COVID-19 comes under control, airplanes fill to capacity, businesses reopen, and in-person learning resumes, there is legitimate concern that the indignation and other motivations prompting renewed interest in anti-racism will wane, or diversity as an end goal will stymy systemic change (Ore, Wieser, and Cedillo 2021). These concerns grow in the wake of legislation banning Critical Race Theory (CRT) in K–12 education and conservative efforts to block Nikole Hannah-Jones, renowned Pulitzer Prize–winning journalist and progenitor of the groundbreaking 1619 Project, from receiving tenure.

Considering the potential for declining interest in, increasing distraction from, and continuing opposition to anti-racist work, this chapter asks, How can attention to anti-racism and commitments to racial justice extend beyond moments of national outcry? In the context of writing centers, what can administrators and tutors do to keep racial justice at the forefront of tutor education and praxis? Building upon the premise that tutor education should center anti-racist pedagogy (Greenfield and Rowan 2011; Aikens 2019; Jordan 2020), I argue that the training seminar is the foundation but not the endpoint for cultivating a tutoring staff equipped to engage race(ism).

Following a reflection on anti-racist praxis in Stanford's writing tutor seminar, I share examples of ongoing professional development designed to enrich tutors' racial literacy and critical awareness of their ability to promote racial justice through dialogic interplay with writers. These pedagogical offerings, including workshops and community events, not only encourage tutors to make anti-racism and racial justice a regular part of their everyday practice but also illustrate to the university community a more expansive narrative about what writing and speaking centers can and should do. We are not the place that protects English grammar from bastardization or that treats language in the academy and beyond as somehow unaffected by racism, sexism, xenophobia, and other social ills. Rather, we are a space where all writers and speakers learn how to communicate justly in an increasingly diverse world.

ANTI-RACIST WORLD-BUILDING THROUGH WRITING TUTOR EDUCATION: STANFORD'S REQUIRED SEMINAR

At Stanford, I have been working to recruit and train a diverse tutoring staff that embraces anti-racism and racial justice as foundational to their tutoring praxis. When writers engage with tutors from a variety of racial and linguistic backgrounds, we disrupt the commonplace narrative that writing tutors are white and people of color are deficient writers in need of their help. When tutors have a critical understanding of language bias and the hegemony that often disadvantages BIPOC students, they can develop an ethic for promoting racial justice and resisting linguistic oppression. In this sense, I resonate with the National Education Association's understanding that "racial justice—or racial equity—goes beyond 'anti-racism.' It is not just the absence of discrimination and inequities but also the presence of deliberate systems and supports to achieve and sustain racial equity through proactive and preventative measures" ("Racial Justice in Education Resource Guide" 2021, 2).

In the writing tutor seminar, which all undergraduate and graduate writing tutors take before they begin tutoring at the Hume Center for Writing and Speaking, I start introducing anti-racist praxis on day one. Becoming a Hume writing tutor, I tell them, requires more of you than knowledge of writing and writing instruction. Conversations about language, whether written or spoken, are inherently about identity, culture, and power. What counts as "good," "effective," and/or "academic" communication, and who makes those determinations, reflects the hegemonic ideologies and norms that have historically oppressed BIPOC and multilingual students. Those norms shape misperceptions of what writing centers do—correct "bad" grammar or, worse, fix bad writers. We have a different understanding of our shared mission, I exhort.

Through one-to-one dialogic exchanges, we contribute to the formation of a racially just campus and world (Jordan 2020).

As one can imagine, the new writing tutors are often both inspired and a bit overwhelmed by this kind of a writing center—one that recognizes how centers are implicated in "the institutional racism that shapes . . . higher education," as well as the agency that centers have to "actively resist injustices" (Greenfield and Rowan 2011, 124–125). Tutors may initially worry about their ability to intervene, since they are not yet "theorists of race and racism" (García 2017, 49). What can they do to disrupt racist standpoints during a tutorial or racist practices sustained by powerholders beyond the center's purview? While it is unrealistic to expect that we can eradicate prejudicial worldviews and systemic racism through a single tutor training or writing tutorial, there are things that we can do to advance a racially just future.

Womanist ethics, as I have written elsewhere (Jordan 2020, 2021), is the anti-racist framework guiding my approach to racially just tutor education and praxis. Deriving its epistemological grounding from Black women's experiential knowledge of interlocking oppression (i.e., racism, classism, and sexism), womanist ethics asserts the moral right of Black women to create worlds in which they can flourish. This world-building, as inspired by Alice Walker's (1983) poetic revolutionary paradigm (xi), reflected in Stacey Floyd-Thomas's (2006) distillation of womanist tenets (6), and embodied in Barbara Holmes's (2021) delineation of "Womanist Futures," can be captured in these three principles: reclamation of self through authentic and loving personhood, recovery of Black culture and its true nature through the (re)telling of Black experience, and redemption of Black futures through unabashed resistance of white supremacy.

While womanism centers Black women's epistemologies, its liberatory methods extend to all oppressed peoples. As the Combahee River Collective (1977) opined years before Walker coined the term "womanist," "If Black women were free, it would mean that everyone else would have to be free since our freedom would necessitate the destruction of all the systems of oppression." Therefore, womanist world-building principles can apply to all BIPOC and oppressed people and are beneficial for everyone regardless of their racial identity.

My womanist world-building ethic not only shapes my characterization of writing tutoring as anti-racist, racial justice work but also informs how I structure the training seminar. Tutors move through a series of carefully curated readings and scaffolded assignments to help them critically examine their preconceptions about language, identity, and writing tutoring. They learn that as a community of practice, we can commit to interrogating our own language attitudes, to unlearning "standard language ideology" (Lippi Green 2012) and the presumed superiority of "Standard English" (Greenfield 2011, 35), to increasing our knowledge of and appreciation for language diversity (Greenfield 2011; Martínez 2018), and to making conversations about race(ism) a normal part of what we do as writing tutors (Johnson 2011).

Promoting racial justice in one-to-one tutoring, they learn, can look like inviting writers to (1) critique their assumptions and the potential impact their rhetoric may have on others, (2) examine racist or problematic language use and patterns of reasoning, (3) consider readers' perspectives and counterclaims, and (4) continue learning about race and difference after the tutorial. To build up beleaguered writers who have experienced language bias and discrimination, tutors learn to validate the inherent communicability of all languages (Greenfield), celebrate linguistic heritage as an asset to one's educational journey, empathize with the difficulties of joining new discourse communities (Johns 1997), make visible a variety of linguistic and rhetorical options (Micciche 2004; Greenfield 2011), and acknowledge that challenging hegemonic linguistic norms can have complex outcomes.

By the end of the quarter-long course, through reading reflections, small group discussions, tutoring observations, practice tutoring, discussion of writing samples, development of tutoring strategies, and more, tutors have gained theoretical and experiential knowledge of anti-racist writing tutoring praxis. Because anti-racism and racial justice work require an ongoing investment, I encourage tutors to see their collaborations with writers as planting seeds of racial justice that others will water and watering seeds that others have planted (cf. 1 Corinthians 3:6). I also encourage them to expect the same internal growth process as they open themselves to learning from and with writers and commit to recurring anti-racist and racially just tutor education.

ONGOING ANTI-RACIST, RACIALLY JUST TUTOR EDUCATION: A WOMANIST APPROACH

Building upon the training seminar, ongoing anti-racist tutor education aligns with the womanist principles mentioned earlier: reclamation of self, recovery of Black culture and its true nature, and redemption of Black futures. I offer below representative examples of pedagogical workshops and community programming in these areas.

Reclamation of Self through Authentic, Loving Personhood

Linguistic racism and racist assessment practices can diminish writer's self-confidence and appreciation for their own languages and rhetorical traditions, not to mention disadvantage their academic achievement (Inoue 2015; Baker-Bell 2020). Recurring tutor education in this category is broadly designed to provide strategies for supporting BIPOC students' writerly confidence and/or fostering appreciation for BIPOC and other marginalized linguistic traditions, which benefits all writers and tutors. Such strategies begin with cultivation of racial literacy.

In January 2018, I facilitated the workshop "Cultivating Racial Literacy in the Hume Center" for lecturers in Stanford's Program in Writing and Rhetoric (PWR). In addition to teaching writing requirement and advanced rhetoric courses, PWR lecturers also tutor weekly in the Hume Center. Newly hired PWR lecturers participate in a three-hour training on Hume pedagogy and thereafter can elect to participate in "cross-tutor" workshops typically offered two to three times per quarter and open to all Hume tutors, including drop-in peer writing tutors, appointment-based graduate writing tutors, appointment-based undergraduate and graduate oral communication tutors, and PWR lecturers who hold appointment-based sessions. As Pittock and Cirrillo-McCarthy (2019) describe, prior to 2017 some cross-tutor workshops broadly addressed matters of "inclusion" and "difference." Since my appointment, I have endeavored to make anti-racist praxis a more explicit, centralized part of tutor education.

My 2018 workshop for PWR lecturers was an outgrowth of a lecturer working group in September 2017 on racial literacy. At my recommendation, a small subset of PWR lecturers read Johnson's (2011) "Racial Literacy and the Writing Center," which invites all "literacy instructors," including writing center tutors, to interrogate how race and racism are perpetuated through language (211). This call to action is predicated upon two needs: support for students "mak[ing] meaning of race while writing" and the dearth of critical, productive dialogue about race (211). To continue the dialogue about racial literacy and sustained reflection as strategies for cultivating radically inclusive, anti-racist discourses in the Hume Center, I invited lecturers to critique H&M clothing advertisements featuring a Black male child wearing a green hoodie with the slogan, "Coolest Monkey in the Jungle" and a white male child wearing an orange hoodie with the slogan, "Survival Expert."

Drawing upon Johnson's definition of racial literacy and Stuart Hall's (1996) theorization of "race as a floating signifier," we discussed how the meanings of the controversial H&M advertisements were shaped by both the language and the history of US anti-Black racism and derogatory epithets. Many found "monkey" to be an offensive and racist label on a Black body, while "expert" on a white body reinforced notions of white superiority. Our ability to interrogate how racism functioned through language in the advertisements is a part of racial literacy.

Next, we considered opportunities for cultivating racial literacy in tutoring when student writing explicitly engages race. In small groups, lecturers discussed how they would respond to the following tutoring scenario based upon a Health Policy Class that Mya Poe (2016) describes in "Reframing Race in Teaching Writing Across the Curriculum" (87). I have used this same tutoring scenario as a role-play exercise for undergraduate and graduate student writing tutors during bi-quarterly professional development meetings:

> In discussing the ethics of using a patient's cells, a white student argues that taking the cells of an African American cancer patient and using the cells without her consent was acceptable "because it was legal at the time." The student comes to you with a first draft and asks for help with "flow." Indeed, there are some issues with cohesion and transitioning between ideas. How would you respond and why?

After sharing ways of responding to this scenario, we then noted that we can cultivate racial literacy even when student writing does not explicitly reference race or race-related topics because work with language is always already raced.

I concluded the workshop with the metalogues of womanist theologian Katie Cannon (1998)[2] as a model for transformative reflection, and I provided these questions to help lecturers interrogate normative language attitudes and practices:

- How do race, gender, embodiment, and sexuality shape the ways my language practices are or have been received in the academy?
- If my language practices are well received, why is that? What is it about the norms of the academy that position my communication practices as "academic," accepted and valued? If my language practices are challenged or problematized, why is that? What is it about the norms of the academy that position my communication practices as less academic and worthy of the academy?

2. Cannon (1998) defines "metalogue" as "highly organized or specialized forms of logic, designating new but related disciplines that can deal critically with the nature, structure, or behavior of the original discourse, talk, performance, or recital" (136). The metalogues that I used in the workshop were an amalgam of those provided in Cannon's 2014 *Freedom Narratives* course at Emory University and described by Townes (2006) in the *Encyclopedia of Women and Religion in North America.*

- Reflecting on my tutoring and conferencing, what language practices do I tend to interpret as academic or nonacademic?
- How might my responses to different language practices and grammars do violence to our students?
- How do/could my responses intervene in systems of oppression or repair the violence done to student writers and speakers?
- For other racial literacy workshops, I have used popular texts as conversation starters.

The "All-Tutor Dialogue on Bias and Racial Justice" that I facilitated virtually in October 2020 focused on Imani Perry's (2020) essay in the *Atlantic*, "Racism Is Terrible. Blackness Is Not." I chose the essay because of the "resilience" it evoked and Perry's refusal to "reduce" Black experience to "grief." It felt like what we all needed as we embarked upon a fully online year with the dual pandemics still raging.

Having asked tutors to read the short piece ahead of time, I provided the twenty-eight undergraduate and graduate student writing and oral communication tutors in attendance with the following prompt: "Using Imani Perry's 'Racism Is Terrible. Blackness Is Not' as a point of departure, share your thoughts about or experiences with bias and racial injustice. Offer your hopes and ideas for how we can promote racial justice through tutoring." The tutors' responses, offered orally, in a Padlet (a digital whiteboard), and in the Zoom chat, included the following:

- Commentary on excerpts and their rhetorical impact, like the shift from "pitying" to "empowering the Black community" that Perry's quoting of Zora Neale Hurston encourages
- Connections with other authors, like resonance between Perry's ideas and Ibram X. Kendi's discussion of assimilationism and James Baldwin's reflection on the white gaze
- Identification of thought-provoking passages and their invitation to readers, such as how Perry encourages allyship in Black joy: "exhilaration in black life is not to mute or minimize racism, but to shame racism, to damn it to hell [. . .] If you join us, you might feel not only our pain, but also the beauty of being human"
- Naming of anti-racist tutoring practices, like "valu[ing]" "Black language"; "affirming tutees' language, expression, and experiences"; "holding space for tutees to be committed to their own voice"; and avoiding the "erasure" that can happen when we become "fixers" rather than "collaborators"

Through my own commentary, I sought to reinforce concepts shared during the writing tutor seminar, such as tutoring as participation in a larger democratic project, appreciation for linguistic diversity, learning with and from tutees, and being open to critique. I closed the dialogue with this exhortation:

> What we share [with writers and speakers] is our humanity: I see you. I value you. I welcome you. I want to join with you and celebrate the richness of who you are and what you bring. It may be different from my experience, but I know enough to know there is inherent beauty in all forms of communication. Let's work together and enhance what you already have. We are helping all kinds of people. We enjoy collaboration. We also need to pay attention to bias, racism, and the ways they can sneak into our experience.

Recovery of Black Culture and Its True Nature through the (Re)telling of Black Experience

American history as traditionally taught in K–12 public schools and in higher education often excludes, minimizes, and whitewashes BIPOC histories, cultures, and contributions, as well as the brutal realities of American racism from the transatlantic slave trade to the continuing impact of widespread systemic racism on BIPOC life outcomes and opportunities. Therefore, recurring tutor education in this category recognizes BIPOC and other rhetorical traditions as valuable and efficacious for learning. Events in this category were open to the entire Stanford community. Representative examples include "'Acting Womanish': An Expressive Arts Workshop on Black Women's Sermonic Traditions," and a Toni Morrison and Wole Soyinka Read-In.

In January 2019, just a few days after the Dr. Martin Luther King Jr. national holiday, I facilitated a campus workshop on womanist preaching. Nearly seventy students, faculty, and staff signed up, and about half were able to attend. The workshop was the second in a Hume Center series on expressive arts designed to showcase and celebrate the synergies between writing and speaking. Focusing on womanist preaching was an opportunity to expand the university community's knowledge of Black rhetorical traditions and to highlight the ways that Black women have been advancing a social change movement through womanist biblical interpretation, scholarship, and homiletics.

As attendees gathered, I played *Ella's Song,* sung by Sweet Honey in the Rock. The refrain, "We who believe in freedom cannot rest. We who believe in freedom cannot rest until it comes" and verses like "Until the killing of Black men, Black mothers' sons, is as important as the killing of white men, white mothers' sons," evoked the Black Lives Matter Movement and the life-sustaining activism embodied in womanist proclamation. The song also served as the musical selection before the opening word, a short homily of my own (excerpted below) based on 2 Kings 7:3 (NIV):

> "Why stay here until we die?" It's the question the four lepers asked themselves when they were stuck between a rock and a hard place. The evangelist tells us in 2 Kings chapter 7 that invaders had laid siege on the capitol city of the Northern Kingdom of Israel and a famine arose in the land. According to religious custom, the lepers were outside the city gates, because anyone with their skin condition was cast out, marginalized from society. If they stayed where they were, they would die from famine. If they went into the city, they would die from famine. If they went into the invaders' camp, they might be killed, but there was a slim chance that their lives might be spared. So instead of accepting a sure death, they reasoned that they had nothing more to lose, but everything to gain, and became players in their own destiny.

The homily was an apt segue to womanism, as it conveyed the spirit of resistance in the face of death-dealing subjugation that womanist foremothers embodied when they recognized their exclusion from feminism, which focused on white women's oppression, and from Black Liberation Theology, which focused on Black men's oppression. There was no place for expressing, theorizing, and resisting the racism, sexism, and classism that Black women experienced in the church, in the academy, and in the world at large, so they created their own.

Following the homily, I offered definitions of womanism and womanist preaching and then introduced participants to some early "womanish" voices and contemporary womanist preachers: Jarena Lee (1783–1864), the first Black woman to preach the Gospel in the thirteen colonies; Sojourner Truth (c. 1797–1883), an evangelist, abolitionist, women's rights activist, and former slave; Julia A. Foote (1823–1900), an evangelist and the first woman to be ordained a deacon in the African Methodist Episcopal (AME) Zion Church; Anna Pauli Murray (1910–1985), the first Black woman to be ordained by the Protestant Episcopal Church; Prathia Hall (1940–2002), a womanist theologian, Civil Rights leader, activist, and Christian Ethics professor; Katie Geneva Cannon (1950–2018), a womanism trailblazer and the first Black woman ordained in the United Presbyterian Church; Gina M. Stewart, a womanist theologian and the pastor elect of the 4,000+ member Christ Missionary Baptist Church in Memphis, Tennessee; and Dominique A. Robinson, a millennial womanist and youth pastor at Shaw Temple AME Zion Church in Atlanta, Georgia.

We read selected sermonic excerpts by several of the women that challenge gender and race discrimination and then listened to portions of Rev. Dr. Gina M. Stewart's "An Uncompromised Commitment" and Rev. Dr. Dominique A. Robinson's "You Have the Right to Remain Silent." As participants listened carefully, I invited them to use the womanist tenets and chart provided to identify womanish elements in the sermons. After participants shared their observations and questions, I concluded the workshop with a reference back to 2 Kings 7:3 and the power of language and purposeful action to create more equitable futures.

Other events, such as the Morrison and Soyinka read-in, have encouraged community-building around the intellectual contributions of BIPOC writers. Co-sponsored by the Hume Center and the Program in Writing and Rhetoric, the Morrison and Soyinka read-in was held in celebration of the Toni Morrison Society's twenty-fifth anniversary. We joined other universities and organizations across the country in hosting a read-in of the works of poet laureates Toni Morrison and Wole Soyinka. The two-hour event held in the Hume Center lounge attracted forty-five students, staff, and faculty. With copies of the authors' publications on hand, we invited attendees to sign up to read a favorite passage, something compelling or important to them, or to just listen and reflect upon the legacy of the authors' literary works.

Redemption of Black Futures through Unabashed Resistance of White Supremacy

This third principle for womanist world-building recognizes that racially just futures come about through deliberate, unconventional action that resists white supremacy. Recurring tutor education in this category looks like supporting BIPOC innovation, creativity, and agency as tools for envisioning futures where everyone flourishes. Two primary examples in this category include a virtual student event, "In Conversation with the Inaugural Poem: Shaping the Future with Language," and a new tutor education workshop series, "Pop-Up Conversations on Anti-racist Tutoring."

In March 2021, inspired by Amanda Gorman's Inaugural Poem, the Hume Center and the Program in Writing and Rhetoric co-sponsored a virtual student write-in/speak-in. As reflected in the call for student submissions, our hope was to facilitate a space for creative engagement with Gorman's poem and to encourage students to recognize the power of their own voices to articulate new futures for Stanford and beyond.

> Amanda Gorman's brilliant Inaugural Poem reminded us all of the power language has to call us to reckon with our past, seek greater connection with each other, and build collective futures big enough for us all. The Program in Writing and Rhetoric and Hume Center for Writing and Speaking invite you to share your messages to Stanford and to the nation

> in conversation with the poem. We will share your responses on our website and social media platforms, and you will be invited to share in a virtual event for the campus community.
>
> You may submit in any of the following genres:
>
> A poem or other written response (200–500 words)
> A 1–2 minute spoken piece (speech, poem, or other genre)
> An image slide deck of 8–10 images
> A playlist of 8–10 songs
>
> You might offer a response to the poem itself or share your own ideas about this new moment in conversation with the poem.

Out of seventeen students who submitted pieces, six were available to participate in the live virtual event. Their submissions included four original poems, one video poem, and an image slide deck. Additionally, A-lan Holt, Director of Stanford's Institute for Diversity in the Arts, agreed to share original poetry, and a PWR 2 second-year writing class submitted a curated playlist.

As attendees entered the event webinar, they heard the first selection on the PWR 2 playlist, "BROWN SKIN GIRL," by Blue Ivy, SAINt JHN, Beyoncé, and WizKid, intoning the beauty and value of Black women. The URL for the full class playlist was included on the event landing slide, so attendees could explore the other selections as they waited for the event to begin. The program's Faculty Director Adam Banks provided the welcome and framing for the event, noting that Amanda Gorman's "work with words touched our common humanity, gave us all space to tell our truths individually and collectively, to reckon with the depths and details of our past, and to allow us to imagine and build and work for futures that are more just, that are more human, and that connect us together in ways that honor us all." Banks also referenced the Hume Center as a space where students can bring not only course assignments but also "their voices to all of the issues that matter to them in their own individual journeys and in the ways that they want their work and words to have impact in the world." This framing made a powerful case for racially just futures, for the agency of students to participate in its creation, and for the writing and speaking center as a place that cultivates that work.

Stanford president Marc Tessier-Lavigne graciously accepted my invitation to attend the write-in/speak-in and shared with attendees his "enthusiasm" for the event and the "opportunity" that it gave students to "think through the ideas that arose around the inauguration, ideas about our responsibilities as citizens and the meaning of our democracy." He went on to note how moved he was when he heard Gorman's poem "The Hill We Climb" and recited some of the lines that he found especially "meaningful."

These lines, said President Tessier-Lavigne, convey "a call to reflection and action to all of us." By drawing upon Gorman's words and her implicit call to action, Tessier-Lavigne suggested that the Stanford community has a collective duty to work toward racial justice.

After A-lan Holt recited an original poem, I introduced the six student presenters. Their presentations moved listeners from poetic critiques of the nation, to lament for murdered Black men and women, to a visual argument conveying hope for a better humanity, and finally to episodic reflections on ways that time and light shape our reality. We closed the event with another selection from the PWR 2 playlist, "Free if We Want It" by Nothing But Thieves. The refrain reminded listeners that we all can take part in building a better world: "We can be free if we want it, or we can stay in this lane all alone."

Other events in this category, like "Pop-Up Conversations on Anti-racist Tutoring Practices," a new workshop series for all Hume Center writing and speaking tutors, explore anti-racist tutoring practices in greater depth. The first session in the new series, held in May 2021, focused on "nam[ing] the elephant in the room," which is principle seven in Mandy Suhr-Sytsma and Shan-Estelle Brown's (2011) heuristic, "How Tutors and Writers Can Challenge Oppression through Attention to Language" (22). After reviewing the reasons why attendees registered for the workshop (e.g., "unlearn my own racist practices"; "talk with others about building actively anti-racist practices"; "continue growing as an anti-racist tutor!"), I invited the eight participants, an intimate group of undergraduate and graduate writing and oral communication tutors and PWR lecturers, to share occasions for talking about race(ism) that have emerged in their own tutoring. Then, reflecting upon principle seven, I posed this question from Suhr-Sytsma and Brown (2011): "How can tutors better identify and challenge the everyday, often subtle, language of oppression in their own discourse and in that of other tutors and [students] in writing [and speaking] centers" (13–14)? We ran out of time before I could guide tutors in discussion of a tutoring scenario, so the work shall continue another day.

CONCLUSION

Recurring education, Julia Bleakney (2019) contends, helps writing tutors develop a reflective practice for responding to new tutoring situations. The absence of ongoing tutor education can prompt writing tutors to revert to old or untheorized practices. Intuitively, we also know this to be true of anti-racism training. Ongoing education for anti-racist, racially just tutoring is necessary to help writing tutors and the institutions in which they reside unlearn linguistic bias and gain new knowledge and appreciation for BIPOC languages and rhetorical traditions. Without recurring opportunities to increase one's ability to talk about race and racism, to recognize and challenge oppression, and to envision new realities that are life giving to us all, we will default back to the normative behaviors that perpetuate racism.

The tutor education and community events that I shared illustrate some of the ways, imperfect and unfinished, that we are meeting this challenge at Stanford. Through racial literacy workshops, anti-racist tutoring workshops, and community events foregrounding BIPOC rhetorical traditions, we are shifting the narrative about what writing and speaking centers can and should do. We recognize that tutoring is about much more than revising prose and presentations for class assignments. Dialogic interplay about language creates opportunities to see ourselves and others and to interrogate how our language and worldviews give rise to the racism that traumatizes Black, Brown, and other marginalized bodies. This work is year-round, extending beyond moments of national outrage, and it is vital to our collective liberation.

REFERENCES

Aikens, Kristina. 2019. "Prioritizing Antiracism in Writing Tutor Education." In *How We Teach Writing Tutors: A* WLN *Digital Edited Collection*, edited by Karen G. Johnson and Ted Roggenbuck. https://wlnjournal.org/digitaleditedcollection1/.

"Amanda Gorman Write-in/Speak-in PWR 2 with Dr. J Playlist." 2021. Spotify. Last modified February 13. https://open.spotify.com/playlist/3sCjAam12UkAeF2q2pbJWp?si= 84f89c6933ff4312&nd=1.

Baker-Bell, April. 2020. *Linguistic Justice: Black Language, Literacy, Identity, and Pedagogy.* New York: Routledge.

Belli, Brita. 2020. "Racial Disparity in Police Shootings Unchanged over Five Years." *Yale News*, October 27. news.yale.edu/2020/10/27/racial-disparity-police-shootings-unchanged-over-5-years.

Bleakney, Julia. 2019. "Ongoing Writing Tutor Education: Models and Practices." In *How We Teach Writing Tutors: A* WLN *Digital Edited Collection*, edited by Karen G. Johnson and Ted Roggenbuck. https://wlnjournal.org/digitaleditedcollection1/.

Cannon, Katie G. 1998. *Katie's Canon: Womanism and the Soul of the Black Community.* London: Bloomsburg Publishing.

Chavez, Nicole. 2021. "An Estimated 2600 Latinos Were Killed by Police or in Custody in the Past Six years, Preliminary Report Says." CNN. May 28. www.cnn.com/2021/05/28/us/latinos-police-brutality-report/index.html.

Combahee River Collective. 1977. "The Combahee River Collective Statement." Accessed June 13, 2021. https://www.blackpast.org/african-american-history/combahee-river-collective-statement-1977/.

Floyd-Thomas, Stacey M. 2006. *Mining the Motherload: Methods in Womanist Ethics.* Cleveland: Pilgrim Press.

Foster-Frau, Silvia. 2021. "Latinos Are Disproportionately Killed by Police but Often Left out of the Debate about Brutality, Some Advocates Say." *Washington Post,* June 2. https://www.washingtonpost.com/national/police-killings-latinos/2021/05/31/657bb7be-b4d4-11eb-a980-a60af976ed44_story.html.

García, Romeo. 2017. "Unmaking Gringo Center." *Writing Center Journal* 36, no 1: 29–60. JSTOR. https://docs.lib.purdue.edu/wcj/vol36/iss1/4/.

Greenfield, Laura. 2011. "The 'Standard English' Fairy Tale: A Rhetorical Analysis of Racist Pedagogies and Commonplace Assumptions about Language Diversity." In *Writing Centers and the New Racism: A Call for Sustainable Dialogue and Change,* edited by Laura Greenfield and Karen Rowan, 33–60. Logan: Utah State University Press.

Greenfield, Laura, and Karen Rowan. 2011. "Beyond the 'Week Twelve Approach': Toward a Critical Pedagogy for Antiracist Tutor Education." In *Writing Centers and the New Racism: A Call for Sustainable Dialogue and Change,* edited by Laura Greenfield and Karen Rowan, 124–149. Logan: Utah State University Press.

Gorman, Amanda. 2021. "The Hill We Climb." *Inaugural Poem.* https://youtu.be/Wz4YuEvJ3y4.

Hall, Stuart. 1996. *Stuart Hall: Race—The Floating Signifier.* Produced by Sut Jhally, Joanna Hughes, and Mike Spencer. Media Education Foundation.

Holmes, Barbara. 2021. "Womanist Futures." Keynote address. Katie Geneva Cannon Center for Womanist Leadership Virtual Conference, "The Future Is Womanist," April 9.

"In Conversation with the Inaugural Poem: Shaping the Future with Language. A Student Write-in/Speak-in." 2021. A virtual event co-sponsored by the Hume Center for Writing and Speaking, and the Program in Writing and Rhetoric, March 5. https://drive.google.com/file/d/18hx1BVQkjGvlNMBhqGR1M6L49zIArypf/view.

Inoue, Asao. 2015. *Antiracist Writing Assessment Ecologies: Teaching and Assessing Writing for a Socially Just Future.* Parlor Press. WAC Clearinghouse.

Inoue, Asao. 2021. "Why I Left the CWPA." *Asao B. Inoue's Infrequent Words.* April 18. https://asaobinoue.blogspot.com/2021/04/why-i-left-cwpa-council-of-writing.html.

Johns, Ann M. 1997. *Text, Role, and Context: Developing Academic Literacies.* Cambridge: Cambridge University Press.

Johnson, Michelle T. 2011. "Racial Literacy and the Writing Center." In *Writing Centers and the New Racism: A Call for Sustainable Dialogue and Change,* edited by Laura Greenfield and Karen Rowan, 211–227. Logan: Utah State University Press.

Jordan, Zandra. 2020. "Womanist Curate, Cultural Rhetorics Curation, and Antiracist, Racially Just Writing Center Administration." *Peer Review* 4, no. 2 (October). http://thepeerreview-iwca.org/issues/issue-4-2/womanist-curate-cultural-rhetorics-curation-and-antiracist-racially-just-writing-center-administration/.

Jordan, Zandra. 2021. "Flourishing as Antiracist Praxis: An Uncompromised Commitment to Black Writing Tutors." *WPA* 44, no. 3 (Summer): 33–37.

Lippi Green, Rosina. 2012. "Language Ideology and Language Practice." In *Language in the USA: Themes for the Twenty-first Century,* edited by Edward Finegan and John R. Rickford, 289–304. Cambridge: Cambridge University Press. https://doi.org/10.1017/CBO9780511809880.017.

Lockett, Alexandria L., Iris D. Ruiz, James Chase Sanchez, and Christopher Carter. 2021. *Race, Rhetoric, and Research Methods.* WAC Clearinghouse. https://doi.org/10.37514/PER-B.2021.1206.

Martínez, Ramón Antonio. 2018. "Beyond the English Learner Label: Recognizing the Richness of Bi/Multilingual Students' Linguistic Repertoires." *Reading Teacher* 71, no. 5: 515–522.

Micciche, Laura R. 2004. "Making a Case for Rhetorical Grammar." *College Composition and Communication* 55, no. 4 (June): 716–737.

Ore, Ersula, Kimberly Wieser, and Cristina Cedillo. 2021. "Special Issue CFP! Diversity Is Not an End Game: BIPOC Futures in the Academy." *Present Tense: A Journal of Rhetoric in Society.* March 22.

Perry, Imani. 2020. "Racism Is Terrible. Blackness Is Not." *Atlantic,* June 15. https://www.theatlantic.com/ideas/archive/2020/06/racism-terrible-blackness-not/613039/.

Poe, Mya. 2016. "Reframing Race in Teaching Writing Across the Curriculum." In *Performing Antiracist Pedagogy in Writing, Rhetoric and Communication,* edited by Frankie Condon and Vershawn Ashanti Young, 87–105. WAC Clearinghouse. https://doi.org/10.37514/ATD-B.2016.0933.2.04.

Pittock, Sarah, and Erica Cirrillo-McCarthy. 2019. "Let's Meet in the Lounge: Toward a Cohesive Tutoring Pedagogy in a Writing and Speaking Center." In *How We Teach Writing Tutors: A* WLN *Digital Edited Collection,* edited by Karen G. Johnson and Ted Roggenbuck. https://wlnjournal.org/digitaleditedcollection1/.

"Racial Justice in Education Resource Guide." 2021. *National Education Association.* https://www.nea.org/professional-excellence/student-engagement/tools-tips/racial-justice-education-resource-guide. Accessed June 21.

Stuart Hall: Race—The Floating Signifier. 1996. Lecture on DVD. Produced by Sut Jhally, Joanna Hughes, and Mike Spencer, Media Education Foundation.

Suhr-Sytsma, Mandy, and Shan-Estelle Brown. 2011. "Theory In/to Practice: Addressing the Everyday Language of Oppression in the Writing Center." *Writing Center Journal* 31, no. 2: 13–49.

Townes, Emilie M. 2006. "Womanist Theology." In *Encyclopedia of Women and Religion in North America,* edited by Rosemary Skinner Keller, Rosemary Radford Ruether, and Marie Cantlon, 1165–1173. Bloomington: Indiana University Press.

Walker, Alice. 1983. *In Search of Our Mother's Gardens: Womanist Prose.* San Diego: Houghton Mifflin Harcourt.

6

ADDRESSING RACIAL JUSTICE THROUGH RE-IMAGINING PRACTICUM TO PROMOTE DIALOGUE ON CAMPUS

Lindsay A. Sabatino

The writing center should have an active voice in campus conversations around diversity, equity, inclusion, and accessibility (DEIA). We can engage in meaningful racial justice through tutor education and promoting dialogue across campus. As Geneva Smitherman (2002) stated in her proposal to work toward a national public policy on language, "All that is required for oppression to take hold is for good and well-meaning folk to do nothing" (168). Writing centers cannot be silent. We are positioned to influence change through foregrounding anti-racist practices, modeling inclusion, and fighting for linguistic justice.

As we all aim to create centers that are inclusive and welcoming, Wonderful Faison (2018) reminds us that "if a writing center is supposed to be open and inclusive, race, language, and identity cannot be ignored." The writing center field has been slow to respond to the calls to address issues of racism and linguistic injustices. While some question whether this is the place of the writing center, others have made significant progress, such as East Carolina University's Writing Center's Consultants Advocating for Linguistic Justice and Demand for Change,[1] or the Conference on College Composition and Communication (CCCC) Special Committee's 2020 Demand for Black Linguistic Justice. While these statements and demands for action are increasing, they have deep-rooted histories, including the 1974 Students' Right to their Own Language, reminding us how slow our change has been. We need to establish anti-racist activism and practices on our campuses. I recommend that directors discuss with their tutors how they see race, gender, sexuality, disabilities, culture, and so on being represented and/or

1. See Johnson, Johnson, and Caswell, chapter 10 in this collection.

https://doi.org/10.7330/9781646424573.c006

silenced or oppressed on their campuses. We can learn a lot from our students' lived experiences.

Due to the importance of addressing racial and linguistic injustices as well as accessibility, I have designed tutor education with the purpose of promoting dialogue on my campus. My goal with this chapter is not to tell directors where they should be putting their focus—as I recognize that each campus's and center's needs are different—instead, I share how I revised both our credit-bearing tutor course and our ongoing practicum to address DEIA initiatives. In doing so, others may be inspired to take aspects of my approach and make them their own. In this chapter, I outline how I lay a foundation to address linguistic justice in our tutor course. Then, I discuss the process of creating a social justice ongoing practicum and share the tutors' reflections. Last, I provide a brief look forward as I am revising the tutor course with a civic engagement component. By preparing tutors to engage in anti-racist practices as well as recognize and promote DEIA initiatives, my hope is that the tutors will help influence the culture on campus but, more important, have a greater impact on society.

WRITING INTENSIVE TUTORING COURSE: ACCESSIBILITY, LINGUISTIC, AND RACIAL JUSTICE

In this section, I outline the ways that apprentice tutors—called students throughout this section—engage with concepts of linguistic justice and accessibility along with foundational tutoring practices. All students who work in the writing center are required to take our credit-bearing tutoring course, which I teach. The students also have the option to take the course for zero credits, removing the financial burden if the course does not add to their college requirements. The course typically enrolls between ten and fifteen students every spring semester, with students from majors across the college.

For context, I am the Director of a writing center at a small liberal arts college in New York. We are a predominately white institution (PWI) with approximately 30 percent students of color. There are currently about seventeen writing center tutors, who are all undergraduate students and vary in discipline, race (slightly higher than the college demographics), sexuality, class, and disability status. The one area we are lacking in diversity is gender, as our staff is predominately women.

I have designed the tutoring course around three major concepts (see figure 6.1): (1) working with writers, (2) writing and research processes, and (3) digital rhetoric and multimodality. In this chapter I

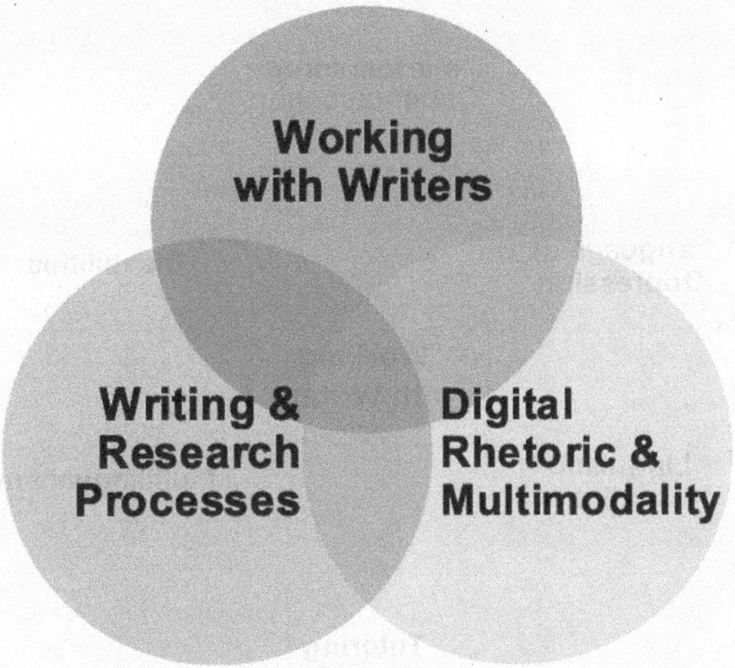

Figure 6.1. The three major concepts in the Writing Intensive Tutoring course.

focus on the first concept. The concepts addressed under the category of working with writers include multiple areas that are interconnected, such as interpersonal communication, tutoring practices, disabilities, multilingual writers, linguistic justice, and language of oppression (see figure 6.2). While the course follows particular themes, this chapter is a snapshot into my course but not the whole picture, as the course changes to prioritize campus needs. The course is an excellent place to create a foundation for establishing anti-racist practices.

The course starts with a focus on interpersonal communication, active listening, collaboration, and agenda setting, as listed in table 6.1. Students are challenged to analyze what it means to be a peer tutor and collaborate to generate knowledge. Students dissect concepts of collaboration and learn that a writing session aims for collaboration where power is balanced, goals are clearly defined and equally distributed, and hierarchy is rejected (Lunsford 1991). It is vital for students to understand that their role is one of collaborator because the writer has their own voice, agency, and valuable knowledge set.

Active listening is an imperative foundational practice for tutoring sessions and anti-racist practices with the goal of listening to understand,

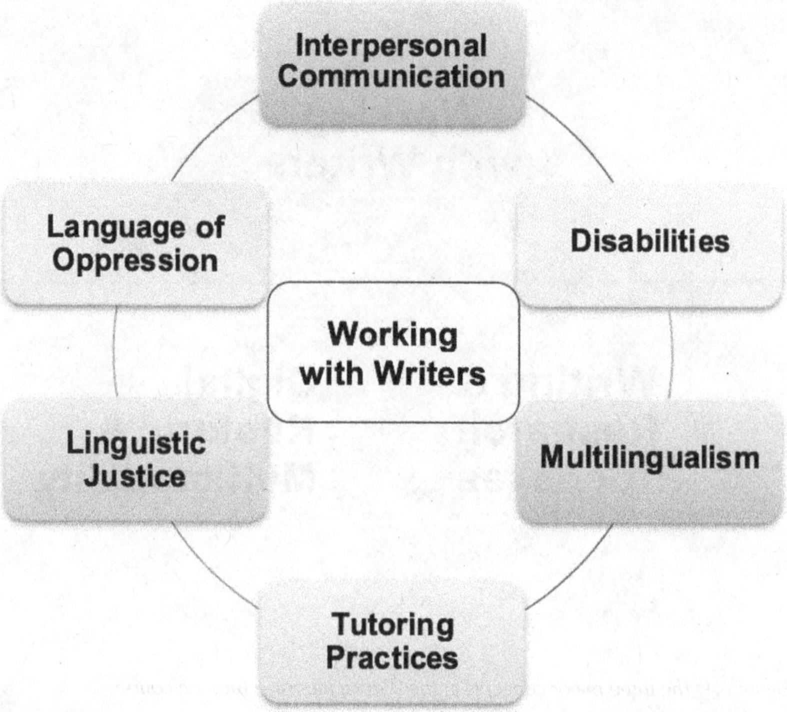

Figure 6.2. The six major areas of study within the category of working with writers.

instead of listening to respond. Active listening also entails listening for total meaning, responding to feelings, and being aware of both verbal and nonverbal cues (Rogers and Farson 1957). These approaches allow students to engage writers without preconceived notions of what they intend to convey. This focus on active listening follows a similar understanding to dialectic organizing, as Moira Ozias and Beth Godbee explain, "to suspend judgment, listen deeply, look for the unseen, and recognize our own positions and assumptions" (Ozias and Godbee 2011, 162). By modeling this level of listening, we are also encouraging others to be active listeners and creating an expectation for open dialogue. As Carl R. Rogers and Richard Evans Farson (1957) state, "People who have been listened to in this new and special way become more emotionally mature, more open to their experiences, less defensive, more democratic, and less authoritarian" (2). Active listening is paired with Isabelle Thompson's (2009) "Scaffolding in the Writing Center" to more closely discuss verbal and nonverbal tutoring strategies. Additionally, students complete a listening self-assessment that I modified from

Table 6.1. Ways instructors could structure foundational principles in their tutoring course

Focus areas	*Sample scholarship*	*Activities*
Active listening Collaboration	Lunsford (1991), "Collaboration, Control, and the Idea of a Writing Center." Rogers and Farson (1957), "Active listening."	Active listening self-assessment Improv Drawing understandings of main concepts
Interpersonal communication Scaffolding Negotiating priorities	Fitzgerald and Ianetta (2015), *The Oxford Guide for Writing Tutors: Practice and Research.* Thompson (2009), "Scaffolding in the Writing Center: A Microanalysis of an Experienced Tutor's Verbal and Nonverbal Tutoring Strategies."	Defining and applying main terms Analyzing nonverbal cues Improv Reflecting on session observations
Setting an agenda	Macauley (2005), "Setting the Agenda for the Next Thirty Minutes."	Mapping the arc of a session

Harvard ManageMentor Coaching Tools' (2004) "Active Listening Self-Assessment." The exercise provides a reflection on their own experiences with active listening and encourages students to recognize their strengths and areas of improvement.

The chapters in Lauren Fitzgerald and Melissa Ianetta's *The Oxford Guide for Writing Tutors* are used to dissect tutoring practices, such as setting an agenda, negotiating priorities, asking open-ended questions, offering praise, reading body language, scaffolding, and wrapping up a session by reviewing goals. We then use improv to engage in areas of interpersonal communication in a low-stakes environment. Additionally, tutors observe sessions to examine these practices in action. While most of the concepts just outlined are fairly accepted in the writing center field as important practices, we need to reflect on how these practices can translate into anti-racist practices and in which situations these strategies may create further marginalization instead of assistance. My goal is to establish this underpinning for the students at the beginning of the course that we can then apply and scrutinize through varying lenses throughout the semester. Therefore, after we have discussed the different tutoring practices and interpersonal communication strategies, we focus on disabilities, multilingual writers, linguistic justice, and language of oppression (table 6.2).

Disability should be addressed in any conversations about diversity and inclusion. I recommend that all directors and instructors work with their disabilities service officer or department to learn more about the student population on campus. I have been fortunate to build a very

Table 6.2. Ways instructors could structure pedagogy with a focus on disabilities, multilingual writers, linguistic justice, and language of oppression

Focus areas	*Sample scholarship*	*Activities*
Disabilities—ADHD, dyslexia, anxiety	Anglesey and McBride (2019), "Caring for Students with Disabilities: (Re)Defining Welcome as a Culture of Listening." Babcock (2015), "Disabilities in the Writing Center." Babcock and Daniels (2017), *Writing Centers and Disability*. Garbus (2017), "Mental Abilities in the Writing Center." Murphy (2020), "Dyslexia in the Writing Center: Multimodal Strategies." Neff (2008), "Learning Disabilities and the Writing Center." Rinaldi (2015), "Disability in the Writing Center: A New Approach (That's not so New)." Ryan, Miller, and Steinhart (2017), "Informed Practices." Winton (2020), "d/Deaf Culture and Translingualism in the Writing Center."	Define and apply main terms (specifically, the different ways disabilities are defined from medical to social and cultural) Examine the writing center space, both physical and virtual Practice using multimodal tools (e.g., whiteboards, manipulatives, etc.) Review policies and scenarios Improv Presentation or collaboration with the disabilities service specialist on campus
Multilingual Writers	Bruce and Rafoth (2016), *Tutoring Second Language Writers* Praphan and Seong (2016), "Helping Second language Writers Become Self-Editors." Rafoth (2014), Multilingual Writers and Writing Centers Severino (2009), "Avoiding Appropriation." Severino and Prim (2016), "Second Language Writing Development and the Role of Tutors: A Case Study of an Online Writing Center 'Frequent Flyer.'" Staben and Nordhaus (2009), "Looking at the Whole Text." Stanley (2013), "Noticing the Way." Truscott (1996), "The Case against Grammar Correction in L2 Classes." *Writing Across Borders* (2011).	Define and apply main terms (specifically, identity construction; classification of "error;" etc.) Map out challenges international students face when writing for American colleges Cultural values self-assessment Examine institutional values Identify discourse communities Improv Plagiarism scenarios Comparing and contrasting tutoring strategies across scholarship

continued on next page

close relationship with the disabilities service specialist on our campus as we work together to best support students. Some of the writing tutors are also employed by her office, creating even stronger collaboration opportunities.

Over the years, I have fine-tuned the reading selection so that the works are chosen specifically to address our current student population. Depending on the semester, we have used a range of scholarship from *Writing Centers and Disability* (Babcock and Daniels 2017) and others (table 6.2). Our discussions center on defining and redefining disabilities, recognizing ways we may create unintentional barriers, and

Table 6.2.—*continued*

Focus areas	*Sample scholarship*	*Activities*
Linguistic Justice and Anti-racism	Faison (2018), "Black Bodies, Black Language: Exploring the Use of Black Language as a Tool of Survival in the Writing Center."	Define and apply main concepts (specifically, Standard English ideologies, oppression, racism, prejudice, discrimination, etc.)
	Green (2018), "Moving beyond Alright: And the Emotional Toll of This, My Life Matters Too, in the Writing Center Work."	Unpack values perpetuated around "Standard English"
	Greenfield (2011), "The 'Standard English' Fairy Tale: A Rhetorical Analysis of Racist Pedagogies and Commonplace Assumptions about Language Diversity."	Language values self-assessment
	Greenfield (2019), *Radical Writing Center Praxis: A Paradigm for Ethical Political Engagement.*	Improv
	Krall-Lanoue (2013), "'And Yea I'm venting, but hey I'm writing isn't I': A Translingual Approach to Error in a Multilingual Context."	Dissect "masked" racist practices in insistence of "Standard English"
	Lu and Horner (2013), "Translingual Literacy, Language Difference, and Matters of Agency."	Analyze and apply position statements to the classroom, college, workplace
	Meacham (2002), "The Clash of the 'Common Sense': Two African American Women Become Teachers."	List and identify areas of linguistic oppression
	Suhr-Sytsma and Brown (2011). "Theory in/to Practice: Addressing the Everyday Language of Oppression in the Writing center."	Practice and discuss approaches for addressing linguistic oppression
	Young (2011), "Should Writers Use They Own English?"	Analyze popular culture examples
		Apply translingual approach to writing samples

learning strategies for working with different types of learners (e.g., visual, auditory, tactile, kinesthetic). Additionally, we read Julie Garbus's (2017) "Mental Abilities in the Writing Center," where she discusses her own experiences with disclosure and uses them to discuss the policies around disclosure. In addition to providing students with strategies and approaches, my overall goal is to remove the stigma surrounding disability.

Tutors also engage with writers from various racial, cultural, and linguistic backgrounds. Through the documentary *Writing Across Borders* (2011), students learn the challenges international students face when writing for American colleges. We explore aspects of language acquisition and strategies for working with multilingual writers. Similar to completing the active listening assessment, the students are asked to fill out forms about their cultural values and discourse communities (DeVries 2005). Through these reflective tools, the students are encouraged to examine how culture and institutions have influenced their own values. The conversation helps us understand others' perspectives. We apply those values to a writing center session and consider how the values may influence the ways the student tutors interact with writers. We also work to demystify the Eurocentric views of plagiarism and develop an understanding of how plagiarism came to be part of American culture through copyright laws. By taking a cultural approach to understanding plagiarism, the students can more effectively and compassionately help writers navigate the academic honesty codes at the college.

With this foundation, we move into topics about linguistic justice and racial oppression. Table 6.2 shows an overlap in scholarship between the focus areas of multilingual writers and linguistic justice—some of the sample scholarship could have been placed in either category. Given the need to unpack the racism that can be rooted in approaches for supporting multilingual writers (such as appropriation, removing accents, etc.), I have found it particularly helpful to scaffold these two areas together to highlight the intersections and emphasize anti-racist practices.

Specifically, students dissect the roots of racism and power associated with the insistence of "Standard English" (Greenfield 2011). The students engage in a reflective writing prompt to work through their own thoughts and experiences. I ask students what Rosina Lippi-Green (1997) means by "all spoken languages are equal in linguistic terms" (as cited in Greenfield 2011, 35) and why people believe that "Standard English" needs to be taught. We analyze how the insistence on "Standard English" perpetuates racism and racist systems. For example, the US Department of Health, Education, and Welfare (1970) study involved videotapes of three children—Black, white, and Mexican American—and dubbing over the speech with the same voice. The teachers in the study rated the white child's speech as superior. As the students and I review this study, we examine how the perceptions of the children's speech were rooted in preconceived expectations of the teachers based on the children's racial backgrounds. We also analyze the situation presented by Shuaib Meacham (2002) explaining a scenario where an African American student was presumed to have plagiarized due to the sophistication of her writing, which shows that "Standard English" does not protect students from experiencing racism. With this example, I share my own experiences as a Director receiving similar inquiries from faculty questioning the writer's work and either the tutor's or my role in assisting the writer. In order to dismantle structures that perpetuate racism, we need to have conversations with our students about practices on our campuses and our classrooms that uphold these systems.

The students are prompted to analyze their own personal biases about language and "Standard English"—what they had been taught, who taught it, and for what purposes. Self-reflection is a key step in working toward establishing anti-racist practices.[2] After analyzing their own biases, the students dissect position statements released by our college or other organizations. The students analyze what it would look like to enact it at our college and center. One way to change the culture on campus is through a grassroots approach with our students. The students need to be a vital voice in the process of generating ideas to tackle issues on campus and moving those plans forward. By preparing students with the tools to understand the complexities of racial literacies, multilingualism, and the impacts of language, my hope is that we can address oppression, create a place of inclusion, and celebrate diversity.

An important aspect of writing is learning the power of language, specifically how rhetorical choices impact the narratives we tell and how language shapes our perceptions of the world. Therefore, we study strategies for how to address language choices that perpetuate oppression (Suhr-Sytsma and Brown 2011). We start by defining oppression: "systemic inequalities and discrimination based on sites of difference such as race, ethnicity, religion, class, gender, sexuality, and or (dis)-ability" (Suhr-Sytsma and Brown 2011, 15). Then, we turn to popular culture and the media for examples. We see oppressive tactics employed regularly, for example, victim-blaming rape survivors or demonizing Black Hurricane Katrina survivors. Additionally, I play clips from media outlets where women leaders are called "bossy" and the veiled racism present when people of color are told how articulate they sound. Students are asked to share their own examples. Some language of oppression is so ingrained in our modes of communication that we do not even recognize the detrimental consequences as they shape how we understand society. As instructors of writing and as we are preparing tutors to have conversations about writing, I believe it is our job to help students to be more critically aware of their language choices.

We discuss strategies to address language of oppression. By recognizing approaches they are comfortable using, analyzing how to use them, and practicing using those approaches, the students are more prepared for when they encounter oppressive language. As Mandy Suhr-Sytsma and Shan-Estelle Brown (2011) state, "When writing centers do not make time to address oppression, they miss an opportunity to enrich the people as well as the discourses that occupy their spaces" (19). Students need to be prompted to self-reflect on how they may contribute to oppressive behaviors even when that is not their intent; and, we can provide them with strategies to engage in tough conversations with

2. See Haltiwanger Morrison in chapter 9 in this collection for examples of self-reflection activities to promote racial justice.

others. Additionally, I inform the students that they are not required to remain present in a session that makes them feel uncomfortable or unsafe. Haltiwanger Morrison, in chapter 9 in this collection, emphasizes the importance of a tutor's being able to leave a session without consequences and offers detailed guidance for (writing center administrators) WCAs.

Vershawn Ashanti Young (2011) calls us to teach "how language functions within and around various cultural perspectives" (165); therefore, students learn to adopt a translingual approach, which engages writers in conversations about language choices, the negotiation of meaning, and the writer's goals when composing (Krall-Lanoue 2013). Through understanding cultural perspectives, students are encouraged to use the translingual approach in order to not see difference as error. Instead, understanding that an error, as outlined by Suresh Canagarajah, "is not miscommunication; it is not breaking a rule. Instead, *error* is those items one or both members of the interaction refuse to negotiate" (2013, 233). As tutors, we cannot assume that we know what the writer intended to write, but instead, we need to be open to dialogue about language choices and meaning by reading the text on the page. Therefore, without discussion, written error correction is not effective for improving accuracy in student writing (Truscott 1996, 2007), and taking such an approach may misrepresent the writer's ideas and appropriate a writer's text.

A translingual approach emphasizes the importance of active listening and to read with patience, respect difference, and support the writer so that the writer's voice is clearly heard. For a more detailed discussion of translingualism, see Rachael Shapiro and Celeste Del Russo discussion, in chapter 7 of this collection.

As a Director at a PWI, I find that many of my students have not thought about the ways language is weaponized to perpetuate oppression. Our conversations around "Standard English" have been heated at times, as students are working through their own implicit biases. In some instances, these discussions also lead to a clicking together of pieces for students being able to name the oppression or prejudices they have previously faced. These conversations are typically powerful and difficult, especially as we dissect what this means for the writing center working within an institution with certain expectations. Opening up space for these hard conversations is necessary. Therefore, when engaging in these conversations, as instructors, we need to be willing to be vulnerable as well. Do not force students of color to be the spokesperson for their race—their experiences are theirs to share if and when they choose; they should not be expected to pour out their souls for us to believe that there are racist practices occurring on our campuses.

By engaging in these discussions in the space of our classroom, the students have established the foundation that they can build on during our ongoing practicum—if hired as a tutor—and initiate conversations across campus. Anecdotally speaking, tutors have told me that this course was the most influential course that they took during their college career; it changed their previous perceptions and in some ways their paths in life. My hope is that these conversations stay with them and evolve long after their time in the course.

ONGOING TUTOR PRACTICUM

Overview

Ongoing tutor practicum is equally as important at the course in addressing racial justice. While the course is designed to provide tutors with foundational practices, the ongoing practicum can be designed with a broader and outward focus. Recognizing that each center has different resources, staff composition, and functions on campus, I share in the text that follows how I have revised our ongoing practicum to a less traditional model that maintained tutor education while maximizing our ability to impact our campus through DEIA initiatives. My goal in revising the practicum model was to be more tutor driven, be more intentional with what we study, strengthen partnerships on campus, and broaden our reach.

In fall 2018, I revamped our tutor education to a theory into practice model that not only educates tutors but also informs broader conversations with our campus (table 6.3). In small groups, the tutors self-select a specialized area to study, such as digital rhetoric, disabilities, multilingual writers, or social justice. The practicum group on social justice purposefully remains broadly defined to recognize intersectionality and injustices associated with race, class, gender, sexuality, culture, and so on. As the group consistently changes, so will the priorities and direct needs of our campus. Additionally, the tutors are welcomed to propose their own area of study. In the fall, the tutors read scholarship about their area, respond to discussion forum questions, and meet with me. The tutors typically read about five pieces of scholarship and respond to discussion posts and each other throughout the fall semester—approximately every two weeks. In the spring, they host an event to engage the campus community in dialogue. Before hosting the event, each group submits an event proposal that asks them to describe their event, identify their

Table 6.3. Theory into practice practicum model (yearlong)

Fall	*Spring*
Survey to determine practicum groups	Beginning of semester, all-tutors practicum meeting where each practicum group brainstorms event ideas
Beginning of semester, all-tutors practicum meeting where each group determines their focus	Submission of event proposals
Biweekly readings with discussion posts	Meeting with Director to discuss and review event proposals
Interactive discussion responses	Revisions of event proposals, if necessary
Tutor-led practicum group meetings (1–2 a semester), with Director to review concepts, organize activities, and discuss tutoring	Event
Brainstorm event ideas	Reflective writing on event, practicum, and tutoring

audience, think through logistics, connect the event to the scholarship they read in the fall, and identify campus partnerships. The events are not meant for tutors to present themselves as experts but, instead, to initiate conversations with the campus.

The theory into practice model was inspired from conversations at the spring 2018 International Writing Centers Association (IWCA) Online Collaborative, "Stories from the Center: Activism, Outreach, and Research." While the outline above has generally remained the same, I have made modifications since its inception. For example, the first year I designed this practicum, I determined the emphasis of each group. Now, the tutors decide what they want their focus to be, making the practicum tutor driven. Before our first meeting at the beginning of each fall semester, the tutors fill out a survey where they rank-order their preferences or can offer a suggestion of another area to study. At our first meeting, the students are placed into groups and tasked with identifying what they want to study and why, resulting in greater tutor investment.

Moreover, I modified what constitutes as an event. From being required to have a live presentation, now the tutors can choose to conduct a live discussion or prepare digital resources, workshops, or empirical-based research papers, and so forth. This flexibility has opened the tutors to more opportunities to engage the campus. While this tutor practicum is entering its fourth iteration, due to COVID, the spring 2020 events were cancelled. Therefore, we have had two years of campus engagement through this tutor education model.

In Action—Event Examples

Before they can host their events, the tutors need to compose an event proposal, meet with me to discuss it, and reach out to campus partners for collaboration. A main aspect of designing their event is determining their intended audience. All events are open to the campus, but the tutors are prompted in their proposal to determine specifically who they hope will attend and what they want their audience to learn. These events typically have been aimed at students on campus. The first social justice practicum event in 2019, described later in this section, was aimed at all members of the campus as they were hoping that students, faculty, and staff would have an open dialogue together about oppression and linguistic justice. For directors looking to promote tutor-driven events, I recommend making sure the goals of the event are clear, partnering with other groups on campus, and knowing what else is happening on campus to avoid duplicating efforts.

To date, our writing center has conducted five events, one empirical research project, and digital resources for our website under this practicum model. For the sake of this chapter, I am only going to highlight a few of the events our writing center has hosted. In spring 2019, the social justice practicum group hosted an event focused on racial and linguistic justice. As described in their proposal: "We, as [tutors], will present our stance on the topic of discriminatory rhetoric and breaking stereotypes in the context of writing, speaking, and collaboration." The tutors' event focused on language as a form of oppression and breaking stereotypes and other forms of oppression in writing, communication, and writing center practice.

The tutors started the event with a brief presentation about linguistic diversity and discriminatory rhetoric. Then, the tutors talked personally about some of their own experiences as tutors and instances when they have either personally experienced oppression in the center or had to address it in a student's writing. For example, three women from various racial backgrounds shared how they experienced verbal oppression when tutoring men writers. They explained that sometimes the writers would treat them like they are incapable to tutor or would mansplain to them. Others would expect the tutor to do the work for them. When they opened the floor for discussion, one participant shared an example of reading a friend's paper that argued African Americans should just listen to the police to solve the issue of police brutality. He then asked the tutors what they would do in the situation. Using an approach outlined by Suhr-Sytsma and Brown (2011), one tutor explained that she would first clarify the writer's meaning to check to see if the oppression was intentional or unintentional. She would ask questions to understand the writer's goals and explain how the piece reads to her. Another tutor shared that she would look up articles with the writer to examine instances where police brutality has taken place, discuss the complexities of the situation, and hope to engage in an open dialogue. She also shared that she would see if the writer had any sources or clear evidence to back up his claims, emphasizing the importance of credible scholarship. The conversation evolved to discussing strategies for promoting dialogue. The event was fairly successful and sparked ongoing dialogue.

For spring 2021, the social justice and multilingual writers practicum groups partnered together to host a video-submission event titled "A Rise in Voices." The tutors wanted to create a positive and creative outlet for everyone to share their feelings, experiences, culture, language, and passions. The tutors asked students, faculty, and staff to submit a video of themselves reading or performing a literary work (e.g., poetry, a quote, or an excerpt) that speaks on a social justice issue they are passionate about, or that is representative of their culture. They welcomed submissions in any language. Unfortunately, they received no submissions. We hope to relaunch this event in the future.

Also in spring 2021, the disabilities practicum group held an event to increase a general understanding about disabilities and offer strategies for preparing for finals. With the focus on finals, their intended audience was students. They started the event with a fun Kahoot! quiz, where the participants were presented with facts about d/Deaf culture, dyslexia, anxiety, and depression. After the quiz, the participants were encouraged to ask questions. One tutor disclosed her own experiences with dyslexia and approaches she was personally using to make writing papers during finals go smoother. With the encouragement of our disabilities service specialist, who was in attendance, the tutors also emphasized that the students do not need to disclose any disabilities or accommodations they receive in order to seek assistance from the writing center. The event was very well attended, and the dialogue was lively. Our hope is that in addition to providing strategies for writers, by having regular conversations about disabilities we can help normalize seeking assistance and de-stigmatize disabilities.

REFLECTIONS AND IMPACT

As part of the requirement for the practicum, each tutor is provided with a series of reflective questions about their event, their role, and how both have impacted their tutoring. The tutors shared that they had a better understanding of the complexities of oppression and prepared to address it directly. They also recognized the importance of addressing oppression from the bottom up, especially when institutions fail to do so. The new practicum model helped them change their perspectives as tutors: they do not solely see themselves only supporting someone's writing, and they can have an impact beyond the walls of the center. Additionally, their commitment to social justice is an ongoing commitment to society.

Writing centers cannot wait any longer to implement anti-racist practices. Those of us who come from privileged positions need to use them to make change. As Neisha-Anne Green (2018) stated in her IWCA/NCPTW keynote, "I wanted to remind them [those with more privilege] that the disadvantaged had been telling them how to help and that it just wasn't fair to keep expecting us to" (30). Here I share a final tutor reflection that succinctly synthesizes the impact these types of actions can have on their campus as she reflects on the event held in spring 2019:

> I think what changed my perception the most was the feedback we received from the audience. Personally, I was a little nervous about the reception we would receive for our event. Since our college is a PWI and the students of color on campus are incredibly active in their respective clubs and organizations (Black Student Union, Alma, etc.), I was scared that we would face backlash on both ends of the spectrum, by the white students who don't like being called out for their microaggressive tendencies and from and by the students of color for overstepping our boundaries as a (mostly) white team. However, I was pleasantly surprised that neither one happened at the event . . . The students of color who came expressed gratitude that someone besides themselves was trying to do work on campus educating the community about oppression and stated that they were willing to partner with us in the future to help further spread the message to campus. Likewise, the faculty and administrators in the room, most of whom were white, were incredibly supportive of our work and stated that they would love to help us continue with these types of education events at an institutional level.

As this tutor points out, one of the most powerful statements during the event was the feedback from a student of color thanking the tutors for initiating this dialogue. Our commitment to anti-racist activism does not go unnoticed and neither does our silence. The following year the Black Student Union hosted an "Excellence Study Jam," and a member of BSU approached me about having tutors support the event. Creating partnerships is integral to changing institutional oppressions and promoting DEIA initiatives. While I still get emails from some faculty complaining about grammar errors in student writing, the campus has started to view the writing center and its role in a different light. The tutors now recognize that they can be integral in making change and its part of their role to actively work against injustices. Overall, I recognize that these steps may seem small, but we must start somewhere, and progress will build over time.

Moving forward, the social justice practicum group received college funding to invite a presenter, who specializes in diversity training and inclusion in professional settings, to conduct a workshop in spring 2022. The speaker will collaborate with the tutors to host an event focusing on tools for anti-racist practices. These practicum events will continue to advance our campus's DEIA initiatives and ongoing support. Additionally, the students in the tutor course will partner with the writing center tutors to focus on access to education and racial inequality through the Andrew W. Mellon Periclean Faculty Leader Grant I was awarded. The course will add a civic engagement component that will take place in partnership with a local high school. The college students will collaborate with the tutors to develop and conduct workshops for the high school students. The focus of the workshops will be determined based on what the high school identifies as their needs; the high school students will learn ways to advance their writing for beyond their high school careers. Additionally, we will be using the Project Pericles Voting Modules to reflect on how voting impacts education access and racial literacies through examining why voting matters. My goal is to establish a sustainable partnership between the high school students and our writing center beyond the initial semester.

REFERENCES

Canagarajah, Suresh, ed. *Literacy as Translingual Practice: Between Communities and Classrooms.* New York: Routledge, 2013.

Combahee River Collective. 1977. "The Combahee River Collective Statement." www.blackpast.org/african-american-history/combahee-river-collective-statement-1977/.

DeVries, Basma Ibrahim. 2005. "Values Clarification." Wiki, Educational Heritage Project.

García, Romeo. 2017. "Unmaking Gringo Center." *Writing Center Journal* 36, no 1: 29–60. https://www.jstor.org/stable/44252637.

Greenfield, Laura, and Karen Rowan. 2011. "Beyond the 'Week Twelve Approach:' Toward a Critical Pedagogy for Antiracist Tutor Education." In *Writing Centers and the New Racism: A Call for Sustainable Dialogue and Change,* edited by Laura Greenfield and Karen Rowan, 124–149. Logan: Utah State University Press.

Hall, Stuart. 1996. *Stuart Hall: Race—The Floating Signifier.* Lecture. Produced by Sut Jhally, Joanna Hughes, and Mike Spencer. Media Education Foundation.

Harvard Business Publishing. 2013. "Harvard ManageMentor: Coaching." Harvard Business Publishing, December 18. https://hbsp.harvard.edu/product/7108-HTM-ENG.

Johnson, Michelle T. 2011. "Racial Literacy and the Writing Center." In *Writing Centers and the New Racism: A Call for Sustainable Dialogue and Change,* edited by Laura Greenfield and Karen Rowan, 211–227. Logan: Utah State University Press.

Jordan, Zandra. 2021. "Flourishing as Antiracist Praxis: An Uncompromised Commitment to Black Writing Tutors." *WPA* 44, no. 3 (Summer): 33–37.

Lippi Green, Rosina. 2012. "Language Ideology and Language Practice." In *Language in the USA: Themes for the Twenty-first Century*, edited by Edward Finegan and John R. Rickford, 289–304. Cambridge: Cambridge University Press. https://doi.org/10.1017/S0047404507070765.

Lunsford, Andrea. 1991. "Collaboration, Control, and the Idea of a Writing Center." *Writing Center Journal* 12, no. 1: 3–10. https://doi.org/10.7771/2832-9414.1252.

Perry, Imani. 2020. "Racism Is Terrible. Blackness Is Not." *Atlantic*, June 15. https://www.theatlantic.com/ideas/archive/2020/06/racism-terrible-blackness-not/613039/.

Poe, Mya. 2016. "Reframing Race in Teaching Writing Across the Curriculum." In *Performing Antiracist Pedagogy in Writing, Rhetoric and Communication*, edited by Frankie Condon and Vershawn Ashanti Young, 87–105. WAC Clearinghouse. https://doi.org/10.37514/ATD-B.2016.0933.2.04.

Rogers, Carl Ransom, and Richard Evans Farson. 1957. *Active Listening*. Chicago: Industrial Relations Center of the University of Chicago.

Suhr-Sytsma, Mandy, and Shan-Estelle Brown. 2011. "Theory In/To Practice: Addressing the Everyday Language of Oppression in the Writing Center." *Writing Center Journal* 31, no. 2 (2011): 13–49. https://doi.org/10.7771/2832-9414.1732.

Truscott, John. "The Case against Grammar Correction in L2 Writing." *Language Learning: A Journal of Research in Language Studies* 46, no. 2 (1996): 327–369. https://doi.org/10.1111/j.1467-1770.1996.tb01238.x.

US Department of Health, Education, and Welfare, Office of Research. 1970. Effects of Visual Cues of Ethnicity upon Speech Ratings. https://files.eric.ed.gov/fulltext/ED046938.pdf.

Walker, Alice. 1983. *In Search of Our Mother's Gardens: Womanist Prose*. San Diego: Houghton Mifflin Harcourt.

7

WORKING TOWARD RACIAL JUSTICE IN THE WRITING CENTER

Five Strategies for Translingual Tutoring

Rachael Shapiro and Celeste Del Russo

INTRODUCTION

While many writing centers promote an ethos of inclusion and diversity, the idea of nondominant forms of English or linguistic diversity as valuable writing forms remains hard for many writing center staff and university administrators to accept. In this chapter, we hope to support and hasten the shift toward understanding language diversity as a central social justice issue for writing center space, mission, and pedagogy. We join scholars such as Romeo García, Laura Greenfield, and Ellen Camarillo who challenge the idea of a seemingly "neutral" writing center space in their mission of transforming their centers to provide more racially and linguistically just spaces for student learning, where a "multilingual worldview" is valued and impactful (Olson 2013). We concentrate our efforts on what Nelson Flores and Jonathan Rosa (2015) have termed "raciolinguistic ideologies," the connection between standard language ideologies and racial ideologies through which "conflate certain racialized bodies with linguistic deficiency unrelated to any objective linguistic practices" (150). Further, we agree with the authors that therefore "anti-racist social transformation cannot be based solely on supporting language-minoritized students in engaging in the linguistic practices of the white speaking subject but must also work actively to dismantle the hierarchies that produce the white listening subject" (167).

Challenging raciolinguistic ideologies is essential work for writing centers that wish to work toward racial justice. We believe that to disrupt the pattern of a hollow racial neutrality that in actuality sustains what Asao Inoue (2015) calls "White language supremacy" requires the shift to a raciolinguistic justice paradigm. April Baker-Bell demonstrates this important work with her "linguistic justice approach" that serves Black students by "dismantling Anti-Black Linguistic Racism and white

https://doi.org/10.7330/9781646424573.c007

linguistic hegemony and supremacy" (2020, 7). Indeed, it's essential to continually develop pedagogies that meet the specific needs of particular racialized communities as Baker-Bell does. However, many writing centers, like ours, serve racially diverse groups of linguistically minoritized students and must also work toward a broader raciolinguistic approach to challenge the misconceptions about language that allow practitioners to too readily settle their language pedagogies in the ruts of a standard language ideology underwritten by white supremacy. We see a translingual approach to tutoring writing, in which tutors value difference as an asset to literacy and disrupt the equation of language difference with deficiency (Horner et al. 2011), to be one way forward for writing centers to work toward raciolinguistic justice.

Some common tutoring practices already shuttle translingualism's potential to decenter white linguistic norms through dialogue, such as the tactic we think of as "responding like a reader, rather than an editor." In this way, tutors respond to student writing through a lens of curiosity; rather than moving straight to the naming of a tutor-identified pattern (e.g., "I noticed a pattern of comma splices in this piece"), the tutor might move to an example of a comma splice in context and walk the author through the ways they interact with the instance as a reader, stopping to ask questions about intended meaning. Opening dialogue between tutor and tutee establishes a space of co-determination, the sharing of authority in diagnosis of "error," and the design of meaning. Such dialogue may implicitly draw from a translingual lens to promote negotiation between the tutor-reader and the student-writer. As Suresh Canagarajah writes in "Negotiating Translingual Literacy," in linguistic contact zones, speakers across difference must come together with a shared responsibility for co-constructing meaning; thus, "interlocutors are supportive and consensus-oriented as they strive to achieve their shared objectives through their divergent codes" (2013, 43). In order to serve language-minoritized students in the writing center, tutors may embody the interlocutor and support their tutees in negotiating moments of contact, or linguistic features that do not match Standardized (white) academic English, together. And in some writing centers today, like our own, tutors are trained to understand this work as anti-racist linguistic advocacy.

In our own center, although we found tutors to be engaged in the main tenets of translingualism and its work in challenging monolingualism and linguistic oppression, they still struggled to implement practices in their tutoring. Greenfield argues there are two reasons for tutors and directors to maintain anti-racist linguistic pedagogy: they are either "convinced of [Standard English]'s superiority or more often reject its superiority but are stuck about how to imagine and put into practice an alternative" (2011, 40). We provide these five strategies as a way to get "unstuck."

We understand translingual tutoring approaches to be one significant way in which writing centers can take up social justice work by actively countering racist and monolingualist ideologies. The five strategies we describe in this chapter work to challenge the seeming neutrality (García 2017; Camarillo 2019) of process-oriented writing center strategies that have previously solely worked to help students assimilate to the hegemonic expectations of Standardized English in academic writing. In what follows, we define translingualism and how it can actively challenge monolingualist attitudes in the university. Next, we name and describe our five strategies for translingual tutoring, as we introduce them to our own tutors during orientation and in professional development sessions throughout the year. For each strategy, we explore common best practices or recommend tutor moves that may be new to many readers through the lens of translingual theory and anti-racist and decolonial approaches. While some practices may be old hat to some readers, we hope new framing can give trusty tools a more political edge. For tutors new to writing center work or the field of Writing Studies, we offer what we believe will be a useful synthesis of translingual theory and anti-racism as it's evolved in our discipline. Finally, we conclude by situating these translingual practices as moves that open up space for a more socially just writing center that disrupts monolingual bias and assumptions that privilege monolingual practices.

TRANSLINGUAL TUTORING AS ANTI-MONOLINGUAL, SOCIAL JUSTICE PEDAGOGY

Translingualism has been understood as an orientation, an approach, a theory, and more; it has been reduced to languaging practices and criticized as misnamed, undertheorized, or misunderstood (Canagarajah 1994; Matsuda 2013, 2014; Lee 2018; Gevers 2018; Schreiber and Watson 2019). Nevertheless, those who study and write about translingualism generally agree upon some central tenets of language: language variation is the norm, not the exception; linguistic difference is a resource, and not a deficit; all languages are fluid, hybrid, emergent, and change over time; language difference is situated and political; and language users regularly negotiate across linguistic contexts. While much of the research that informs these foundational concepts emerge from fields like second language writing and linguistics, there are also very deep roots for such sophisticated understanding of language theory and practice in Rhetoric and Writing Studies, going as far back as the late 1960s and early 1970s in the era of open admissions and the Students' Right to their Own Language movement brought to us by Geneva Smitherman and other dedicated teacher-scholars. Whereas much contemporary work in translingualism focuses on languaging practices such as code-meshing and translation in exploration of form, function, and strategy, we consider the most pressing thread of translingual theory to be that which works to destabilize, confront, and actively dismantle monolingualism in all its forms, and particularly as standard language ideology (Watson and Shapiro 2018).

Specifically, translingualism fights monolingualism by welcoming, practicing, and advocating for language difference. In the writing center, while there has been some significant work in challenging harmful language ideologies (much of which is referenced throughout this article), scholars and practitioners have not yet identified particular strategies for integrating translingualism to support our tutees across their diverse linguistic assets, goals, and contexts. In "Twenty-first Century Writing Center Staff Education: Teaching and Learning towards Inclusive and Productive Everyday Practice," Sarah Blazer (2015, 19) outlines three ways in which her visibly diverse tutoring center still witnessed well-intentioned tutors working to "manage" linguistic variation according to three monolingual myths: that language diversity is an aberration rather than the norm; that there is a single, correct form of Standard English to which all speakers should conform—what Bruce Horner and John Trimbur referred to as "a tacit policy of unidirectional English monolingualism" (2002, 594)—and the harmful misconception that non-standard language practices or presence of students' L1 in English-based communication contexts will interfere with their ability to acquire standardized forms of academic English (Blazer 2015, 21) (see also Watson and Shapiro 2018). Counter to such ideologies of language, which are distinct from observations in linguistics, TESOL, and second language writing scholarship, as well as translingualism, Blazer argues that "advancing a transformative ethos for writing centers requires rejecting these premises that justify *managing* difference" (2015, 21, emphasis added). Helping tutees investigate monolingualism is one path forward.

Translingualism also demands that we confront harmful language ideologies and harness the agency and resources of speakers of diverse linguistic varieties. When we can understand how monolingualism may unsuspectingly muddy the waters of our well-intended work in supporting student writers, we can work toward anti-racist language practices to participate in the building of a more socially just landscape of higher education. It is our hope that the guidelines we propose for tutors in this will stand alongside a rich tutor education curriculum, such as the one offered in chapter 5 in this collection, Zandra L. Jordan's "Beyond the Tutor Training Seminar: A Womanist Approach to Ongoing Education for Racially Just Writing Tutoring." Such a curriculum can reveal and work against the violence of raciolinguistic ideologies, offering an activist and informed application of translingualism's advocacy and allyship with students of color, international students, students from working-class backgrounds, undocumented students, and other language-minoritized students for whom standard language ideology bears real, material consequences.

After all, monolingual attitudes have continually harmed English Language Learners (ELLs), international students, students of color, and students who are speakers of non-standard varieties of English (Shaughnessy 1977; Smitherman 1977; Fox 1990; Gilyard 1991; Villanueva 1993; Horner and Trimbur 2002; Lu 2006; Lippi-Green 2012; Wilson 2012; Matsuda 2013; Inoue 2015; Baker-Bell 2020; etc.). Whether through economic impact, such as higher tuition or additional remedial and non-credit-bearing courses, or psychological impact, like the countless microaggressions from teachers and peers, or the underrepresentation of mentors who look and sound like themselves, these students face daily consequences of monolingual attitudes that can erode their writerly confidence. By fighting for language rights, however, our translingual pedagogies can be transformative for those who are harmed by monolingualism, especially ELLs, immigrants, and people of color. Further, dismantling harmful language attitudes serves white speakers by helping them to confront internalized racist perceptions of difference and to open them to wider repertoires of meaning making. As an institutionally embedded space of support, the writing center is especially well positioned to serve language-minoritized students; a translingual approach to tutoring is thus a natural progression for writing center professionals who are already committed to such work.

FIVE STRATEGIES FOR TRANSLINGUAL TUTORING

We present the five translingualism-inspired tutoring strategies as ways that tutors and writing center administrators can work against harmful and racist monolingualist ideologies in and beyond writing center sessions with language-minoritized students. In each strategy, we offer context and describe a small range of possible tactics that illustrate practical applications.

Strategy 1: Where First You See "Error," Look for Intention

The first strategy we propose invites tutors to reframe their approach to "error" in student work as potentially an informed and strategic writerly choice. As Bruce Horner explains, error is socially constructed and is best understood as a disagreement between writer and audience, or a failure "to negotiate an agreement" about the conventions of language (1992, 174). Thus, behind much of what we perceive as error there is intention—a choice a writer has made to accomplish their purpose according to their linguistic tools, purposes, values, and desires. Training writing center tutors to cultivate an orientation of curiosity for the intention in students' writing can keep present the sociality of difference. This work also makes space for negotiation, such as what Canagarajah calls "interactional strategies," wherein "readers and writers align with each other in the fullest ecological context to produce meaning when they can't assume shared language norms" (2013, 50). Having taken on the stance of reader, rather than editor, as described in the introduction, tutors are well prepared for such collaborative production of meaning.

Rashi Jain (2014) offers an example of how, in a U.S. context, we use the preposition "on" to describe riding the bus (e.g., "she got on the bus"). When such a reader hears a World English speaker use the phrase "in the bus," they may perceive the phrasing as an error; however, some speakers are from countries "where the available resources are inadequate for the size of the population, and people are often forced to (or sometimes prefer to) travel on bus-tops" (500). For such speakers, to write "in the bus" would not be a matter of error, but rather a reflection of clarity. Tutors who are reading like an editor may automatically identify and attempt to "correct" such a construction, forcing it to conform to a more common American English expression. However, if we take the opportunity to consider that what we notice as different might in fact be an intentional construction rather than a mistake, we preserve the writer's agency and honor their experience and their ability to express it without flattening their realities with the rigidity of Standard White English, Academic Discourse, Edited American English, and so on. As Bobbi Olson (2013) writes, simply asking a writer about their intention may allow tutors to "engage more consciously with multilingual writers in ways that attend to the realities of the intersections between language, power, and identity."

To understand linguistic variation as a moment for learning and negotiation between writer and audience is to take a translingual approach because the tutor comes to the session with an expectation that difference is the norm and a resource for all writers. In this way, as Rebecca Lorimer Leonard and Rebecca Nowacek argue, linguistic deviations can be understood as "a norm of language-in-practice, one of its meaning-making functions" (2016, 261). During a session, a tutor might locate an unfamiliar language construction and respond like a reader, noting: "This is an interesting construction—I'm not sure I quite know what you mean here." The tutor might explain what they understand about the context, the passages immediately surrounding the unique phrase or passage, and describe how they take the writer's meaning in that section to relate to the larger purpose of the project. In this way, tutor and tutee can ensure agreement or mutual understanding of the surrounding content in relation to the overall composition. Next, the tutor might say, "Can you tell me more about your choice to use this term here?" Or, "How do you understand the comma in this location to be serving your writerly goal in this sentence?" These questions can welcome the tutee into a dialogue surrounding meaning that disrupts a prescriptivist role for the tutor and dispels standard language ideologies.

Grounded in our rich professional development, tutors in our Writing Center understand that asking for intention helps them understand a student's goal for their own writing—especially when it comes to "grammar" or sentence-level support. Students might be writing intentionally in a home language or a non-standard variety of English. Looking for intention means tutors don't assume the student even wants to write in Standardized English. As our tutor, Nicole, writes, "If what tutees are saying makes sense, has meaning, and it is their intention to write in this way, we can have a conversation about that." Thomas, one of our multilingual tutor coordinators says, "If I see something that stands out in terms of syntax, and I've had to read through it several times to try and understand the meaning, usually I just ask, 'what is it that you want to say in this phrase here?' Often what is happening is an attempt at a colloquialism that doesn't translate well to English. If that's the case, I'll ask, 'ok, so what is the phrase in your language?' and we open up a conversation about idioms and colloquialisms in both English and their home language." From there, tutees can work with students to help them decide on whether or not they wish to leave the idiom untranslated or to switch it out with one that might work in English—a tutor-tutee negotiation of language and meaning that bolsters writerly agency over an imagined audience member's expectation of Standardized English.

Strategy 2: Situate Standardized English as Political

To explicitly contend with the racialized and disparate harms of monolingualist ideologies, we can train tutors to support writing center visitors in understanding Standardized English as an ideological construction rather than a factual set of rules. As Laura Greenfield writes in "The Standard English Fairy Tale," "our assumptions about language are guided more often by a rhetoric that feeds on our unconscious racism than they are by our intellectual understanding of linguistic fact" (2011, 34). When we consider the vast range of variation commonly accepted as Standard English when spoken by white tongues, Greenfield concludes that rather than a discrete code, Standardized English is "any variety of English that has not been associated historically with resistance by communities of color" (2011, 43). Rather, Standard English is a construction rooted in white language supremacy (Inoue 2015). As linguist Rosina Lippi-Green explains, the racialized and racist expectations for a particular form of "accentless" English are a manifestation of standard language ideology, or "a bias toward an abstract, idealized homogeneous language, which is imposed and maintained by dominant institutions" (2012, 64). Because we can understand Standard English as a construction rather than a factual linguistic system, we join the many scholars who refer to it as "Standardized English" to emphasize the political nature of the variety.

Tutors can acknowledge the political nature of Standardized English effectively once they have, following the first translingual tutoring strategy, made space for inquiry and negotiation of students' linguistic choice. As we work with students to negotiate their writing, we will inevitably reach moments where linguistic features do not align with Standardized English, at which point we have opened a junction. When we acknowledge to a language-minoritized student that the conventions of Standard English are not objective rules that necessarily result in clear communication—so much as they are socially constructed expectations that are infused with particular culture-, race-, and power-informed values—the student may cultivate a more authentic position of agency from which to negotiate their language choices. From here, tutors are able to present a range of options to the writer, who might minimize risk by adopting a Standardized English construction in place of their own; maintain the original construction as a point of style reflecting their positionality, personal history, intersecting identities, and purpose; or perhaps revise the text around the nonconforming feature to prepare readers for how to understand the construction and to better situate its purpose in the larger work through parentheticals, footnotes, or exposition. All are valid choices, but it may only be in conversation with the tutee that a sense of choice emerges at all.

In addition to helping language-minoritized students see beyond and critique the inherent authority of Standardized English, drawing attention to the political nature of these constructions with their rootedness in histories of the white academy can work to disrupt the hegemony of Standardized English in academic writing, making space for other ways of being and knowing.

Tutor education following the translingual tutoring strategy of situating Standardized English as political, then, will explicitly challenge white language supremacy by exploring ways to productively critique Standardized English with students. As Kristina Aikens points out, we can help tutors explore how their own linguistic assumptions may "have been shaped by White supremacy and other hegemonic systems" (2019, sec. 4, para. 13). Thus, anti-racist tutor education combats monolingualism and directly examines the political nature of Standardized English; this is complex work that attends to the matrix of power, language, and the writing center's location in the institution. Of course, training tutors to situate Standardized English as political does not necessarily mean that students will leave sessions having challenged the norm with texts full of non-Standard English linguistic features. Rather, as Brooke Schreiber and Missy Watson describe, such a translingual orientation "can acknowledge that language boundaries and standards are socially constructed and permeable without overlooking communicative expectations and without denying the power that adhering to standards can afford in students' lives" (2018, 95). This translingual tutoring strategy can be enacted in small gestures that make choice feel more accessible by dispelling the myth that Standardized English or academic discourse broadly writ are the sole means for clear or correct communication, that Standardized English is the "pure" form of English, or that instances of non-standard or non-English varieties can only be unintelligible. Students may then weigh their purpose, their context, and other essential concerns more fairly when deciding whether to conform to or subvert standardized expectations in university writing.

Listening to tutors talk about how they apply this strategy demonstrates the importance of training around how to contest standard language ideology. Tutor Bianca shares her experience in initiating conversations about the politics of language: "In the past I've framed this strategy by talking to students about their 'voice.' I'd say things like, 'I can really hear your voice in this paragraph. This is how you write, let's keep this.' I wasn't so good about situating language as political, but since attending workshops around language diversity and working more intensely with ELL students, I feel more equipped to help students make writerly choices because I have the language to address the power dynamics at play. It has helped me to say, 'you have options.' "

Tutors also acknowledge that it's a privilege to challenge any system. As peer-tutor Thomas shares, "usually when this [a conversation about language and power] happens it's a conversation about a grade. Students will say, 'I need you to check my grammar. I need this to read correctly.' " GPAs, as students are aware, have real material impact, and tutors using Strategy 3 might consider ways they can provide space to invite students into this conversation while acknowledging the material stakes. Asking students to consider their own personal writing goals in addition to those of the assignment is a place to begin parsing out student agency and assignment expectations, teacher directive, and institutional power.

Strategy 3: Complicate Your Idea of "Audience"

One common way that folks have responded to calls for honoring linguistic diversity is to respect linguistic difference in informal settings, while teaching students that Standardized English is what's expected in formal contexts. Such strategies seemingly take a commonsense rhetorical approach to helping writers make informed choices about their linguistic practices, helping them navigate complicated everyday communication with a sophisticated linguistic repertoire. But such strategies often rely on a limited understanding of audience and context, framing most school-based and other formal settings as those in which linguistically diverse students' organic language practices are simply inappropriate, and in which a "formal," standardized variety of English is preferred. In these moments, teachers and tutors, together with students, imagine their audience to be "the racist over there," rather than working to conceive of a reader who can engage with complex linguistic constructions in nuanced and responsive ways.

In 2018, co-author and Rowan Writing Center Director Celeste helped to bring the regional Mid-Atlantic Writing Centers Association's annual conference to our campus, where we were honored to host keynote speakers Vershawn Ashanti Young and Frankie Condon. Their talk was moving, addressing linguistic racism and our roles as literacy educators; but one of the most striking moments, for us, happened during the Q&A. An audience member had asked a common question in response to translingual and code-meshing scholarship about how we balance the need to work against linguistic racism while also supporting students in navigating the expectations of Standardized English in courses with "less woke" professors around the university or employers down the road. dr. vay (as he's known) replied that we have to be cautious about becoming a "proxy racist." If we teach racist pedagogy to prepare students for when they come into contact with racists down the road, he explained, we embody the racist we say we deplore. Such acts, as dr. vay argues, put us in the position of proxy racist as we invoke the attitudes of the most narrow-minded reader, rather than the most responsive. We need not continue to identify *this* reader as the imagined audience, and thereby continue to constrain students' linguistic choices, opting for standardized varieties over personal preference, organic practice, community and heritage features, embodied and racialized codes, and the like.

In order to train tutors to avoid the pitfalls of proxy racism in service of the "nameless, faceless people" (Schreiber and Wordon 2019) we fear will judge or reject our students' non-standard language variety, in this strategy we invite readers to consider how we might complicate the idea of audience. After all, rarely are we writing solely for an audience of red-pen-toting, old English professor-types. Rather, a translingual perspective recognizes that our audience necessarily includes speakers of non-standard or non-English languages, people of color, and multilingual speakers in addition to white, Standardized English speakers who welcome variety in their reading experience. To complicate our idea of audience, we must throw off what Flores and Rosa call "the White gaze" (2015), helping students imagine audiences that include those who have an orientation of openness to our fuller linguistic repertoire. Otherwise, we are likely to deliver code-switching pedagogies, which fail to understand the connection between language and racial identity, imagining that one can simply overcome racist reactions to a speaker by changing the speaker's language practices (Baker-Bell 2020; Young 2007). We are not, of course, suggesting that tutors enact what can be characterized as a caricatured and misunderstood version of translingualism that ignores audience and, as Zhaozhe Wang describes, consists of "unwarranted and unsubstantiated linguistic novelty in the name of challenging discursive conventions" (2018, sec. 5, para. 2). Rather, when we teach tutors to help their writers consider audience, we may invite them to consider how a racially and linguistically diverse audience, rather than a Standardized English–only audience, might respond to particular choices.

Tutors Nicole and Julian, for instance, help Rowan students expand their idea of audience by coaching them with questions such as: Who else can you imagine reading this paper (besides your professor)? What would you want this audience to understand? What message would you want them to receive? In what ways does your language shift for that audience? These questions can open up conversations about language use, and rhetorical context, and can further engage conversations about language and power. Tutor Anthony describes how framing audience around experimentation and play can engage students in thinking beyond the limits of specific course assignments and imagine new audiences for their writing. This can help students consider the expectations of the assignment while also imagining alternatives to shaping their writing for a range of audiences—audiences that include non-white speakers of a variety of languages, as inevitably most audiences will.

Strategy 4: Address Internalized Monolingualist Ideologies

While it may feel like a big ask, in Strategy 4, we suggest that writing center staff can work with the writers who visit us to address their internalized monolingualist ideologies. Internalized monolingualist ideologies appear when we doubt the value of our linguistic differences and perceive our accented or otherwise different organic language varieties as features to be overcome in order to be "fit" for academic writing.

White students are systemically taught that their language and literacy practices are welcome and suited for academic learning, according to April Baker-Bell, but when Black students use Standardized English, "they are often are met with symbolic linguistic violence," as well as "linguistic microaggressions—bias and negative messages such as 'you are really articulate;' 'you speak very well;' 'you speak intelligently'—that imply that they should sound a certain way based on their race" (2018, 101). In the writing center and in our classrooms, we often hear our Black students as well as other language-minoritized students say, "I can't write," or "I suck at grammar." These are moments we can see as a trauma response, wherein accumulated microaggressions have persuaded students that their language practices define them as outsiders, unwelcome, not good enough, or otherwise unfit for the university. As a translingual practice of countering monolingualist ideologies, tutors can use such moments as an opening for healing and change.

Writing center practitioner Nancy Effinger Wilson recalls her own experience of exclusion in "Stocking the Bodega: Towards a New Writing Center Paradigm," wherein she was told (and believed) that she did not belong in higher education. Wilson's story is, sadly, not uncommon. We hear similar tales from our students, in writing center sessions, and from colleagues in our field who have described their own experiences of racialized linguistic oppression in and beyond the classroom (Gilyard 1991; Villanueva 1993; Baker-Bell 2020). But according to Wilson, tutors can either sustain harmful linguistic attitudes, or they can help students understand their linguistic difference as an asset: "Had I visited a writing center back then, perhaps someone would have contextualized this new discourse for me—stressing that my home discourse had value and legitimacy, even if rhetorically ineffective given my professors' requirements" (2018, sec. 7, para. 3). We would, however, suggest that tutors can use the translingual and anti-racist strategies we offer here to move beyond mere acknowledgment of the value of language variety; we can and should transform the very structures of linguistic violence within our universities and help to attend to their harm upon our students.

One concrete way writing centers can accomplish this tall order is to train tutors to understand and teach tutees about standard language ideology. A tutor training curriculum that works for raciolinguistic justice might include readings like selections from Rosina Lippi-Green's *English with an Accent,* Young's "Should Writers Use They Own English," and June Jordan's "Nobody Mean More to Me than You and the Future Life of Willie Jordan," or even the video of Asao Inoue's 2019 Conference on College Composition and Communication (CCCC) chair's address. Once tutors understand standard language ideology for themselves, as Liliana Naydan suggests, they may begin to "look inward to unearth the languages that they speak and the means by which those languages position them as prospective agents of change who can work to counter monolingual hegemonic thinking" (2016, sec. 3, para. 2). In understanding standard language ideology as it infuses our educational and cultural institutions, our day-to-day interactions, and even our personal thoughts, we can position ourselves to better support multilingual and language-minoritized students in confronting and healing their own internalized monolingualism.

Of course, racial tensions continue to shape our language and literacy work and our students' experiences at the university as they seek to assimilate to expectations in academic writing. For García, who describes raciolinguistic conflict in joining the academy, "What was at a stake, among other things, was being an accomplice to my own degradation" (2017, 31). But writing centers, the primary location of support for language-minoritized students in the university, can serve as a space for disruption and culture shift as tutors work closely with students to unveil ideologies like white language supremacy that circulate through our institutions. García suggests tutors could become "decolonial agents," and we believe we can get them there by engaging in anti-racist professional development that helps them situate the context of language difference during a session in which a tutee has disclosed a sense of their language as inferior, a sign that they do not belong. Tutors might also keep handy examples of published academic writing that showcase linguistic diversity and code-meshing in print. As Nancy Bou Ayash writes in "Conditions of (Im)Possibility," placing such "academic literacies on display and making their production, mode of emergence, and manifestation available for scrutiny can be a first step toward harnessing more informed representations" (2016, 573). To highlight examples of published academic work featuring non-English languages or non–Standardized English varieties would help students challenge their internalized monolingualist ideologies and received notions of which languages count and what insiderness looks like in the academy.

One way of opening spaces for healing and change is, as tutor Nicole notes, "leaning into the things that students do well in their writing and helping them to see how they can be successful at different stages of the writing process." When tutors collaborate with students to identify their successes throughout the writing process, they can then address internalized monolingualism by encouraging writers to generate ideas, speak, and write in whatever language they find is most comfortable for them. Anthony shares his experiences working with a student whose home language is Farsi: "We were working on an outline together for a lab report. She was speaking English with me and writing the outline in English, but it seemed like she was struggling with the outline part. I suggested she make her outline in Farsi if she wanted to, and she tried that. We worked together to talk through those ideas in English for her draft." In order to productively draw from her Farsi as a valid linguistic resource, this student had to first confront her reluctance to do so. In this way, she practiced noticing, then overcoming, internalized monolingualism as a barrier.

Finally, encouraging the use of students' full range of linguistic resources in the writing center means we must foster a writing center culture that values and appreciates language variation. Piper and Thomas are two tutors in our center who talk about this connection of learning Japanese and their experience in tutoring multilingual writers. Thomas shares, "Learning a new language can be a humbling experience. It's this desire to learn something new and to put yourself in uncomfortable situations to do so. I've never had a Japanese student actually visit me in the writing center, but the experience of learning a language is so translatable to tutoring any student through a lens of linguistic diversity." To empathize with multilingual and non-standard language users' internalized monolingualism, and to notice it in their own thinking, tutors—including so-called monolingual tutors—can experience language learning on the path to better supporting all writers. Addressing internalized monolingualism in these ways is successful because it empowers critical self-reflection in tutors and tutees and demonstrates that many of the same principles we value—conversation and collaboration—can happen in many languages and across language differences.

Strategy 5: Advocate for Language Difference beyond Individual Sessions in the Writing Center

The final strategy we offer for translingual tutoring acknowledges that we cannot change institutional cultures merely by supporting students' use of non-English and non-standard languages in one-on-one writing center sessions with students. Rather, we must help shift harmful misconceptions of linguistic difference around the university. In committee work, in emails where faculty write to seek support for their students who "can't write," in professional development workshops for faculty around the university, in working to push against standardized testing in admissions processes—here lies our responsibility and our opportunity to build institutions free of raciolinguistic discrimination.

We can begin by helping faculty across the university to better understand the value of linguistic variation and the complex realities of language learning. Fortunately, many faculty *want* to learn how to better serve their language-minoritized students. According to Schreiber and Wordon, the "nameless, faceless" faculty around our campuses most often don't report the attitudes toward error that we imagine they might (2019, 68). Rather, they find, faculty who adhere to strict expectations for particular conventions often do so out of a desire to support students in meeting expectations of professional audiences outside of the university. These realities suggest the need for increased and continued programming to acquaint faculty across the university, as well as more public audiences, with the problem of language bias and linguistic oppression that we all may be sustaining only for fear that others will.

There are many specific tactics writing centers might take to help educate our colleagues and prepare them to better serve our language-minoritized students. For instance, we might become more explicit in our mission, vision, and policy statements that we support language diversity and that we use our language work toward building an anti-racist university. And we can and should circulate these statements to a wider audience of students and faculty. We can also use the common practices of tutor- and administrator-facilitated workshops to share the center's vital mission of valuing language diversity. Programming for multilingual support might be extended to include an audience of both faculty and student multilingual writers, supporting dialogue around challenges and strengths of their language and literacy experiences at university. Such faculty-student collaborations, drawing from translingual theory's central tenet that variation is the norm and an asset, would work to challenge the monolingualist ideologies framing linguistic difference as deficit. See Lindsay A. Sabatino's discussion in chapter 6 in this volume for more interesting ways tutors can offer events to intervene in language and social violence across campus.

Another way that tutors actively advocate for students beyond the writing center space is to help student-writers craft an email to their professor or prepare a script for a conversation about their own or others' language diversity. Recently in our center, a worried student and dedicated writing center visitor shared a very strict grading policy on grammar that dropped grades by a certain number of points for each "error." One of our tutors sat with him to craft an email to the professor about his concerns from his position as a multilingual writer. Regardless of the outcome, this is the kind of advocacy we hope to see our writing centers doing. Thus, we see administrators and tutors as sources of creative leadership potential for taking our translingual, anti-monolingual, anti-racist, and raciolinguistic justice pedagogy out of the writing center and into our wider institutions to meet monolingualist ideologies where they prevail.

CONCLUSION

The five strategies shared here are an invitation to become more critical of monolingual ideologies and to listen to and learn from our linguistically diverse students about what their language means to them. Listening to multilingual students' attitudes about writing support at our own university, we found that students shared the many ways they view their linguistic difference is a source of writerly strength, such as one student who comments, "I feel that I'm definitely more creative. My metaphors and similes are my strong suit because I can refer to my mother language." Another student writes, "I have a different background than most of my peers. I think that this really separates my writing as it's not like anyone else's." They also identify how being multilingual allows them to be more reflective of their writing experiences, with one student writing, "I definitely think about my writing more and synthesize it carefully." These comments suggest that multilingual students already use translingual strategies that disrupt deficit thinking around language difference. If featured in tutor training sessions, our five strategies for translingual tutoring may allow tutors to engage language diversity as a resource in their daily sessions, where it matters.

While no theoretical orientation to language pedagogy or series of strategies is a magic wand to cure the social ills that pervade higher education, we can nevertheless use our language and literacy pedagogy to work against harmful attitudes toward our language-minoritized students. It is not enough to simply change our vision and mission statements, although this is an important step to culture shift in our centers and universities. Rather, we have to work in practical ways and at the ideological level—in one-on-one sessions, in professional development, with colleagues across the university, and within our larger discipline—to help students produce writing that honors their linguistic agency and identity, to push academic discourse to welcome and honor the gift of many voices, and to eradicate raciolinguistic discrimination as a gatekeeper in the academy. It is our sincere hope that these strategies will serve as a useful starting point for administrators and staff to continue the fight for justice for language-minoritized students, particularly for students of color.

REFERENCES

Aikens, Kristina. 2019. "Prioritizing Antiracism in Writing Tutor Education." In *How We Teach Writing Tutors*, edited by Karen Gabrielle Johnson and Ted Roggenbuck. WLN: A Journal of Writing Center Scholarship. https://wlnjournal.org/digitaleditedcollection1/Aikens.html.

Ayash, Nancy Bou. 2016. "Conditions of (Im)Possibility: Postmonolingual Language Representations in Academic Literacies." *College English* 78, no. 6: 555–577. https://www.jstor.org/stable/44075144.

Baker-Bell, April. 2018. "'I Can Switch My Language, but I Can't Switch My Skin': What Teachers Must Understand about Linguistic Racism." In *The Guide for White Women Who Teach Black Boys*, edited by Eddie Moore, Ali Michael, and Marguerite Penick-Parks, 97–107. Thousand Oaks, CA: Corwin.

Baker-Bell, April. 2020. *Linguistic Justice: Black Language, Literacy, Identity, and Pedagogy*. New York: Routledge.

Blazer, Sarah. 2015. "Twenty-First Century Writing Center Staff Education: Teaching and Learning towards Inclusive and Productive Everyday Practice." *Writing Center Journal* 35, no. 1 (Fall/Winter): 17–54.

Camarillo, Eric. 2019. "Dismantling Neutrality: Cultivating Antiracist Writing Center Ecologies." *Praxis: A Writing Center Journal* 16, no. 2 (Spring): 1–6. http://www.praxisuwc.com/162-camarillo.

Canagarajah, A. Suresh. 1994. "Competing Discourses in Sri Lankan English Poetry." *World Englishes* 13, no. 3: 361–376. https://doi.org/10.1111/j.1467-971X.1994.tb00322.x.

Canagarajah, A. Suresh. 2013. "Negotiating Translingual Literacy: An Enactment." *Research in the Teaching of English* 48, no. 1 (August): 40–67. https://www.jstor.org/stable/24398646.

Flores, Nelson, and Jonathan Rosa. 2015. "Undoing Appropriateness: Raciolinguistic Ideologies and Language Diversity in Education." *Harvard Educational Review* 85, no. 2 (December): 149–71.

Fox, Tom. 1990. "Basic Writing as Cultural Conflict." *Journal of Education* 172, no 1 (April): 65–83.

García, Romeo. 2017. "Unmaking Gringo Centers." *Writing Center Journal* 36, no. 1: 29–60.

Gevers, Jeroen. 2018. "Translingualism Revisited: Language Difference and Hybridity in L2 Writing." *Journal of Second Language Writing* 40 (June): 73–83.

Gilyard, Keith. 1991. *Voices of the Self: A Study of Language Competence.* Detroit: Wayne State University Press.

Greenfield, Laura. 2011. " 'The Standard English' Fairy Tale: A Rhetorical Analysis of Racist Pedagogies and Commonplace Assumptions about Language Diversity." In *Writing Centers and the New Racism: A Call for Sustainable Dialogue and Change,* edited by Laura Greenfield and Karen Rowan, 33–60. Logan: Utah State University Press.

Horner, Bruce. 1992. "Rethinking the 'Sociality' of Error: Teaching Editing as Negotiation." *Rhetoric Review* 11, no. 1 (Autumn): 172–99.

Horner, Bruce, Min-Zhan Lu, Jacqueline Jones Royster, and John Trimbur. 2011. "Language Difference in Writing: Toward a Translingual Approach." *College English* 73, no. 3 (January): 303–321.

Horner, Bruce, and John Trimbur. 2002. "English Only and College Composition." *College Composition and Communication* 53, no. 4 (June): 594–630.

Inoue, Asao. 2015. *Antiracist Writing Assessment Ecologies: Teaching and Assessing Writing for a Socially Just Future.* Fort Collins, CO: WAC Clearinghouse.

Inoue, Asao. 2019. "How Do We Language So People Stop Killing Each Other, or What Do We Do about White Language Supremacy?" Keynote delivered at the Conference on College Composition and Communication, Pittsburgh, PA, March 2019.

Jain, Rashi. 2014. "Global Englishes, Translinguistic Identities, and Translingual Practices in a Community College ESL Classroom: A Practitioner Research Reports." *TESOL Journal* 5, vol. 3 (September): 490–518.

Jordan, June. 1988. "Nobody Mean More to Me than You and the Future Life of Willie Jordan." *Harvard Educational Review* 58, no. 3 (August): 363–375.

Lee, Jerry Won. 2018. *The Politics of Translingualism: After Englishes.* New York: Routledge.

Lippi-Green, Rosina. 2012. *English with an Accent: Language, Ideology and Discrimination in the United States.* New York: Routledge.

Lorimer Leonard, Rebecca, and Rebecca Nowacek. 2016. "Transfer and Translingualism." *College English* 78, no. 3 (January): 258–264.

Lu, Min-Zhan. 2006. "Living-English Work." *College English* 68, no. 6 (July): 605–618.

Matsuda, Paul Kei. 2013. "It's the Wild West Out There: A New Linguistic Frontier in US College Composition." In *Literacy as Translingual Practice: Between Communities and Classrooms,* edited by Suresh Canagarajah, 128–138. New York: Routledge.

Matsuda, Paul Kei. 2014. "The Lure of Translingual Writing." *PMLA* 129, no. 3 (May): 478–483.

Naydan, Liliana. 2016. "Generation 1.5 Writing Center Practice: Problems with Multilingualism and Possibilities via Hybridity." *Praxis: A Writing Center Journal* 13, no. 2. http://www.praxisuwc.com/naydan-132.

Olson, Bobbi. 2013. "Rethinking Our Work with Multilingual Writers: The Ethics and Responsibility of Language Teaching in the Writing Center." *Praxis: A Writing Center Journal* 10, no. 2. http://www.praxisuwc.com/olson-102.

Schreiber, Brooke, and Dorothy Wordon. 2019. "'Nameless, Faceless People': How Other Teachers' Expectations Influence Our Pedagogy." *Composition Studies* 47, no. 1 (Spring): 57–72.

Schreiber, Brooke, and Missy Watson. 2018. "Translingualism ≠ Code-meshing: A Response to Gevers' 'Translingualism revisited.'" *Journal of Second Language Acquisition* 42 (December): 94–97.

Shaughnessy, Mina. 1977. *Errors and Expectations: A Guide for the Teacher of Basic Writing*. New York: Oxford University Press.

Smitherman, Geneva. 1977. *Talkin and Testifyin: The Language of Black America*. Detroit: Wayne State University Press.

Villanueva, Victor. 1993. *Bootstraps: From an American Academic of Color*. Urbana, IL: National Council of Teachers of English.

Villanueva, Victor. 2011. "The Rhetorics of Racism: A Historical Sketch." In *Writing Centers and the New Racism: A Call for Sustainable Dialogue and Change*, edited by Laura Greenfield and Karen Rowan, 17–32. Logan: Utah State University Press.

Wang, Zhaozhe. 2018. "Rethinking Translingual as a Transdisciplinary Rhetoric: Broadening the Dialogic Space." *Composition Forum* 40 (Fall). http://compositionforum.com/issue/40/translingual.php.

Watson, Missy, and Rachael Shapiro. 2018. "Clarifying the Multiple Dimensions of Monolingualism: Keeping Our Sights on Language Politics." *Composition Forum* 38 (Spring). http://www.compositionforum.com/issue/38/monolingualism.php.

Wilson, Nancy Effinger. 2012. "Stocking the Bodega: Towards a New Writing Center Paradigm." *Praxis: A Writing Center Journal* 10, no. 1. http://www.praxisuwc.com/wilson-101.

Young, Vershawn Ashanti. 2007. *Your Average Nigga: Performing Race, Literacy, and Masculinity*. Detroit: Wayne State University Press.

Young, Vershawn Ashanti. 2010. "Should Writers Use They Own English?" *Iowa Journal of Cultural Studies* 12, no. 1 (Fall and Spring): 110–118.

Young, Vershawn Ashanti, and Frankie Condon. 2018. "Performing Agency, Authority, Authenticity and Antiracism in Writing Center Work." Keynote delivered at the Mid-Atlantic Writing Centers Association Conference, Rowan University, Glassboro, New Jersey, March 2018.

8

DISRUPTING SYSTEMS

Anti-racism and Online Writing Center Work

Lisa Eastmond Bell

Online learning was meant to disrupt established educational systems. In 1997, Harvard Business Professor Clayton Christensen introduced the term "disruptive innovation" to describe how businesses might adapt existing products or services by lowering complexity and cost to forge paths into new markets. Christiansen also identified online learning as a potential disruptive innovation. At the time, higher education largely embraced the concept as a way to make postsecondary education available to diverse and underrepresented populations (Stokes 2011). However, by the early 2010s, online education "[was] often taken to task for not having revolutionized higher education enough" (Stokes 2011). Perhaps, online education has failed to fully disrupt established systems because it was never about using new platforms in neutral spaces. Systems, including educational systems, are designed to benefit select participants who adhere to designated perspectives and protocols. Any unrealized potential in online education is not about platforms—it is about systems, people, and power.

Most online education has roots within systems and communities that justify and reinforce racial inequality by defaulting to certain programming and participants. Clear evidence of this is a lack of attention to how online learning impacts the underrepresented communities it held promise to serve. In 2020, as researchers from the National Research Center for Distance Education and Technological Advancements (DETA) and the Wiche Cooperative for Educational Technologies (WCET) set out to "review which digital learning practices most benefit students who identify as Black, African American, Hispanic, Latinx, Latino or Latina, American Indian, Alaskan Native, Indigenous American, Native Hawaiian, or Pacific Islander, they quickly ran into a problem—there wasn't much research to review" (McKenzie 2021). After searching for relevant research, they only identified twelve studies

https://doi.org/10.7330/9781646424573.c008

(McKenzie 2021). If online education were designed with disruption and racial equality in mind, research and assessment would reflect how systems had been altered to best serve a wider range of students. Although online education provides additional access points to higher education, its design and assessment suggest it functions more as a reification than a reinvention of educational systems.

Writing centers have also largely failed to reimagine and research online tutoring or use online programming to disrupt old systems and better serve a wider range of students. If "writing centers are places where inequality—unequal access to educational resources—is made manifest" (Denny, Nordlof, and Salem 2018, 69), then online writing center work likely tells a similar story. As with any system, it is worth asking about those our online programs were built for and who benefits from them. As J. M. Dembsey (2020, 15) reminds us, for more than two decades, the writing center community has failed to frame online writing center work as valuable, although scholars have identified online tutoring as a viable option for many learners, including writers of color, multilingual writers, and Disabled writers. We now understand that "online instruction and tutoring are not deficit models, substandard to onsite instruction and tutoring; rather, they are models of differentiated learning" (Hewett et al. 2019). However, many of us within the writing center community have spent too many years trying to replicate in-person tutoring systems and stories during online tutoring instead of studying and structuring online writing center work with social justice in mind.

This chapter invites writing center communities to disrupt established systems through anti-racist online writing center work. This is not the first invitation, and such calls will likely continue until we admit that "the inequality that stubbornly pervades the rest of the American education system also shapes writing center work" (Salem 2016, 161) and we purposefully reexamine our online work. As someone involved with online writing center work for two decades and having developed online tutoring at two large universities, I am still learning and see anti-racism as providing an essential lens for researching and revising the online writing center spaces and systems I help design and maintain. The concepts presented in this chapter are not a template, since anti-racism and online writing center work are by nature contextual and complex (see acknowledgment). However, while anti-racist online writing center work is not a series of easy answers, addressing racism in our work is central to advancing our local and larger writing center communities. In exploring the complicated intersections of anti-racism and online writing center theory and practice, we should do so with optimism, knowing that "if humans can create unjust systems, they can also change those systems" (Greenfield 2019, 62). Since the daunting task of disrupting systems of racial inequality can itself be a roadblock to anti-racism, this chapter limits its focus to understanding people and power, becoming data-driven, and addressing access in online writing center work. It also provides ideas for practical application and acknowledges that anti-racist online education is a process that is dynamic and ongoing.

UNDERSTANDING PEOPLE AND POWER

Anti-racist online writing center work is about people and power dynamics more than platforms. In both in-person and online tutoring sessions, writers and tutors take on roles and relationships that often seem predetermined. In most cases, these are not organic roles but the result of established systems. Within most academic systems and writing center programs, power and expertise are ascribed to tutors, and learning and deficit models are often aligned with writers, particularly writers of color. Using Lev Vygotsky's constructivist model of scaffolding learning, writers are guided through the learning process by "*more capable peers*" [italics in original] (Vygotsky and Cole 1978; Vygotsky 1986). Tutors are most often poised as the "more capable peers," helping and supporting writers rather than functioning as co-learners. However, defining tutors this way reinforces and rationalizes problematic power structures and fails to acknowledge the identities and expertise writers bring into tutorials. Rather than disrupting these normed roles, most online writing center work has reinforced them. More ethical and racially equitable structures are possible, but the work of anti-racism in online spaces will involve writing centers relinquishing and sharing power by disrupting identity, reframing roles, and acknowledging ownership.

Disrupting Identity

Disrupting identity markers and power dynamics is essential to anti-racism in online writing center spaces. A 2019 study by Susan Salvo, Kaye Shelton, and Brett Welch reports Black men often preferring online learning environments because they experience fewer microaggressions and feel distanced from racial prejudice and stereotypes. This may be because in online spaces, students have greater control over disclosing their identities, allowing them to engage as writers undefined by other identity markers. Speaking of online tutoring, Ries (2015, 5) notes, "there is empowerment present when students are able to control the perceptions that others have of them." Along with shifting perceptions, online tutoring can reshape power dynamics, particularly in asynchronous sessions that allow writers to choose when and how to interact with tutor feedback and questions. Rather than having a tutor-guided discussion of the writer's work and set expectations for how the writer will engage in the session, the writer maintains control. In this way, "asynchronous sessions distribute power more evenly than face-to-face ones" (Camarillo 2020, 72). By redistributing power and offering writers greater control when discussing their work and identities, online tutoring provides space for racial and relational equity.

Tutors also benefit from controlling the disclosure of their personal identities in sessions. Describing their in-person tutoring experience, Alexandria Lockett (2019, 27) explains how writers "may decide to decline services from non-white or non-American tutors because they automatically dismiss the very idea that they could speak or write 'better English' than their white colleagues" (see also García 2017). Certainly, discrimination also occurs online. Writing centers should not strip tutors of their identities, but as with writers, providing tutors of color with options for how they engage or show up in online sessions allows them power over their identities and potential interactions with writers.

Disrupting identity also includes hiring a racially diverse staff to shift perceptions and practice within online writing center spaces. Hiring a more diverse staff and challenging discriminatory hiring practices help rewrite the "enduring narratives about roles, stereotypes, who belongs in our centers, who doesn't, who does the work of our centers" (Jordan 2020; also see Rachel Herzl-Betz, chapter 3 in this collection). However, hiring should not be reduced to representation or tokenism, and having a racially diverse staff means little if employees are trained and managed in ways that reinforce inequitable power structures or colonizing practices of language and literacy common to established educational systems (Inoue 2021). Additionally, tutors of color should not be hired so white tutors can interact with and learn from people of color, forcing tutors of color to perform additional labor to educate their peers in online spaces. If writing centers want to disrupt learning in online spaces and promote anti-racism, then a range of identities, experiences, and perspectives are needed to shape new systems.

Disrupting Identity in Practice

- Retire training materials that reinforce or position specific racial groups as outside the norms of typical students or sessions.

- Allow writers and tutors control over their identities by not requiring use of cameras in online tutorials.
- Give staff choices about how their image or other identity markers are used on writing center websites or in online writing center spaces.
- Offer asynchronous online tutoring options to allow students more control over how they receive and interact with tutor feedback.
- Hire online tutors from different racial and cultural backgrounds and normalize sharing new perspectives rather than expecting staff to embrace established norms.

Reframing Roles

Making systems, roles, and relationships visible in online writing center work is central to aligning anti-racist theory with practice. As Nancy Grimm (2009, 16) explains, "Significant change in any workplace occurs when unconscious conceptual models are brought to the surface and replaced with conscious ones." In online settings, it is particularly important for tutors and administrators to clarify roles and relationships. In person, tutors can signal their role as learner through active listening, pausing to think, taking notes, sharing facial expressions, and adjusting body language. However, in online tutoring sessions, whether cameras are on or off, signally learning may be more difficult. Fortunately, decreased nonverbal communication may encourage tutors to clarify roles and name themselves as readers, peers, listeners, and learners and explicitly name writers as owners of their work (Bell 2019). In addition to defining roles and relationships in online spaces, tutors should make systems visible. This may be as simple as a tutor noting that they understood the writer's ideas and casual language, while also explaining that a professor may expect a more formal tone. The tutor and writer can explore options and potential outcomes to help inform the writer's revision choices. Being explicit about both expectations and options for writers helps online tutors and writers develop a better understanding of how participants' race and culture may privilege or complicate their learning within traditional academic systems. Ideally, this would also encourage critical conversations needed to disrupt and reshape systems of inequality.

These critical conversations should also be present in online tutor training and praxis. In discussing inequality and inclusion in online learning, tutor and administrator education should be ongoing and move from conversation to concrete action. As Sarah Blazer (2015, 19) suggests, "writing center staff education must unfold such that all involved have dynamic and varied opportunities to unpack assumptions, engage with new perspectives, and imagine and perform praxis." Essentially, anti-racist learning should be actionable (Smalling 2020, 7). Speaking of writing center work generally, Frankie Condon (2007, 31) explains that "moving beyond an ethics of good intentions to an ethics of responsibility will require us to bracket questions of sincerity in order to engage with questions of impact and effect." For instance, in one of my online tutor training meetings, this shift from awareness to action occurred as tutors reflected on violence against our Asian American Pacific Islander (AAPI) community. After giving staff space to feel and reflect, we shifted the conversation to identify action we could take in online tutoring to support AAPI students. Tutors suggested and committed to starting each online tutorial by learning and correctly pronouncing each student's name. While a small move, it was a disruptive one designed to increase respect, facilitate tutor learning, and shift power dynamics within online tutorials.

Reframing Roles in Practice

- Make roles, power dynamics, and systems visible online, and discuss how to disrupt systems in favor of empowering students and creating anti-racist learning communities.
- Explicitly train online tutors to avoid deficit thinking and assumptions about students as problems and to understand that the challenges tutors and writers face are most often about navigating and negotiating systems.
- Reframe tutors and administrators as co-learners and guides within anti-racist online learning environments.
- Make online anti-racist writing center education actionable, so tutors and administrators move from discussing to doing the work needed to learn and change.
- Make use of or add to scholarship that reframes and rethinks the possibilities for online writing center work that is more ethical and inclusive.

Acknowledging Ownership

When interacting with writers of color whose power and range of choices are often diminished within current systems, it is vital for online writing center staff to recognize, respect, and reinforce writers' power to make their own decisions about their learning and writing. Writing centers often choose how and when writers access online writing support. In online spaces, writing centers control and reinforce structures of power and privilege when they severely limit hours of online assistance and fail to provide support in more than one form. Since writers have both personal forces as well as external reasons that influence their decisions to use or not use writing center services (Salem 2016), an anti-racist approach to online writing center work requires increasing writers' choices about how they will connect with our programs. Just as we would respect a student's choice to not register for an 8 a.m. seminar or to consider how close a class is to their campus job, we should assume writers can make effective choices about using online writing center services. Kathryn Denton (2014, 108) reminds us that students should be trusted to make decisions about their education, explaining that "students deliberately seek out asynchronous online tutoring not because they consider it a drop-off service, but because it is a format that works for them, and they are seeking feedback that will help to guide their revision process. Asynchronous online tutoring benefits the students who seek it out." We should also consider increasing online options to better serve a range of writers, including offering access to online handouts or chat options for writers to ask quick questions rather than attending full appointments. Online writing center work does not and should not have to replicate in-person interactions. Disruptions to established systems contribute to the work of anti-racism by empowering a diverse range of writers.

In anti-racist online writing center work, students of all cultural and linguistic backgrounds maintain ownership of their language and literacy. As Diane Martinez and Leslie Olsen (2015, 185) remind us, in online writing center spaces, "just like in an onsite writing center, students should remain the agents of their own writing." Whether the writer is present, or tutors only have access to a student's text, since writing is intertwined with identity, tutors and administrators should not make assumptions about what is best for a writer rhetorically or linguistically. Reinforcing writers' ownership disrupts systems of racial inequality by refusing to require writers to conform to what many writing centers, as part of in-person and online dominant educational systems, deem the standard or norm for written language in academia (see Jennifer Martin, chapter 1 in this collection). Allowing writers control of their language and writing choices online provides a more racially responsive and respectful approach to online tutoring.

Acknowledging Ownership in Practice

- Offer options for online writing support, and empower writers to choose the services and programming that best fit their needs and preferences.

- Reinforce writers' ownership of their work in online spaces where the presence of participants may be less visible.
- Suggest rhetorical and linguistic options to writers rather than encouraging assimilation of individual's texts.
- Own your role as a member of a local and larger online writing center community, and attend webinars or workshops and collaborate with colleagues on how to develop more anti-racist online writing center services.

BECOMING DATA DRIVEN

In education, including online writing center work, students are often lumped together in terms of experience and identity. Even the term *writers of color*, used throughout this chapter, is problematic since it combines a wide range of learners (see acknowledgment). The same overgeneralization and erasing of identity happen with other student populations, including first-generation, multilingual, nontraditional, Disabled, LGBTQ+, graduate, first-year, and international students. In examining more than two decades of research on learners in online environments, researchers from DETA and WCET (2021, 8) found that in most instances, data for more than one racial group of participants were combined, aggregated, and compared against white, "privileged counterparts." This pattern is common but not particularly useful. Instead, "it is pertinent to consider multiple racial and ethnic groups to identify research-based practices and to be cognizant of the importance of studying groups separately as to avoid the trap of monolithic stereotyping in research" (DETA and WCET 2021, 8). While there may be similarities among some groups of students in online learning environments, similarities do not equate to sameness.

Knowing the Writers We Work With

When writing center administrators fail to identify and understand the writers using online services, we risk reinforcing systems of racial inequality. Although we train online tutors to work with writers as individuals, there is danger in seeing only the personal and not the larger social context writers bring with them into writing center spaces (Villanueva 2006; Salem 2016). Even more troublesome are the ways in-person and online writing center communities racialize *average* as white by problematically providing training in terms of typical (i.e., white) sessions and *atypical* tutorials with one-hour trainings or single readings on different demographics of students (English Language

Learners [ELL], LGBTQ+, Disabled, working-class, BIPOC). This does little more than maintain systems of whiteness at the center of our programs.

Anti-racist online writing center work requires research about the writers we see regularly as well as those who do not feel the writing center serves or suits them (Wilson 2012; Salem 2016). As we learn more about students, we see how " 'one size fits all' is not the most effective approach" (Gallagher and Maxfield 2019). When we address the needs of all online learners generically, the approach equates to an "all lives matter" approach that fails to recognize or rectify racial inequalities for student populations disenfranchised and marginalized by dominant educational systems.

Assessment data and research in online writing center usage provide a vantage point that makes both anti-racist programming and individual tailoring of services possible (Aguilar 2018). After piloting online tutoring at a previous institution, two tutors and I examined participant data from over 21,000 tutoring sessions to better understand student preferences for online writing center support. Results revealed that a larger number of working students, caregivers, and multilingual, international students were participating in asynchronous online tutoring. Given the writing center's busy in-person schedules, we had assumed we were adequately serving a range of students, but there were specific groups of students for whom our in-person services were less accessible. Actual data revealed that our online tutoring disrupted time, space, and methods of feedback in ways that made our services more accessible and equitable for a wider range of students (Bell, Brantley, Van Vleet 2022). While online tutors primarily work with students one-on-one, looking at larger datasets provides needed insight into how online writing center programming and resources may disrupt writing center norms and more fully serve students in diverse contexts and cultural or racial backgrounds.

Knowing the Writers We Work with in Practice

- Use data collected by your program and institution to better understand the writers who use online writing center programming and services.
- Compare the demographics of writers using different types of tutoring—in-person tutoring, in-person appointment-based tutoring, synchronous online tutoring, asynchronous online tutoring, and so on. If there are notable differences, learn more about writers' access, identity, and experiences.

- Rather than relying on general student satisfaction surveys to assess online writing center work, actively seek input from specific demographics and those who do not use the programs or resources offered.
- Be intentional and specific about the data you collect—instead of having a focus group for BIPOC students, talk to graduate students who identify as Mexican American or first-year writers who are international students.
- Partner with other offices to combine surveys and reduce survey fatigue and to reduce inequitable and additional labor asked of certain student populations.

The Need for Narratives

In addition to empirical research, real voices are needed to shape antiracist online writing center work. Understanding specific, local student demographics should not reduce students to numbers and writing center usage patterns. In addition to learning *about* the writers we work with online, we must learn *from* them. Although the data my tutors and I collected for our study revealed usage trends, it was the stories of the writers we worked with that ultimately shaped our online tutoring. After identifying usage patterns related to demographics, it would have been easy to develop our own stories about why certain students used online tutoring. To author students' stories would have allowed us to remain in control of the outcomes and authority, but it would not have positioned us to understand or respond to the needs of these writers. Diane Martinez et al. (2019) remind us that "online literacy educators still do not know much about student needs from the student point of view." Not only do online participants' perspectives help triangulate data and qualitatively explain findings, but they provide counterstories challenging writing center assumptions and complicating online work in ways that help disrupt inequitable systems.

The Need for Narratives in Practice

- Couple research with real voices. Let participants help you understand their data and provide purpose to the patterns you find. Do not assume you understand why and how writers use online services; listen and learn.
- Instead of distributing online surveys, host focus groups and compensate participants to access a wider range of students and stories.
- Amplify marginalized voices on behalf of those who speak, not solely for the performance and profit of the writing center.
- Use the qualitative and quantitative information you gather from participants to disrupt traditional systems and serve writers and tutors online in new and more effective ways.

Data Use and Anti-racism

What writing centers choose to do online with people's data and stories must also align with anti-racism. When posting on social media, writing centers should amplify and not appropriate students' data and stories. If students register for online tutoring, know who has access to registration data and how it is protected, since data loss or exposure "might disproportionately impact students who already experience marginalization" (Downs 2021). Since collecting demographic data also reduces writers' and tutors' control over their identities, narrative, and online footprint, writing center administrators should decide whether to collect additional data or share data with third parties or offices on campus. Additionally, since writing and identity are intertwined, beyond demographic data, the work of writers and tutors, both their intellectual property and life experiences, should be protected. For online tutorials, tutors' and writers' identifying information should be treated intentionally (e.g., title pages, paper headers, names associated with comments on papers). To protect those using online tutoring, papers and videos from online sessions should be deleted after a reasonable amount of time. Protecting online tutoring participants is crucial, particularly when we know that many systems are not reliable in protecting against identity and data loss online.

Data Use and Anti-racism in Practice

- Make sure employees receive training on how to protect data. Training should be tailored to your context but may include FERPA or cybersecurity training.
- Know how data are collected, stored, and protected. If tutors are commenting on drafts of student papers, be intentional about where those drafts are saved, who can access them, and for how long.
- Give registering participants options about how they identify. Note whether your registration process provides ways to opt out of demographic questions or fully identify.
- Design online writing center spaces in ways that allow tutors to choose and change how they show up in terms of race, gender, age, and so on.
- Know if third-party providers share or sell user data and if employing third-party providers or programs increases the digital footprint of tutors and writers. If so, notify participants and offer alternative options.
- Identify offices or individuals on campus that can help you learn more about anti-racism and ethical approaches to data collection and storage.

ADDRESSING ACCESS

Access and online writing center work are intrinsically connected. As Martinez and Olsen (2015, 188) explain, "providing inclusivity and accessibility grounds all of the OWI principles and should be considered at the onset of developing solutions instead of as an afterthought" (see also Conference on College Composition and Communication [CCCC] Position Statement on OWI).[1] As a writing center community, we know that online tutoring can help students access learning support. In fact, many learners—including writers of color, busy students, caregivers, working students, language learners, Disabled writers, and many students identifying in intersectional ways—prefer online tutoring for the ways in which it reconfigures space, time, interactions, and identity (Martinez and Olsen 2015; Ries 2015; Denton 2017; Bertucci Hamper 2018; Prince et al. 2018; Hewett et al. 2019; Camarillo 2020; Dembsey 2020; Bell, Brantley, and Van Vleet 2022). We also know online tutoring can evolve and facilitate learning in new ways. Two decades ago, collaborating on a Google Doc or conducting a video or screencast tutorial was not possible. Social media had not yet amplified the ways in which conversations continue despite gaps in time and space, and readily accessible closed captioning and transcription were only wish list items in online education. As technology and online learning develop, so should access to online writing center programming and resources.

Despite the benefits of online learning, issues of access can further digital and racial divides. Inequality in online education often persists because "neighborhoods that were previously redlined, rural areas, and a significant portion of Tribal Lands, lack high-quality access to the internet. While the digital divide is not strictly race-based, as there are white people who live in places with poor access to the internet including rural areas who face their own issues around internet access, historical racism has a significant impact on where internet connectivity issues exist" (Downs 2021). Access also relates to ownership of the personal technology used to learn online. The Pew Research Center (Perrin and Turner 2019) notes that Black and Hispanic adults often rely on smartphones for internet access, with 25 percent of Hispanics and 23 percent of Black respondents identifying a smartphone as their only personal access point for online interactions. The implications of this study multiply the digital divide, since smartphones offer less access to files such as PDFs and data tables, and phones make completing forms or writing large amounts of text difficult (Downs 2021). Challenges for online

1. https://cdn.ncte.org/nctefiles/groups/cccc/owiprinciples.pdf.

learners also include limited data plans, shared devices, and unreliable access to Wi-Fi. Such barriers have led to calls for increased funding to "ensure that every student in our country has the resources he or she needs to be able to equitably access online offerings" (DETA and WCET 2021, 22). Additionally, access is not solely a problem for underrepresented or marginalized students; tutors and contingent writing center staff may also be impacted by limited technology and resulting digital divides (Simpson et al. 2021).

Digital literacy, technology training, and experience are also needed for online learning to be accessible (DETA and WCET 2021). According to a 2019 Pew Research Center study, 46 percent of Blacks and 48 percent of Hispanics (in contrast to 20 percent of white respondents) desired technology training to increase their confidence and decision making (Perrin and Turner 2019). Similarly, for Black males taking online courses technology training has been linked to course completion (Salvo, Shelton, and Welch 2019). Martinez et al. (2019) found in their research of online tutorials that students often need additional technical support when using unfamiliar and new technology. Consequently, tutors and administrators need technology training and experience to help writers navigate online spaces via a range of devices. Administrators also need ongoing education and practice to design tutor education and online programming. However, many administrators lack time or resources to develop or participate in technology training, which further complicates the work of building more equitable and accessible online writing center options. The effectiveness of online writing center programming and resources is mediated by issues of access, since all participants—writers, tutors, and administrators—need access to adequate technology and training or experience to fully engage in online learning.

Applications for Addressing Issues of Access

- Provide writers and tutors with information about accessing technology (e.g., links to campus offices that check out laptops and hotspots or fliers about computer classrooms on campus).
- Include digital literacy and technology practice in online tutor training.
- Provide digital literacy resources and assistance to writers using online or in-person writing centers services (e.g., learning how to attach or upload papers or how to print papers on campus).
- Encourage tutors to discuss session length with writers and be flexible in tutorials. (e.g., If a writer is joining a session while at work, while caregiving, or in a setting not conducive to learning, the tutor

can address the writer's pressing questions and then follow up asynchronously with additional resources or feedback.)

- Recognize that many administrators lack the resources (i.e., time, staff, funding) to explore and implement more inclusive and accessible forms of online writing center work, so share training resources, publish scholarship via open access publications, and share information about low-cost or no-cost platforms for online writing center work.
- Collaborate with tutors and administrators who can teach you more about technology.
- Provide online services in multiple forms to meet the access needs of writers and tutors.
- Work with campus-accessible and technology offices to design inclusive services and resources (e.g., handouts in accessible formats, asynchronous workshops, or tutoring platforms compatible with mobile devices).
- Commit financially to anti-racism, knowing that some initiatives (e.g., additional services or hours of operation) will require an investment or redistribution of resources.

CONCLUSION: ANTI-RACISM AS A PATH, NOT A PLACE

As we embrace anti-racist paradigms and practices for online writing center work, intentionally disrupting systems of inequality is possible, but it is also challenging. Like learning, writing, and tutoring, anti-racism is inherently social work and more of a path than a static solution. Jessica Williams (2020) reminds us that "we must see anti-racist equity work as both an outcome and a process in the development of digital learning tools and practices. Additionally, we must regularly challenge ourselves to evaluate how we are engaging; who we are listening to; how we are processing; and who we are bringing to the table." Although the work may be daunting and will never be done, we can focus on starting points for disrupting inequitable systems of online learning, including acknowledging and addressing people and power dynamics in online writing center work, using data in multiple forms to address the real needs of real learners, and designing online services and resources with access in mind. Certainly, anti-racism in online writing center work is cyclical and slow, but it is also critical if our writing center communities are to move beyond the systems that have shaped us and build programs and places where all people are not just included and treated equitably but where we all belong.

Acknowledgment. In writing this chapter, I want to acknowledge and address my context and use of terms. The ways we discuss race are complex. Words often fail us, and we must learn to do better. Whiteness is a social construction that protects and privileges certain groups of people, myself included. In using this term, I am not seeking to reinforce legitimacy of this construction, but I use the term to simplify and group people privileged within our systems due to their skin color. Similarly, phrases such as "people of color" or "writers of color" are reductive and fail to fully represent a wide range of people with varying cultures and life experiences, but these terms are used to streamline the discussion and help it mirror language used in other scholarship. Again, rather than reify racial constructs, these terms are used to talk about systems of racial inequality and anti-racism. As a white writing center administrator, I am actively seeking to engage in anti-racism, while also hoping my work can amplify the work of writing center colleagues who have long engaged in this work and not always received the recognition and resources deserved. I have been purposeful in citing many of them in this chapter and know their words and ideas will be a thread throughout this collection. So, read this chapter as a way of entering a larger conversation found in the citing of scholarship and the workrooms of our writing centers.

APPENDIX 8.A

Understanding People and Power

Disrupting Identity in Practice

- Retire online tutor training materials that reinforce or position specific racial groups as outside the norms of typical students or sessions.
- Allow writers and tutors more control over their identities in online spaces by not requiring the use of cameras in online tutorials.
- Give staff choices about how their image or other identity markers are used on writing center websites or other online writing center spaces.
- Offer asynchronous online tutoring options to allow students more control over how they receive and interact with tutor feedback.
- Hire online tutors from different racial and cultural backgrounds and normalize sharing new perspectives rather than solely expecting new staff to embrace established norms.

Reframing Roles in Practice

- Make roles, power dynamics, and systems visible online, and discuss how to disrupt systems in favor of empowering students and creating anti-racist learning communities.
- Explicitly train online tutors to avoid deficit thinking and assumptions about students as problems and to understand that the challenges tutors and writers face are most often about navigating and negotiating systems.
- Reframe tutors and administrators as co-learners and guides within anti-racist online learning environments.
- Make online anti-racist writing center education actionable, so tutors and administrators move from discussing to doing the work needed to learn and change.
- Make use of or add to scholarship that reframes and rethinks the possibilities for online writing center work that is more ethical and inclusive.

Acknowledging Ownership in Practice

- Offer options for online writing support, and empower writers to choose the services and programming that best fit their needs and preferences.
- Reinforce writers' ownership of their work in online spaces where the presence of participants may be less visible.
- Suggest rhetorical and linguistic options to writers rather than encouraging assimilation of individual's texts.
- Own your role as a member of a local and larger online writing center community, and attend webinars or workshops and collaborate with colleagues on how to develop more anti-racist online writing center services.

Becoming Data Driven

Knowing the Writers We Work with in Practice

- Use data collected by your program and institution to better understand the writers who use online writing center programming and services.
- Compare the demographics of writers using different types of tutoring—in-person tutoring, in-person appointment-based tutoring, synchronous online tutoring, asynchronous online tutoring, and so on. If there are notable differences, learn more about writers' access, identity, and experiences.
- Rather than relying on general student satisfaction surveys to assess online writing center work, actively seek input from specific

demographics and those who do not use the programs or resources offered.

- Be intentional and specific about the data you collect—instead of having a focus group for BIPOC students, talk to graduate students who identify as Mexican American or first-year writers who are international students.
- Partner with other offices to combine surveys and reduce survey fatigue and to reduce inequitable and additional labor asked of certain student populations.

The Need for Narratives in Practice

- Couple research with real voices. Let participants help you understand their data and provide purpose to the patterns you find. Do not assume you understand why and how writers use online services; listen and learn.
- Instead of distributing online surveys, host focus groups and compensate participants to access a wider range of students and stories.
- Amplify marginalized voices on behalf of those who speak, not solely for the performance and profit of the writing center.
- Use the qualitative and quantitative information you gather from participants to disrupt traditional systems and serve writers and tutors online in new and more effective ways.

Data Use and Anti-racism in Practice

- Make sure employees receive training on how to protect data. Training should be tailored to your context but may include FERPA or cybersecurity training.
- Know how data are collected, stored, and protected. If tutors are commenting on drafts of student papers, be intentional about where those drafts are saved, who can access them, and for how long.
- Give registering participants options about how they identify. Note whether your registration process provides ways to opt out of demographic questions or fully identify.
- Design online writing center spaces in ways that allow tutors to choose and change how they show up in terms of race, gender, age, and so on.
- Know if third-party providers share or sell user data and if employing third-party providers or programs increases the digital footprint of tutors and writers. If so, notify participants and offer alternative options.
- Identify offices or individuals on campus that can help you learn more about anti-racism and ethical approaches to data collection and storage.

Addressing Issues of Access

Applications for Addressing Issues of Access

- Provide writers and tutors with information about accessing technology (e.g., links to campus offices that check out laptops and hotspots or fliers about computer classrooms on campus).
- Include digital literacy and technology practice in online tutor training.
- Provide digital literacy resources and assistance to writers using online or in-person writing centers services (e.g., learning how to attach or upload papers or how to print papers on campus).
- Encourage tutors to discuss session length with writers and be flexible in tutorials. (e.g., If a writer is joining a session while at work, while caregiving, or in a setting not conducive to learning, the tutor can address the writer's pressing questions and then follow up asynchronously with additional resources or feedback.)
- Recognize that many administrators lack the resources (i.e., time, staff, funding) to explore and implement more inclusive and accessible forms of online writing center work, so share training resources, publish scholarship via open access publications, and share information about low-cost or no-cost platforms for online writing center work.
- Collaborate with tutors and administrators who can teach you more about technology.
- Provide online services in multiple forms to meet the access needs of writers and tutors.
- Work with campus-accessible and technology offices to design inclusive services and resources (e.g., handouts in accessible formats, asynchronous workshops, or tutoring platforms compatible with mobile devices).
- Commit financially to anti-racism, knowing that some initiatives (e.g., additional services or hours of operation) will require an investment or redistribution of resources.

REFERENCES

Aguilar, Stephen J. 2018. "Learning Analytics: At the Nexus of Big Data, Digital Innovation, and Social Justice in Education." *TechTrends* 62, no. 1: 37–45. https://doi.org/10.1007/s11528-017-0226-9.

Bell, Lisa. 2019. "Examining Tutoring Strategies in Asynchronous Screencast Tutorials." *Research in Online Literacy Education* (*ROLE*) 2, no. 2: http://www.roleolor.org/examining-tutoring-strategies-in-asynchronous-screencast-tutorials.html.

Bell, Lisa Eastmond, Adam Brantley, and Madison Van Vleet. 2022. "Why Writers Choose Asynchronous Online Tutoring: Issues of Access and Inclusion." *WLN: A Journal of Writing Center Scholarship* 45, nos. 5–6: 3–11.

Bertucci Hamper, Maggie. 2018. "The Online Writing Center Is about Equity for Students (and You Too)." *Another Word* (blog). University of Wisconsin-Madison Writing Center. February 5. https://dept.writing.wisc.edu/blog/the-online-writing-center-is-about-equity-for-students-and-for-you-too/.

Blazer, Sarah. 2015. "Twenty-First Century Writing Center Staff Education: Teaching and Learning towards Inclusive and Productive Everyday Practice." *Writing Center Journal* 35, no. 1: 17–55.

Camarillo, Eric C. 2019. "Dismantling Neutrality: Cultivating Antiracist Writing Center Ecologies." *Praxis: A Writing Center Journal* 16, no. 2: 69–74. http://dx.doi.org/10.26153/tsw/2673.

Camarillo, Eric C. 2020. "Cultivating Antiracism in Asynchronous Sessions." *South Central Writing Centers Association* (blog). April 30. https://writingcenter08.wixsite.com/scwcaconference/post/cultivating-antiracism-in-asynchronous-sessions.

Condon, Frankie. 2007. "Beyond the Known: Writing Centers and the Work of Antiracism." *Writing Center Journal* 27, no. 2: 19–38.

Dembsey, J. M. 2020. "Naming Ableism in the Writing Center." *Praxis: A Writing Center Journal* 18, no. 1: 8–18. https://doi.org/10.26153/tsw/11322.

Denton, Kathryn M. 2014. "Beyond the Lore: A Research-Based Case for Asynchronous Online Writing Tutoring." PhD diss., University of New Mexico, Albuquerque.

Denton, Kathryn M. 2017. "Beyond the Lore: A Research-Based Case for Asynchronous Online Writing Tutoring." *Writing Center Journal* 36, no. 2: 175–203.

Denny, Harry, John Nordlof, and Lori Salem. 2018. " 'Tell Me Exactly What It Was That I Was Doing That Was So Bad': Understanding the Needs and Expectations of Working-Class Students in Writing Centers." *Writing Center Journal* 37, no. 1: 67–100.

Downs, Lindsey Rae. 2021. "Racism in Educational Cyberspace" *WCET Frontiers* (blog), *WICHE Cooperative for Educational Technologies.* April 23. https://wcetfrontiers.org/2021/04/23/racism-in-the-educational-cyberspace/.

Faison, Wonderful, Katie Levin, Jasmine Kar Tang, Talisha Haltiwanger Morrison, Elijah Simmons, and Keli Tucker. 2019. "Potential for and Barriers to Actionable Antiracism in the Writing Center: Views from the IWCA Special Interest Group on Antiracism Activism." *Praxis: A Writing Center Journal* 16, no. 2: 4–11. https://doi.org/10.26153/tsw/2675.

Gallagher, Dan, and Aimee Maxfield. 2019. "Learning Online to Tutor Online: How We Teach Writing Tutors." *How We Teach Writing Tutors: A* WLN *Digital Edited Collection*, edited by Karen Gabrielle Johnson and Ted Roggenbuck. https://wlnjournal.org/digitaleditedcollection1/GallagherMaxfield.html.

García, Romeo. 2017. "Unmaking Gringo-Centers." *Writing Center Journal* 36, no. 1: 29–60.

Greenfield, Laura. 2019. *Radical Writing Center Praxis: A Paradigm for Ethical Political Engagement.* Louisville: University Press of Colorado.

Grimm, Nancy M. 2009. "New Conceptual Frameworks for Writing Center Work." *Writing Center Journal* 29, no. 2: 11–27.

Hewett, Beth L., Megan Boeshart, Sarah Prince, and Beth Nastachowski. 2019. "Bridging the Gap: Online Writing Centers and Online Writing Tutoring." *ROLE (Research of Online Literacy Educators)* 3, no. 1. http://www.roleolor.org/editorrsquos-introduction.html.

Inoue, Asao. 2021. "Episode 2: A Conversation with Asao Inoue." *Slow Agency* (podcast), *WLN: A Journal of Writing Center Scholarship.* March 29. https://www.wlnjournal.org/blog/2021/03/asao-podcast-1/.

Jordan, Zandra. 2020. "Racial Justice in Virtual Tutoring: Considerations for Antiracist Online Writing Center Praxis." *Global Society of Online Educators (GSOLE)* (webinar). August 30.

Lockett, Alexandria. 2019. "Why I Call It the Academic Ghetto: A Critical Examination of Race, Place, and Writing Centers." *Praxis: A Writing Center Journal* 16, no. 2: 20–33. https://doi.org/10.26153/tsw/2679.

Martinez, Diane, and Leslie Olsen. 2015. "Online Writing Labs." *Foundational Practices of Online Writing Instruction*, edited by Beth L. Hewett and Kevin Eric DePew, 183–210. WAC Clearinghouse; Parlor Press. https://doi.org/10.37514/PER-B.2015.0650.

Martinez, Diane, Mahli Xuan Mechenbier, Beth Hewett, Lisa Melonçon, Heidi Skurat Harris, Kirk St Amant, Adam Phillips, and Marcy Irene Bodnar. 2019. "A Report on a US-Based National Survey of Students in Online Writing Courses." *Research in Online Literacy Education* 2, no. 1. http://www.roleolor.org/a-report-on-a-us-based-national-survey-of-students-in-online-writing-courses.html.

McKenzie, Lindsay. 2021. "Is Ed Tech Ready to Help Students of Color?" *Inside Higher Education*. May 18. https://www.insidehighered.com/news/2021/05/18/how-can-ed-tech-help-students-color.

The National Research Center for Distance Education and Technological Advancements (DETA) and the Wiche Cooperative for Educational Technologies (WCET). 2021. *Research Review of EdTech and Student Success for Certain Racial and Ethnic Groups*. https://wcet.wiche.edu/frontiers/2021/05/17/new-report-research-review-of-edtech-student-success-racial-and-ethnic-groups/.

Perrin, Andrew, and Erica Turner. 2019. "Smartphones Help Blacks, Hispanics Bridge Some—but Not All—Digital Gaps with Whites." *Fact Tank* (blog). Pew Research Center. Accessed August 20, 2019. https://www.pewresearch.org/fact-tank/2019/08/20/smartphones-help-blacks-hispanics-bridge-some-but-not-all-digital-gaps-with-whites/.

Prince, Sarah, Rachel Willard, Ellen Zamarripa, and Matt Sharkey-Smith. 2018. "Peripheral (Re) Visions: Moving Online Writing Centers from Margin to Center." *WLN: A Journal of Writing Center Scholarship* 42, no. 5–6: 10–18.

Ries, Stephanie. 2015. "The Online Writing Center: Reaching Out to Students with Disabilities." *Praxis: A Writing Center Journal* 13, no. 1: 5–6. http://hdl.handle.net/2152/62621.

Salem, Lori. 2016. "Decisions . . . Decisions: Who Chooses to Use the Writing Center?" *Writing Center Journal* 35, no. 2: 147–171.

Salvo, Susan G., Kaye Shelton, and Brett Welch. 2019. "African American Males Learning Online: Promoting Academic Achievement in Higher Education." *Online Learning* 23, no. 1: 22–36. https://doi.org/10.24059/olj.v23i1.1390.

Simpson, Jollina, Torrie Marin, Brittany Cox, Janet Oliver, José-Angel Corral Rodríguez, and Sandy Vasquez. 2021. "Fighting to Work in the Writing Center." Panel presentation, Rocky Mountain Writing Centers Association, Tutor Con, online, March 6.

Smalling, Susan E. 2020. "Overcoming Resistance, Stimulating Action and Decentering White Students through Structural Racism Focused Antiracism Education." *Teaching in Higher Education*: 1–14. https://doi.org/10.1080/13562517.2020.1725880.

Stokes, Peter. 2011. "Is Online Learning a Disruptive Innovation?" *Voices in Education: The Blog of Harvard Education Publishing* (blog). April 14. https://www.hepg.org/blog/is-online-learning-a-disruptive-innovation.

Villanueva, Victor. 2006. "Blind: Talking about the New Racism." *Writing Center Journal* 26, no. 1: 3–9.

Vygotsky, Lev Semenovich. 1987. *The Collected Works of LS Vygotsky: Problems of the Theory and History of Psychology*. Vol. 3. New York: Springer Science & Business Media.

Vygotsky, Lev Semenovich, and Michael Cole. 1978. Mind in Society: Development of Higher Psychological Processes. Cambridge, MA: Harvard University Press.

Williams, Jessica Rowland. 2020. "As We Build New Digital Learning Spaces, Let's Leave Behind the Racism of the Old." *Times Higher Education* (blog). July 3. https://www.timeshighereducation.com/blog/we-build-new-digital-learning-spaces-lets-leave-behind-racism-old.

Wilson, Nancy Effinger. 2012. "Stocking the Bodega: Towards a New Writing Center Paradigm." *Praxis: A Writing Center Journal* 10, no. 1: 1–9. http://hdl.handle.net/2152/62149.

9

TUTORS MATTER, TOO

Supporting Writing Tutors through Racial Justice

Talisha Haltiwanger Morrison

As noted in the introduction of this collection and in several of its chapters, writing center scholars and practitioners have been talking about race and racism for decades, and while most of our conversations have centered on student writers, recent scholars of color have also noted the absence of conversations about writing tutors or consultants of color and their experiences in the center.[1] They have also begun filling in this gap by telling of their own experiences (Faison and Treviño 2017; Alvarez 2019; Lockett 2019; Haltiwanger Morrison 2019). In one of my own contributions to this area, "Being Seen and Not Seen: A Black Female Body in the Center" (2019), I detail a moment in which I was physically uncomfortable during a session, in which I felt my identity as a Black woman was pulled into the session in a way I had no agency over. Since then, and since becoming a Director, I've thought about that moment differently, and come to some sort of answer about how I might handle the situation differently, and how I might want or expect my own staff to handle similar situations should they arise. I believe it is imperative that tutors, not just writers, have a choice and guidance on how to proceed through difficult sessions.

Others have also tried to address this matter. For example, Leigh Ryan and Lisa Zimmerelli's *Bedford Guide for Writing Tutors* (2010), a commonly assigned tutor education text, offers advice on how new tutors might handle writers who are aggressive or unresponsive, or whose work is offensive. And, more recently, Hohjin Im, Jianmin Shao, and Chuansheng Chen (2020) studied how tutors cope with emotionally laborious sessions. Neither text gives much explicit attention to race. Ryan and Zimmerelli do not consider that a tutor might be *personally*

1. At the OU Writing Center, student employees are called "consultants." In this chapter, I use "consultant" when speaking about my own staff and "tutor" as a general reference to writing center tutors.

https://doi.org/10.7330/9781646424573.c009

offended by a racist paper because the tutor identifies with the race being described. In fact, the authors state explicitly that tutors should not "take writers' viewpoints or language personally" (102). But writing center work can be very personal. Tutors do not pick and choose which of their identities will be salient for them that day, and most tutors of color do not have the option to concealing their raced identity/ies. From working with my own staff and from my conversations with tutors at writing centers across the country, I've learned that moments do arise when things are personal and identities are involved. I've also learned that many writing center directors give their staff express permission to end sessions if the session becomes uncomfortable or inappropriate in any way. Less clear from these conversations, however, are *how* tutors should do this. Further, I've heard from many tutors who wish not only for more guidance on how to safely extract themselves from sessions but also for guidance on how to remain in those moments and have the difficult conversations.

Tutors must be prepared to handle difficult moments as they arise in the center. We know as directors that the daily work of both the tutor and administrator are ever changing and can be mentally and emotionally draining. Im, Shao, and Chen's (2020) important article calls attention to some of the emotional labor tutors engage in, even outside of racially charged moments. This labor may be even more burdensome on tutors of color, who face racism both in and out of the writing center (Haltiwanger Morrison 2021). Further, despite experiences of racism, tutors of color do not come ready-made with expertise in facilitating difficult conversations on race, especially with an audience that may be un(der)prepared for the conversation. Uneven distributions of power also make BIPOC tutors more vulnerable in such situations. For these reasons, directors must let tutors, especially those who identify as Black, as Indigenous, or as a person of color, know, unequivocally, that they have their directors' permission to leave a session without risk to their position. As important, tutors need to know *how* to leave a session, particularly since "risk" to employment and to safety is not equally distributed. Alternatively, they also need to know how to proceed in such moments if they decide to engage, which may be a more common decision, provided adequate preparation. Finally, they need ongoing support as tutors and as *whole people doing work.* This last part is essential for tutors, particularly tutors of color and from other minoritized backgrounds, to feel confident, respected, and valued in their work and to minimize stress and burnout. The other chapters in this section have provided some excellent examples of how to prepare tutors to enact racial justice through their role as tutors. I discuss that here as well. However, when I argue that we must support tutors through racial justice, I mean two things: *we must provide support for tutors as they engage in racial justice work, and as directors, we ourselves must lead and support through a racially just administrative approach.*

A racial justice approach to writing center administration acknowledges and values our tutors of color. Through it, administrators offer flexibility and allow for our conceptions of the writing center, especially those in primarily or historically white spaces, to be disrupted. We intentionally disrupt them. A racial justice approach respects the diverse languages, histories, and cultures not just of the writers who use the center but also of the tutors who staff the center. And, it requires us as leaders to continue learning and growing as people committed to *actionable* racial justice. We cannot expect our staff to do the work we are not prepared to do. Nor can we expect tutors, particularly tutors of color, to take on the additional strain of intentional racial justice activism without built-in considerations for their own well-being. Tutors need proper education, clear policies, *and* the support and guidance from their leadership. In the sections that follow, I outline how writing center administrators might engage in racial justice-oriented administration, including establishing clear expectations for tutors, preparing tutors for racial justice work, and supporting tutors in a way that offers flexibility and agency and prioritizes tutor well-being. I conclude with a list of recommendations for putting this advice into action. This advice is pulled from my own experiences as an administrator and from my conversations and workshops with writing tutors at several other institutions.

ESTABLISHING EXPECTATIONS

Many tutors have found themselves in sessions or other situations in the writing center in which their identity is particularly salient. Identities are always "at the table," and there are moments when identities are also, voluntarily or involuntarily, brought into the session. What is a tutor to do when they find themselves working with a writer whose content undermines their humanity? Or triggers trauma related to past (or current) abuse? Are they professionally obligated to work with that student? Directors need to make clear their expectations for their staff. To what extent are tutors expected to remain in a session and try to make it work, and at what point might we expect or permit them to walk away? I do not believe many directors would expect a tutor to remain in a session in which they feel unsafe. But it is important that tutors have guidance on how to make decisions. I want to be clear here because I am not saying it is up to directors to dictate when someone else feels threatened or uncomfortable "enough" to leave a situation. I am, however, acknowledging the gray area between a tutor's responsibility to writers who schedule with them, the job they are being paid to do, and between their right to protect themselves.

Many of the directors and tutors I've spoken to have expressed a desire to engage in difficult conversations around race. They believe fully in the power and potential of anti-racist writing center work. However, many tutors have expressed feeling unprepared to do this work and feeling caught off guard when the moment arises. Tutors have expressed that they appreciate their directors giving them clear and unambiguous permission to exit from any situation in which they might feel uncomfortable. But many have also been frustrated when walking away is presented as the only tool in their toolbox. Further, while they are confident their directors support ending a session, they are less certain if they have support or autonomy to question a writer about the language or ideas in their work or about their discriminatory behavior. These are limited examples, and it is probably safe to say most directors expect our staff to respect writers' ideas and language and to try not to enforce their own viewpoints over those of the writer. However, do we also expect them to confront problematic or offensive arguments? It may be safe to say that many of us expect that as well, although how well we've articulated this to our staff is another matter. Many writing center administrators may have conflicting or complicated expectations. We do want our staff to confront racist ideas when they encounter them. We do not want them to let things go unchallenged. Yet, we also do not want to force our tutors of color into situations that may do them emotional harm, such as talking to an unprepared writer about their racism. We do not want to give white tutors an easy way to avoid difficult conversations because they themselves are uncomfortable, but we do not want unprepared or ill-informed white tutors "taking up the mantle" of racism and potentially perpetuating racist ideologies or silencing the voices of people of color. These positions all make sense, but if we do not clearly articulate them to our staff, helping them to think through in which situations and under what circumstances they might opt out of a session—and how they might do so—we continue to send confusing messages about our expectations and how tutors can take up racial justice in a way that makes sense for them.

I have made it clear to my staff that I respect their positions and trust them to make their own decisions about whether and how to engage writers who might, for example, include racist language or ideas in their work. I both expect and trust them to make reasonable and appropriate decisions about exiting a session or declining to take it from the beginning. For example, when a Black consultant on staff preferred not to work with a student writing about the effect of racism on Black Americans' health, our writing center leadership simply reassigned the student to another consultant. In this case, another consultant, a white male, volunteered to take the session. I am fortunate to work with a team of incredibly supportive and compassionate consultants who gladly step in to help their coworkers. Having someone volunteer to step in when needed is the ideal way to resolve these moments. Other times, the Associate Director or I have taken over a session. Although the process is far from perfect or complete, both I and current and former administrators at my center have worked intentionally to foster a culture of support and respect amongst consultants that leads to these kinds of actions. Below I talk more about the tutor pedagogy and professional development we use to build and retain this culture.

PREPARING TUTORS FOR RACIAL JUSTICE WORK

While tutor education varies from center to center, for many reasons, it is common for tutors to complete some form of education before and/or during their time as a writing tutor. This may include an "internship" of 1–2 weeks, a course bearing 1–3 credits, self-paced modules, monthly or weekly staff meetings, College Reading and Learning Association (CRLA) (or other) certification, or a combination of these and other training and professional development activities. At my center, new consultants complete a semester-long "Introduction to Writing Center Pedagogy" internship. The training begins with a pre-semester orientation, with sessions for new consultants and for the entire staff. During the first two weeks of the semester, new consultants read writing center scholarship and conduct observations of and co-consultations with experienced consultants. They meet two to three times with me and the Associate Director during this period before starting their own sessions in week three. For the remainder of the semester, new consultants complete self-paced readings and activities, visit the center for feedback on their own work, attend a monthly full-staff practicum, attend midsemester and end-of-semester check-in meetings, and have one of their sessions observed by a Director. Graduate consultants also attend a monthly graduate assistant (GA) professional development session.

Many of us are familiar with Laura Greenfield and Karen Rowan's (2011) critique of the "week twelve approach" to matters of racial justice, where conversations about race, if present, are tacked on at the end of the tutor-education curriculum, leaving little time for tutors to engage with the topics and consider how race intersects with other important practical tutoring considerations. Rather, this approach gives the impression that race is separate from these considerations completely. Numerous scholars since Greenfield and Rowan, particularly scholars of color (Green 2016; Lockett 2019; Alvarez 2019; Haltiwanger Morrison 2021), have clearly illustrated that this separation does not exist, and conversations circulate through our professional channels about the importance of centering racial justice and anti-racism in our tutor education. For myself and my staff, I have found it helpful to reject the traditional trajectory of the training curriculum and center conversations about racial, social, and linguistic justice in my tutor education. I ask my staff to read and talk about race from the beginning, including sections from *Writing Centers and the New Racism* (Greenfield and Rowan 2011) and *Out in the Center* (Denny et al. 2019) and articles from journals like *Praxis* and the *Peer Review*.

I arrived at the University of Oklahoma (OU) during the COVID-19 pandemic and was faced with the immediate tasks of transitioning the center online and preparing the staff for remote sessions. I was fortunate enough to inherit a staff that was accustomed to and comfortable talking about race. The center also was (and is) more racially and ethnically diverse than the broader student body.[2] These factors allowed me to better encourage racially just tutoring practices *as* consultants were preparing for and engaging in online work. The attention to racial justice was not new, and it did not feel extraneous to the conversations about remote writing center work because consultants already associated racial justice with writing center work. As a staff, we reinforced the relationship between online tutoring and racial justice by considering and responding to questions like "What does anti-racist online tutoring look like?" or "How can I support/foster/enact racial and linguistic justice in asynchronous sessions?" We spent our first monthly practicum considering what did and did not need to change about our approach to racial justice given the transition to online. Most of the consultants did not have experience giving asynchronous feedback, and they talked about the politics of setting the agenda with little guidance from the writer and making decisions about how to respond to diverse written Englishes. They also asked and answered questions about how to support writers

2. The culture and makeup of the center at my arrival were due in large part to the work of Dr. Anna Treviño, the former Graduate Student Assistant Director of the OU Writing Center.

throughout the pandemic and racial upheaval following the murder of George Floyd,[3] knowing that both societal factors impacted more heavily on Black writers and other writers of color.

Experienced consultants, already oriented to anti-racist writing center work, led much of these conversations at practicum. However, the consultant-led conversation also invited newer consultants to join in and ask questions. I had hired four new consultants for the 2020–2021 school year, in a hurried fashion after getting last-minute clearance to hire in July 2021. Because I want consultants to see racial justice as part of their work, I hire consultants who are open to this, including language in recruitment materials that communicates our values. I assign a race-focused narrative, similar to papers we see for various first-year classes, for applicants to discuss as part of their interview. This process is not perfect, of course. I'm aware of the power dynamics and how my identity as a Black woman and their potential boss may shape applicants' response. But I've found this part of the application process more useful than not, as it allows me to gauge potential hires' openness to learning and engaging with writers of color and to respecting writers' stories and voices. It also reinforces to applicants the *expectation* for them to engage respectfully with writers about their work and identities and to participate in these kinds of conversations. I am not interested in tricking anyone into working at the Writing Center, nor in concealing the type of work that we do here. I believe firmly that applicants should know what they are getting into when they accept a position as a consultant.

When it comes to tutor education, there are some basics about what tutoring is that new tutors need to know. There are foundational texts that many of us, including myself, often turn to. Such works provide important theoretical and practical guidance, but their attention to race and diversity, when present, is often much less direct than we might want in the 2020s. The same is true for many tutoring manuals, which give passing references to "diverse" writers but are not specific or action-oriented about race and identity matters. I've found it helpful to disrupt new consultants' preconceived notions of the writing center by pairing "canonical" texts, when assigned, with more recent pieces by scholars of color and by asking newly hired consultants to work with sample papers about race and identity. Doing so provides consultants early on with the

3. George Floyd, a Black man, was murdered by a white police officer in Minneapolis on May 25, 2020. Video of the white officer kneeling on Floyd's back for almost nine minutes went viral and led to nationwide upheaval over racial justice. Floyd's death followed closely on the deaths (or coverage of the deaths) of other unarmed Black people such as Elijah McClain, Ahmaud Arbery, and Breonna Taylor.

opportunity to imagine themselves in potentially awkward, confusing, or challenging sessions and discuss with others how to navigate the session, drawing on scholarship where appropriate. Consultants ask questions of one another and of the directors and consider how to approach the session, depending on various factors such as the author's intent, the author's openness, and their own identities and comfort levels. As Director, I use this as an opportunity to provide strategies for navigating difficult sessions and assert from the beginning that consultants have the right to extract themselves from any uncomfortable session. This training also includes several opportunities for self-reflection.

Self-Reflection and Application

A vital part of consultants' ability to understand and apply strategies from their reading is self-reflection. I ask my staff to think about what they believe and why. Our tutors do not arrive at the Writing Center bias-free and absent any history or experiences that may have shaped their approach to or interest in writing and literacy. Rather, as Rachel Herzl-Betz demonstrates in chapter 3 in this collection, many potential tutors, particularly white tutors, are drawn to writing centers because their particular literacies have been valued and encouraged throughout their academic careers. I know that I am not the only administrator who has read application letters or conducted interviews in which prospective tutors professed their superior skill in and "love" for writing, their desire to help, or their English-teacher mothers. There is nothing inherently wrong with any of these motivations, but they can indicate a certain orientation toward writing and literacy that warrants consideration. So many of our tutors find themselves in the Writing Center because they themselves have been successful as writers, more specifically, they've successfully demonstrated their ability to communicate in standardized academic edited English (SAEE). Recent scholarship (Denny, Nordlof, and Salem 2018; Groundwater et al. 2021), however, indicates that the students who use the writing center often have less mastery over SAEE and seek out writing center services for support. This makes it even more important for tutors to think carefully about their relationship to SAEE and other dialects. Two activities I've used to prompt self-reflection about orientations to writing and working with writers are literacy timelines and writing center scenarios. Below, I include an overview of each activity. More information about the exercises can be found in the appendices to this chapter.

Literacy Timelines

It is essential for writing tutors (and teachers) to interrogate their ideas about language and literacy and the origins of those ideas. One way to engage in this sort of critical self-reflection is to build a timeline of important moments in tutors' literacy development and education. I first ask participants to identify their significant literacies or discourses (Green 2016) and then to build a "literacy timeline" of specific moments in their lives and *messages they've received* about literacy and language. I offer examples from my own life, such as the positive reinforcement of being selected to read my work aloud for the class in elementary and middle school, and less positive examples, such as being admonished by in a high school English class to use "proper grammar" and being called out by an English professor freshman year for "dropping my 'g's." I share how I internalized, fairly uncritically, these messages and frequently "corrected" others' grammar before learning better.

I have conducted this activity with both mixed audience groups (undergraduate tutors, graduate tutors, and faculty) and graduate-student-only groups and found it has been useful for participants regardless of status. Some participants have shared experiences like mine of having their languages and dialects corrected or diminished. Others talk about being read to as children or being raised by academics. They talk about space and geography and regional dialects they use or have lost. Sometimes they talk about race or nationality, but this has been almost always from a person of color and/or international student. Few of the white Americans I've asked to complete this exercise have considered their race and nationality without prompting from me or another participant. Overall, however, the activity and subsequent discussion have provided opportunities for those who work with writers to consider what ideas about language they hold, where those ideas come from, and how they might show up, for good or bad, in their work with writers.

Tutor-Training Scenarios

Another exercise I've asked tutors to work through involves several scenarios around race adapted from real-life moments in a writing center. Some of the scenarios come from my own centers, others from stories gathered formally or informally from tutors and directors across the country. While it would be possible to invent scenarios, and anyone wishing to adapt this activity could invent scenarios more specific to their context, I've used real-life scenarios to emphasize that such scenarios actually happen, *are happening*. They may have happened in your center, and perhaps not that long ago. Because the scenarios are drawn from real-life events, the individuals witnessing or experiencing the original scenarios come from specific racial, ethnic, and cultural backgrounds. However, when leading tutors through the scenarios, I ask them to imagine the situation from their own positionalities, rather than "putting themselves in another's shoes." I do this for several reasons, the first being that there are very real limits to seeing things from another's perspective. Additionally, this activity is intended to help tutors reflect on their own identities and prepare for similar situations, should they occur. It does tutors no good to pretend to respond from a racial or ethnic identity they don't inhabit. Instead, it leaves them less prepared to consider their own identities and how those identities shape both their reactions and others' responses to their reactions. It also runs the risk of perpetuating harmful stereotypes and misunderstandings.

The scenarios include possible interactions between a tutor and writer, and also between tutors. As I discussed earlier, tutors need to know what kind of conduct is expected of them in their interactions with both writers and coworkers. Being explicit that racism and otherwise discriminatory language and actions are not tolerated *amongst* the staff communicates to BIPOC tutors that you acknowledge their identities and that they should expect to be treated with respect by anyone who enters the writing center, including their coworkers. For example, one tutor-tutor scenario involves the tutor overhearing a Black colleague bring up a recent incident of racism on campus and a white tutor respond, "But aren't we all just people?" In a tutor-writer scenario, the tutor is working with an Asian international student who argues that Asian people are inherently more intelligent than white people. In another, a white student's paper includes stereotypical and irrelevant assumptions about Latina women, whom they paint as homophobic. Participants in this activity have used it as an opportunity to brainstorm specific strategies for navigating such scenarios, including developing specific phrases and developing a reporting system for elevating concerns when necessary.

RACIALLY JUST LEADERSHIP

Everything I have discussed in the previous two sections about establishing clear expectations and providing tutor-education explicitly focused on racial justice and racial literacy supports my overall goal of leading through racial justice. I let my staff know that they will have sessions that involve writers' personal stories and experiences. Sometimes those experiences may resonate with their own. They may encounter writers or arguments they find personally or morally offensive. They may encounter writers or arguments that undermine their humanity. While the latter is (hopefully) a rare occurrence, I do not want staff to be caught off guard, unsure of what is expected of them or what to do. I often remind consultants that "there is a human being at the table" with them. One of the simplest, but most effective, forms of racially just leadership I've found is simply acknowledging to my staff that just like our writers, each consultant is a whole person who brings their experiences and beliefs to the table. Activities such as the literacy narrative, for example, have offered opportunities for BIPOC consultants to reflect on harmful messages they've received about their language or writing and for me, other Writing Center leaders, and their fellow consultants to validate any feelings of hurt or confusion they felt about those messages.

Activities and discussions such as those I've described help foster an environment of support to help retain BIPOC consultants on staff. Other ways I've tried to support my consultants, including those who identify as BIPOC, are things that any writing center administrator should do and that many already are doing. These steps include minimizing or eliminating unpaid labor and acknowledging outside events that affect consultants' lives. For example, following the 2021 mass shooting targeting Asian women in spas in Atlanta, Georgia, I reached out to staff, several of whom identified as Asian or Asian American and offered them time off as they processed the events. Other steps I have planned or am working to implement are growing relationships with campus offices that support BIPOC students and developing programming around cultural holidays and periods such as Black History Month and Native American Heritage Month, which has been difficult in my first few semesters during the pandemic. I am also working with a team of current consultants to develop scripts they might use to exit uncomfortable sessions or invite a director or second consultant to join. These scripts acknowledge that the risk associated in such moments is not the same for everyone and that women, queer people, and BIPOC people may feel less safe stating outright that they are ending a session because the writer has done or said something offensive or inappropriate.

Finally, I am seeking ways to be present and available for my staff and building in additional support. I spent much of my first year at my center gathering feedback from consultants about their needs and experiences. This included both "face-to-face" (Zoom) conversations and survey data, and both identified and anonymous feedback. I met with each consultant to get to know them better and conducted a midsemester check-in about the transition to remote services, asking questions about what kinds of sessions they were having, what issues they were experiencing, and what their biggest struggles were. Unsurprisingly, general fatigue and exhaustion were the main challenge to working remotely during the pandemic. I used information from this feedback to shape some of the monthly training sessions and revise issues with the scheduling platform, WCONLINE, but feedback also indicated a need to be more attentive to consultants' daily schedules, making sure certain consultants weren't booked up while others had entire shifts off and to make sure consultants had time for breaks. I revised the end-of-year survey to better collect information about their experiences over the fall and spring and conducted exit surveys and interviews with outgoing consultants. Finally, I collected anonymous feedback about the tutor education and concerns and suggestions for the next academic year. Gathering feedback from my staff, at different points of the semester and through different means, allows me to adjust both during and between semesters. It communicates to consultants that I care about their perspectives and about what they need to perform their jobs well. I am using their feedback to develop a more targeted training curriculum and provide broader support, for example, through additional professional development for graduate students and social gatherings for the entire staff.

Racial justice-oriented leadership should take into consideration the unique needs of your staff, as well as campus and community contexts. It is challenging and requires constant adaptation and negotiation of priorities and practices, even more so if you are at a center that is under-resourced or on a campus hostile toward anti-racism or critical conversations about race. The suggestions that follow should be adapted for the needs and circumstances of each writing center.

SUGGESTIONS FOR A RACIAL JUSTICE APPROACH TO WRITING CENTER ADMINISTRATION

Recruit and Hire with Intention

Prospective tutors should know what is expected of them as tutors, what kinds of topics they'll be expected to engage in, and how they are expected to treat writers and one another. Part II, "Recruitment, Hiring, and Retention," provides more guidance on a racial justice approach to recruitment and hiring.

Include Statement in Official Policies and Documents

Tutors need to know that their jobs will not be in jeopardy if they decide to exit a session, and that they will be believed about *why* they chose to exit. Putting this in writing in official writing center documents (e.g., tutor handbook) may provide confidence that they can choose to protect themselves in such moments.

Reinforce Values and Expectations

Taking time to remind tutors that you respect their autonomy during staff meetings or class sessions helps reassure them that you respect their personhood. These moments are also a great time to work out some of the nuances in choosing whether to engage in a particular conversation to ensure everyone is aware of important policies.

Develop a "Code of Conduct" for the Writing Center

Create clear expectations for writers about how they should engage with tutors, and make sure this information is easily accessible for both tutors and writers. Alternatively, if your institution has a good code of conduct for students, make clear to both tutors and writers how that the code applies in the writing center. If your center works with community members, make sure they are also aware how they are expected to conduct themselves.

Include Tutors in Developing Policies and Procedures

Including tutor input on writing center policy helps ensure that their lived experiences shape the policies guiding their work. At OU, we are developing scripts that consultants can use to navigate difficult conversations with writers. Other centers might also try this strategy. Directors should set up procedures their tutors can use to deal with racial tension between writers or their coworkers, including how to report an incident to appropriate offices if necessary.

Analyze Identities

Before tutors can engage in much of the work described the preceding sections, they need to reflect on their own identities and positionalities, including those that they do and do not consider relevant to their work as a writing center tutor. This reflection is particularly important at centers and institutions with relatively homogenous staff, or for tutors who come from more homogenous or privileged backgrounds.

Interrogate Privilege

In addition to naming their identities, tutors should also be prepared to consider the privilege inherent in some of their identities. Many tutors (and students) can *name* their identities but do not inherently see those identities as privileged, and they may concede some forms of privilege more easily than others. For example, many of my students have identified able-bodiedness as a privilege more readily than race, gender, or class privilege. Many white students might acknowledge white privilege as a fact but are reluctant to think about what it means for them specifically as a white person. Not all people enter scenarios with the same degree of privilege or vulnerability. This affects how or if they engage with other tutors or writers.

Consider Local Context

Tutor education should take into consideration campus culture and context, including things like faculty attitudes toward writing and the racial and ethnic diversity of your campus. Focused assessments can help you better understand the needs of the students you see and develop outreach to underserved student populations.

Connect with Campus Partners

Offices such as Diversity, Equity, and Inclusion or International Student Services can provide training to help your staff support student writers from diverse races, ethnicities, and nationalities and help you support your tutors who share those identities. Other offices that might provide training or support include Disability and Accessibility Resources, Mental Health Services, and other offices that support first-generation, queer, disabled, international and BIPOC students.

Build in Time to Listen

Directors should build in time to listen to the concerns of their staff. This includes during staff meetings and training sessions and through other means. Time or spatial constraints may make it difficult for us to be physically present in the center as often as we'd like. Directors may consider holding physical and/or virtual office hours for their tutors and encourage tutors to visit. Tutor surveys can also be helpful, but directors should carefully consider what is being "assessed" and if the data collection should be identified or anonymous.

Foster Social and Community Support Systems for Tutors

While it is not necessary for everyone on staff to be friends, it is beneficial for tutors to be friendly and feel supported by one another. Directors should consider what options their local contexts afford for fostering community among their staff, including collaborating on social-cultural events with campus partners or hosting social gatherings in the community.

Reconsider Purpose of Staff Meetings

Relatedly, writing center directors might reimagine what can happen during a staff meeting. These sessions might be dedicated to informal programming, tutor focus groups, or just rant sessions. Reallocating staff meeting time may be particularly useful at centers where time, space, or budgetary constraints prevent hosting supplemental meetings or events.

Educate Yourself

Writing center administrators dedicated to racial justice should take time to educate and prepare themselves to do racial justice work. This requires engaging with scholarship on race and writing centers / Writing Studies, especially scholarship by BIPOC authors, and being willing to lead and facilitate conversations about race, racism, and racial justice. Directors might also seek out local trainings and professional development opportunities around racial and social justice.

APPENDIX A: LITERACY TIMELINES

Note: I begin this activity with context based in works by scholars such as Aja Martinez, Neisha-Anne S. Green, and Deborah Brandt. In adapting this activity, you might draw on the same or other texts.

Guiding Question: How have the messages you've received shaped your literacy identity and your approach to literacy/writing instruction (including tutoring)?

Table 9.1. Literacy timelines overview

Part 1: *Discourse Community Concept Maps (Green 2016)*	
Task: Create a concept map of various discourse communities you belong to. Include the types of languages/discourses involved and the contexts in which you use (or learned) them.	Purpose: Identify our various languages. Consider the relationship between language and identity
Part 2: Literacy Timelines	
Task: Identify significant moments in your writing/literacy development that have shaped your "writerly identity." Build a timeline of these moments.* Connect these, as you are able and feel necessary, to aspects of your identity (race, gender, nationality, sexuality, disability status, language background, etc.)	Purpose: Reflect on (and possibly reconsider) messages we've received about writing throughout our lives. Disrupt notions of writing (and literacy) as neutral and disconnected from identity, interests, and/or lived experiences.
Part 3: Reflection and Response	
1. What are the significant moments from your history? What messages did you receive about writing and writers? Are there any key moments of learning or unlearning messages about writing/yourself as a writer? 2. (How) do your writerly identity and your understanding of writing shape your tutoring or teaching practices?	

* *For comfort and accessibility, I offer participants multiple ways to create the timelines, including pens/crayons and paper, a PowerPoint timeline template, or web-based timeline builders.*

APPENDIX B: TUTOR SCENARIOS

Writer-Tutor Scenarios

1. A white student-writer has brought in a paper for help with grammar. The paper is about welfare, claiming that Black people lazy and don't want to work. Your session is being observed by a Black colleague.
2. During your appointment, a student-writer constantly questions your advice and does not take your input seriously. You begin to feel that this resistance is based on your identity (race, gender, language/dialect, etc.).
3. An Asian international student brings in a paper about education. In the paper they argue that Asian people are inherently more intelligent than white people.

Tutor-Tutor Scenarios

1. During a staff meeting conversation about professionalism, a tutor recommends that all tutors wear their name tags. A white tutor follows up saying, "Yes, because *some* people have *unusual names*," making this comment toward three women of color with non-Western names.
2. Following a racist incident on campus, a tutor of color brings up the incident in the writing center, expressing concern for their and other

students' of color safety. But a fellow tutor responds by saying, "Did you have to bring that up?" and "Aren't we all just people?"

REFERENCES

Alvarez, Nancy. 2019. "On Letting Brown Bodies Speak (and Write)." In *Out in the Center: Public Controversies and Private Struggles,* edited by Harry Denny, Robert Mundy, Liliana M. Naydan, Richard Sévère, and Anna Sicari, 83–89. Louisville: University Press of Colorado.

Brandt, Deborah. 2001. *Literacy in American Lives.* Cambridge: Cambridge University Press.

Denny, Harry, John Nordolf, and Lori Salem. 2018. " 'Tell Me Exactly What It Was I Was Doing That Was So Bad': Understanding the Needs and Expectations of Working-Class Students in Writing Centers." *Writing Center Journal* 37, no. 1. https://docs.lib.purdue.edu/wcj/vol37/iss1/5/

Denny, Harry, Robert Mundy, Liliana M. Naydan, Richard Sévère, and Anna Sicari, eds. *Out in the Center: Public Controversies and Private Struggles.* Louisville: University Press of Colorado.

Faison, Wonderful, and Willow Treviño. 2017. "Race, Retention, Language, and Literacy: The Hidden Curriculum of the Writing Center." *Peer Review* 1, no. 2. http://thepeerreview-iwca.org/issues/braver-spaces/race-retention-language-and-literacy-the-hidden-curriculum-of-the-writing-center/.

Green, Neisha-Anne S. 2016. "The Re-education of Neisha-Anne S. Green: A Close Look at the Damaging Effects of 'A Standard Approach', the Benefits of Codemeshing, and the Role Allies Play in this Work." *Praxis: A Writing Center Journal* 14, no. 1. https://repositories.lib.utexas.edu/handle/2152/62583.

Greenfield, Laura, and Karen Rowan. 2011. "Beyond the 'Week Twelve Approach': Toward a Critical Pedagogy for Anti-racist Tutor Education." In *Writing Centers and the New Racism: A Call for Sustainable Dialogue and Change,* edited by Laura Greenfield and Karen Rowan, 124–149. Logan: Utah State University Press.

Groundwater, Evin, María Carvajal Regidor, Maria Conti Maravillas, and Dominque Clayton. 2021. "Reimagining Support for First-Generation Writers in Writing Centers." Paper presented at International Writing Centers Association Conference: Together Again Apart: Reimagining our Communities of Practice. Virtual. October 21.

Haltiwanger Morrison, Talisha. 2019. "Being Seen and Not Seen: A Black Female Body in the Writing Center." In *Out in the Center: Public Controversies and Private Struggles,* edited by Harry Denny, Robert Mundy, Liliana M. Naydan, Richard Sévère, and Anna Sicari, 21–27. Boulder: University Press of Colorado.

Haltiwanger Morrison, Talisha. 2021. "A Balancing Act: Black Women's Negotiation of Racial Tension in the Writing Center." *Writing Center Journal* 40, nos. 1–2: 119–141.

Im, Hohjin, Jianmin Shao, and Chuansheng Chen. 2020. "The Emotional Sponge: Perceived Reasons for Emotionally Laborious Sessions and Coping Strategies of Peer Writing Tutors." *Writing Center Journal* 38, no. 1. https://docs.lib.purdue.edu/wcj/vol38/iss1/9/203–230.

Lockett, Alexandria. 2019. "Why I Call it the Academic Ghetto: A Critical Examination of Race, Place, and Writing Centers." *Praxis: A Writing Center Journal* 16, no. 2: 20–33. https://doi.org/10.26153/tsw/2679.

Martinez, Aja. Y. 2016. "Alejandra Writes a Book: A Critical Race Counterstory about Writing, Identity, and Being Chicanx in the Academy." *Praxis: A Writing Center Journal* 14, no. 1. https://repositories.lib.utexas.edu/handle/2152/62610.

Ryan, Leigh, and Lisa Zimmerelli. 2016. *Bedford Guide for Writing Tutors.* 6th ed. Boston: Bedford / St. Martins.

PART IV

Engaging with Campus and Community

10

FROM ANTI-BLACKNESS PROFESSIONAL DEVELOPMENT TO PRO-BLACKNESS ACTIONS

Educating Faculty on Harmful Writing Practices

Brianna Johnson, Rebecca Johnson, and Nicole I. Caswell

In spring 2018, the University Writing Center (UWC) at East Carolina University (ECU) released a Social Justice Statement that served as our mission statement. We released the statement on our website with a commitment to continue to educate, explore, discuss, empower, create, challenge, adapt, and respect languages and social identities. We "recognize that writing is inherently tied to culture and identity and that it is also a tool that can perpetuate systemic discrimination as swiftly as it can participate in the transformation of our world." While the drafting and releasing of the statement *felt good*, the UWC was performing allyship rather than holding ourselves accountable. Consultants struggled to implement the Social Justice Statement into their sessions. So, while we wanted to be change agents actively working toward social justice, we were still a Writing Center remaining in our comfort zone—just with a public-facing statement.

The ongoing murders of Black bodies in 2020 pushed us out of our silence. In summer 2020, the administrative team recognized our overt performative allyship and realized that if we really believed in our social justice mission, then we needed to actively do something. We turned to anti-racist and pro-Blackness work as an entry point to revamp consultants' professional development to focus on anti-racist practices in the writing classroom and in the education system. During weekly staff meetings, we unpacked systemic racism in our community. By the end of summer 2020, our ally to accomplice growth included educating, exploring, and discussing changes that the UWC would like to see across ECU's campus (Green and Condon 2020). We continued to focus primarily on staff professional development, but we organized it in a way that would lead consultants to action. We were not sure what the action would be

https://doi.org/10.7330/9781646424573.c010

when we started, but we knew the consultants would know what to do. Consultants decided the next step was to draft a letter to faculty detailing the harmful practices they see in writing, assignment sheets, and grading criteria. Our letter would challenge faculty to engage in linguistic diversity and move away from white mainstream English as the sine qua non for all writing and speaking situations.

Our faculty letter is an example of a writing center using tutor education to engage in faculty outreach. Dispersed throughout this chapter are reflections from a UWC consultant, Brianna, who played a pivotal role in writing and revising the letter, as well as sections describing the process written by the Director and Assistant Director. Taking these discussions together, this chapter details our nine-month process of researching, drafting, and revising a letter to faculty calling for a commitment to racial linguistic justice on our campus. We begin by describing the professional development that prompted the letter and then shift toward the drafting and revising process. We share how faculty responded to the letter being released and, as Directors, reflect on our mishaps and mistakes. We conclude by describing how the letter-writing process allowed us to deliberately target anti-Blackness in our professional development and instead engage consultants in pro-Blackness actions during sessions.

PROFESSIONAL DEVELOPMENT GROUNDWORK

As Director and Assistant Director, we began laying the groundwork for the letter in summer 2020, dedicating our weekly professional development readings and meetings to examining different levels of racism. Consultants started by learning about how systems of power operate, dividing people into dominant and subordinate groups based on race, gender, sexual orientation, age, ability, and religion (Tatum 2017). However, a lot of our time was spent examining racism on the institutional level. We looked at readings on the legal system, including the war on drugs (Alexander 2010), the school-to-prison pipeline (Wise), and abolishing prison systems (Davis 2003). We focused on these topics so that consultants could better understand the Black Lives Matter protests and how they related to our work, even if they didn't necessarily appear to be connected at first. We had the consultants reflect on their own identities and positionalities within these systems (McIntosh 1989). By doing so, we hoped that consultants would better understand how power systems shape our daily lives in big and small ways, even in the Writing Center. We also hoped that this background work would give consultants the language and concepts to include in the letter.

Additionally, the staff dedicated time to thinking about racism and attitudes toward language use, focusing on Black English. After reading Vershawn Ashanti Young (2009), consultants struggled with how to approach code switching in one-on-one sessions. They wanted to celebrate students' diverse languages and dialects, including Black English, but recognized that many professors do not feel the same way. They did not want students to receive bad grades because of them. Consultants' personal feelings about grammar and their experiences with it were a point of tension in our discussions. While they agreed that requiring code switching is bad, some also took great pride in their knowledge about mainstream grammar. As Directors, we emphasized that the ideas we discussed could be surprising to some at first because the education system reinforces code switching at every level. We discussed how there is no such thing as "standard" English and strategies for having conversations about this with students. However, these are topics that the entire staff returned to throughout the school year.

BRIANNA'S BEGINNINGS

When I first began working with the UWC under Dr. Johnson and Dr. Caswell, I didn't know what to expect. I thought I would be helping writers communicate their ideas in a way that is accepted by the university. Prior to joining the Writing Center, I had taken a few linguistics classes and a teaching theory class, and my concentration was in creative writing. I had a lot of ideas on how writers should be able to express themselves in ways that may not be prescribed by the university. The first time I met Dr. Johnson, she asked if I had any experience with doing professional development (PD). I didn't know what it meant until I did one for the first time. It was all about consent and never overstepping boundaries with myself or others. It was necessary to talk about but quite frankly, it was just cute. It didn't change anything major in my life. Then we started looking into things concerning the pandemic and how to navigate working strictly online and how to cope with living through something that felt apocalyptic. Again, that was cute. And then, another Black body was murdered in plain sight for everyone to see. But the UWC did something different. We didn't let it be another missed opportunity. We changed the PD and educated ourselves.

BRAINSTORMING AND BEGINNING THE LETTER

After reading and discussing the UWC professional development, the staff began brainstorming ideas for the letter in the summer. While consultants were eager to do something to effect change on our campus, many were clearly confronting their whiteness and complicity in systems of power for the first time. Some struggled to believe that racism could operate on different levels. Once, a consultant stayed after one of the weekly meetings to discuss how she felt like she was afraid that she didn't have a lot to add to the letter and that she was doing things incorrectly. As the administrative staff, we emphasized that we are going to make mistakes in this process, but the important thing was that she was learning and trying to do better. In a later instance, the consultant mentioned that she was doing research to learn more about everything that we were discussing. She continued by stating that she was looking into microaggressions because it was her nature as a science major to look for hard evidence. We pointed out that some things cannot be quantified, and in those instances, we have to listen to people of color and respect their lived experiences.

As we continued laying the groundwork for the letter, consultants seemed more comfortable having difficult conversations. However, much of the momentum from the beginning of the summer to work on the letter disappeared as time went on. We asked the consultants to reflect on what they wanted to say in the letter, but many were silent during our weekly meetings. The administrative staff tried to figure out what the biggest obstacle was there. When we asked the consultants why they had not written anything, many stated that they just weren't sure how to get started. It felt like some kind of structure for the letter would help to anchor their thinking. The staff read a piece by Barbara J. Love (2018) for our professional development that seemed to resonate with them. In "Developing a Liberatory Consciousness," Love offers a clear outline for addressing racial injustice—awareness, analysis, accountability, and allyship. We decided to use these concepts to structure the letter, and this seemed to make them feel more confident about writing a rough draft.

DRAFTING THE LETTER

At the beginning of the fall semester, the UWC team started the work of drafting the letter. We broke the staff into groups based on Love's four concepts, as well as a group to work on an introduction, directing the consultants to give some background information on each of these concepts and how instructors could implement them in their classrooms. Meanwhile, the Directors looked for ways to build on the same themes from the summer in professional development (Baldwin 1979; Luu 2020). However, one of the biggest inspirations for our letter was "This Ain't Another Statement: This Is a Demand for Black Linguistic Justice" written by members of the NCTE (Baker-Bell et al. 2020). The statement seemed to strike a chord with everyone and gave consultants a sense of what our letter could look like.

As we read through these things, new feelings emerged that created hesitancy to work on the letter among consultants—shame and embarrassment. While some grew more confident speaking up, some grew more and more quiet as they realized that they were complicit in these systems. These feelings rarely popped up in the meetings but mostly consultants' written responses to our weekly readings. A couple consultants' feelings showed up in their weekly PD, where they wrote about how they were embarrassed that they'd been so oblivious to the experiences of others before. Again, we tried to reaffirm that these feelings were part of the process, but the important thing was that they were actually doing something and using their positions on campus to effect change.

DRAFTING FROM BRIANNA'S PERSPECTIVE

Research began by considering how to be more inclusive in the Writing Center. The first PD that mattered to me was about Multilingual writers being recognized as an integral part of the education system (Matsuda et al. 2020). As consultants, we recognized few efforts were taken to include people of color (POC). The expectation was that those of color would either fall in line with the curriculum as it exists or fail at the institution. Not only does this frame of thinking constrict the cultural expression of POC, but it also hinders the learning of non-POC.

My favorite reading and podcast during PD came from "The School-to-Prison Pipeline, Explained" (Nelson and Lind 2015) and "Dismantling School to Prison Pipeline" episode (Wise 2019) of the *Race Capitol* podcast. This subject is dear to me because of hardships that many of my Black male friends have experienced in the education system. These works touched me all the more because of my husband's testimony of an education system that was determined to put him in prison. One of his teachers falsely testified against him to have him incriminated. To this day, what happened with that teacher is still on his record, even though it was false, and he would not sign a plea. He's now an amazing teacher who works to reset the standards of the education system. He wasn't a perfect student in any way, but he needed assistance. His family needed assistance, and the education system almost completely neglected him in the hopes that he could fill a jail cell. I appreciate the UWC for connecting me with information that further informed our Black experiences and called them exactly what they are, an injustice.

As a Black girl at ECU, the process of researching and writing this statement also gave me the privilege to share my experience with other consultants and the Directors. And yes, I do mean privilege. It is assumed that Black student's values are considered and inherently incorporated, but is it? No. I shared that while the institution brags about being a place of diversity, the school is greatly divided, which changes the perspective that I have. Outside of academics, events are tailored toward one group of people or another. Black students identify with a completely different institution all together. We are constantly outnumbered in the classroom, so we lose our confidence in arguing for the curriculum to include the voices of POC. When the classroom is white and the curriculum is white and the teachers are often white, where do we as POC fit into this institution? Where does our voice matter? So yeah, I felt privileged to have my voice heard and considered. I felt privileged to have been given research that backs up how it feels to be Black in America. I felt all the more privileged to be a part of a movement toward regressing the racist systems of the education system.

Once we had a stronger understanding of the institution's climate and what was needed to push it toward revisions, we were able to brainstorm ways that we in the UWC and those teaching at the institution could improve to benefit all students. We broke into smaller groups to work through the chunks of the letter. Much of the drafting process was a reiteration of the research that had been completed. We reminded each other often of what the real issues were to avoid creating useless and cliché solutions that changed nothing. We recognized that it is not enough for an instructor to say that they are not racist or for an institution to say that it is diverse. We needed to create definitions that expose the silent ways that racism still exists in the institution, whether instructors were aware of it or not. We worked to not just suggest temporary solutions but to demand a change that would continue for generations.

MOVING TOWARD POLISHED DRAFTS

Consultants continued reading about systems of power and language use as we drafted, and these resources served as inspiration for the letter. As consultants drafted our first version of the letter, one question that came up repeatedly in our meetings was, How could everyone challenge these large social structures and institutions that we were examining? This seemed to raise feelings of hopelessness at being embedded in systems of power. We, as the Directors, acknowledged the power imbalance between consultants and faculty and how challenging that might be scary. Dr. Kar Tang, one of the speakers at the International Writing Centers Association (IWCA) panel on anti-racism, describes "wiggling" as a way to navigate this issue (Faison et al. 2019). In other words, making large structural changes is often difficult, but people can make small changes that have a cumulative effect over time. Similarly, we emphasized to consultants that their actions can have an impact on campus.

Around midterms, consultants submitted their first draft of the letter. As the administrative team, we took a couple weeks to review the rough draft of the letter and emailed all the groups individually with ideas about how to develop their sections. We also incorporated looking at the letter into our weekly professional development and staff meetings so we could get ideas from each other for revisions. Several points came up as we all worked together. The main point was how to cut down on the length—the letter was about six pages—while refining our ideas. Another issue that needed to be addressed in revisions was overlap between the sections, particularly awareness and analysis. Many of our resources and activities focused on broad systems of power, so the staff also discussed how to focus more on what we see specifically in the Writing Center. We then gave the groups another three weeks to revise their sections.

BRIANNA'S EXPERIENCE REVISING

I enjoyed working in groups where I was generally the only Black voice because no one came to the meetings and thought of me as an angry Black woman. Everyone was willing to listen as well as speak their truth and share their ideas on how we could make a change. No one seemed uncomfortable to face the harder conversations of white privilege and if they were uncomfortable, they pushed through it. Because of this support, I was able to bring the pain of many Black students to a place where it would be heard and taken seriously, to a place where actions were being planned and taken. Again, it was a great privilege to be a part of something that mattered.

The revision process was not as simple as we expected it to be. While we had a clear understanding of what we had to say, it mattered more how we said it. Audience played a big role in how we revised this letter. We understood that we had to meet the attention of our audience quickly and with a declarative tone. This required us to revise language that did not create concrete, objective statements. We wanted to mimic the tone and language that was created in letters like " 'This Ain't Another Statement: This is a DEMAND for Black Linguistic Justice." We loved how the authors addressed their audience directly and made it clear who they were speaking to. We also discussed how effective the visuals were in creating bite-sized statements that created a call to action. We talked about ways that we could make it easy for our audience to read our statement. We reached a final draft as we used the most direct statements in bite-sized sentences that were both brief and poignant.

FACULTY FEEDBACK

Consultants grew more comfortable confronting their privilege and discussing racism in academia after working on the letter. As we moved closer to a final draft, though, in the back of consultants' minds was a hesitancy about how faculty would respond to the letter. Some were afraid of overstepping their boundaries. Our staff is primarily white, and consultants didn't want to speak over the voices of students and faculty of color. As Directors, we wanted to validate their concerns as legitimate. However, we didn't want that fear to prevent them speaking up at all. The UWC staff talked more about the importance of speaking up in difficult situations and how failing to say anything only reinforces racist systems of power, drawing on Ibram X Kendi (2020) and the work of Audre Lorde (1984). This seemed to help some of the consultants realize that the letter was a good opportunity to use their privilege to effect change on campus and start working to challenge these systems. Consultants also expressed worry about what a faculty member might do if they disagreed with the letter, especially if the consultant ended up as a student in that course. Similarly, consultants expressed concern about faculty refusing to tell their students about the Writing Center. The entire staff spent time thinking through these two situations and kept returning to the motivation for writing the letter in the first place. We reminded consultants that there will always be reasons not to do anti-racist work, and institutions will push them toward not doing the work, but in those moments, we need to push back and remember why we are doing the work.

Since our main audience was faculty, we invited six faculty members from across campus to provide feedback to our letter. We invited faculty we knew would be receptive to the overall goal of the letter but would also be critical of the content. The faculty represented different areas of study: Elementary Education, Sociology/Gender Studies, Speech and

Language Pathologies, English, Chemistry, and History. The racial and gender breakdown of our reviewers was 2 Black women, 3 white women, and 1 Indian male. At least two reviewers publicly identified as LGBTQ+. Over the course of three weeks, one faculty member would attend a staff meeting and have a conversation with the consultants about the letter. Five faculty members provided feedback during staff meetings, and one faculty member provided written feedback.

Overall, the faculty was pleased with the letter and the initiative from the Writing Center. Five themes emerged across the feedback: language colonization, code switching, racism to pro-Black, writing, and concrete actions.

- **Language colonization**: Our initial letter did not address English as a globalized language. Through conversation with one faculty member, the staff added a little bit about the history of the colonization of language in the introduction section.
- **Code switching**: Our initial letter advocated for teachers not to promote or teach code switching to Black Students. The Black and Indian faculty members saw where this stance was coming from but pushed back on how code-switching functions for students of color. Our conversations with faculty center around knowing the language of power to break out of the language of power. This particular point brought up old tensions consultants were experiencing when they initially read the code-switching scholarship. But the consultants also knew that they needed to trust the expertise and lived experiences of the faculty of color sharing their stories and rationale. The staff revised our initial code-switching claim that had advocated for code switching not to be required.
- **Racism to pro-Blackness**: When consultants drafted the letter, our focus was on Black students, but we used broad-stroking language such as racism and anti-racist work. Faculty pushed us to narrow our focus. Faculty members thought our letter was trying to be too much to too many. Rather than tackle racism broadly, we should name our work as pro-Blackness practices, since that was our focus.
- **Writing**: Throughout conversations with faculty, the UWC staff shared examples and experiences from the Writing Center. The faculty were moved by our stories and suggested we add those examples to the letter. This was another moment where the faculty thought our letter was trying to be everything to everyone rather than focus in on our writing expertise. As we revised, we paid attention to connecting ideas and examples to what we've seen and experienced in the Writing Center.
- **Concrete actions**: We did not provide too many concrete actions for faculty in the first draft of the letter. Rather, we added multiple questions for reflection to guide them through Love's steps, including "Do you encourage code-switching by reinforcing that black students use 'academic language?' " and "When grading a paper or listening

> to a presentation, do you find yourself taking off points for a student's particular word choice that deviates from 'standard English?'" However, faculty wanted some actions on what they could do now to combat anti-Blackness in the classroom. In our revision, we tried to provide faculty with a range of specific actions they could make in the classroom moving forward.

We appreciate the willingness of faculty across campus to share their time and expertise with the consultants. Through our conversations with faculty, we decided to add a form for faculty to sign and indicate why they are signing the letter. Inviting faculty to respond to the letter eased the consultants' concerns and helped them recognize that this was an important next step for supporting Black students on ECU's campus. After receiving feedback from the faculty, the UWC Directors asked consultants to revise their sections of the letter one more time. We also discussed how and when would be the best time to release it.

BRIANNA'S TRANSITION TO TEACHING

In spring, my assistantship shifted from the UWC to teaching Composition in the English Department. Therefore, I didn't get a chance to help finish the statement, and reading the final draft for the first time left me disappointed. The words said the right things, but the presentation was so long that even I began to skim and snooze on the letter. I believe that there's too much to be said to the institution and the public about this matter. How can we say it all in a way that keeps everyone's attention AND makes them care? I'm arguing for effectiveness, not value. This letter is only a first step that outlines and calls a general public to action. I'm arguing for the UWC to not stop here. It's great to have an outline of expectations to hand out, but how do we make the educational institution responsible for the changes that we expect? This letter is a giant leap to justice, but it won't matter if no one does anything with it. So, as the readers of this chapter and ultimately this book, what will you DO to make a change? I've heard and read a lot and we've written a lot, now let's do more.

RELEASING THE LETTER

The letter was posted on our website, emailed to faculty, and shared with diversity committees across campus.[1] Within minutes of the letter being emailed, one white male faculty member emailed the UWC with a

1. The university removed the letter from our website in December 2022 after a legal review found the letter in violation of North Carolina law.

complaint. The first complaint focused on how the UWC would not have a standard approach for "fixing" student writing. This faculty member was mostly concerned about the linguistic justice letter being used as evidence for students to file a Title IX complaint against him for not grading according to their linguistic preferences. The faculty member asked, "How should faculty proceed if they are accused of ethnic bias because they use the Bedford Handbook etc. to correct a student's grammar the 'wrong' way?" After a few emails, it was clear this particular conversation was going in circles and the email was not a productive venue for having this conversation.

Two other white male faculty members responded to the letter in an anti-racist committee Microsoft Teams chat forum. Both faculty questioned the lack of research, commenting, "Some of the premises about the nature of 'Standard English' seem far from proven." A second faculty member chimed in, agreeing that since so many claims did not have research and citations to support them, the letter could not be trusted. Multiple colleagues called out these faculty members for sidestepping the intent of the letter and demanding research for what is already well documented. One white female faculty member responded, "Many people of color have expressed that they get tired of having to prove that racism exists and asking for citation on a point like this one can seem like one more way of deferring the very real issues at hand (even if you didn't intend that)." The conversation quickly ended.

While those two white male faculty members focused on evidence and citations, two productive critiques did emerge from their comments. One asked if we had shared the letter with the Faculty Senate because of the emphasis of classroom and curriculum changes. The Faculty Senate recently formed a diversity committee, and we plan to share the letter with the diversity committee this summer. The same faculty member also commented that the UWC is asking individuals to take an implicit bias test without any follow-up or support for interpretation or reflection. We are still sitting with this particular productive critique and thinking about next steps. One possibility is a collaborative workshop on implicit bias with our office of equity and diversity (OED). The OED could provide expertise on processing the results, and the Writing Center could provide expertise on how this applies to their classroom teaching.

Positive feedback outweighed the critiques, with thirty faculty signing onto the letter within a few days of its posting. One of the things we regret is only releasing the letter asynchronously. The anti-racist committee Teams chat forum demonstrated a willingness for faculty to have a conversation about the content of the letter.

MISSTEPS AND MISHAPS

Looking back on the letter-writing process, we find a few things that we could have accounted for in our planning to make everything go more smoothly. Namely, we did not expect that it would take so long to write. We initially thought that we might be able to publish the letter for the rest of the campus to read by the end of the fall 2020 semester. However, it became clear that this would not happen, as the consultants struggled with navigating their classes, work, and social lives from their computers. The letter also took much longer to write and revise because many consultants were at different stages of confronting their whiteness. Additionally, the UWC hired several new consultants throughout the fall 2020 semester, and they joined us after we had already started the letter-writing process. Consultant burnout also played a role in how long it took for us to complete the letter. Some reported feeling sad and exhausted as we continued discussing systems of power, and we did not want to retraumatize consultants of color in our continued discussions. To help with burnout, the UWC staff acknowledged consultants' feelings, discussing mental health resources (Harden Bradford 2020), as well as the importance of self and group care (brown 2017; Carruthers 2018).

PRO-BLACKNESS ACTIONS IN SESSIONS/WRITING CENTER

One of the things the UWC staff tried to focus on with the linguistic justice letter was implementing its recommendations into our daily work. We did not want a repeat of the Social Justice Statement, where we publish the statement and then return to our regular practices. Rather, in each session consultants needed to be advocating for linguistic justice and pro-Blackness actions. We continually brought this up in staff meetings, trying to answer, "How do we do this?" One answer was to think about how they could make at least one comment on oppressive language in all sessions. Using Mandy Suhr-Sytsma and Shan-Estelle Brown (2011) as the jumping-off point, the UWC staff held discussions on what this might involve, including some points that were less obvious to consultants, such as "Speaks of oppression as only in the past." If there was no oppressive language, we encouraged consultants to make at least one comment on the diverse and fluid nature of language, especially if a student asked for help with grammar. The consultants hesitated, saying it was too hard to do in online sessions because they didn't know how a writer would respond or that we would be violating writers' consent because they did not ask for that type of feedback. We pushed back, reminding consultants it is easy to find reasons not to do something but that we need to uphold our end of the faculty letter. The staff talked about how we routinely commented on points writers did not ask about. How can a writer ask for something they might not even realize they are doing? We don't always see consultants making this move in their sessions, but it is something that we are providing feedback on when we review appointments and something we are continually pushing consultants toward. We are careful not to codify this into a rule because we don't want consultants to be searching for oppressive language as the only way to engage in linguistic justice. Rather, we use oppressive language, grammar, and other rhetorical moves as entry points on how to disrupt the white, heteronormative, male practices of the academy.

After the difficulty of bringing new hires into the drafting process, we, as the Directors, realized that we needed to have a baseline knowledge of anti-racist work in writing centers. While we can never re-create conversations that happen in staff meetings, we can ensure that all consultants start their work in the Writing Center with a working knowledge of anti-racist work and practices. We added an online anti-racism module to our onboarding process, covering a lot of the concepts that the staff discussed previously. It guides consultants through examining different levels of racism, including systemic, institutional, interpersonal, and personal levels. By adding an anti-racism module to our onboarding, we are communicating to new hires that this is a central part of UWC work, not an add-on initiative.

To continue to reinforce our commitment to linguistic justice and to further our own knowledge, we designed a new professional development unit around Black English. During the research phase of the letter process, the consultants expressed interest in knowing more about the grammatical structures of Black English. They were not necessarily sure what they would do with the knowledge, but they knew it was an area where they lacked. As part of the professional development unit, we will take the knowledge we gain through learning about Black English to curate campus resources. Faculty have routinely asked for handouts and workshops on grammatical concepts, but we have resisted creating these materials. By learning about Black English, we will be able to create grammatical campus resources that value multiple grammars. Our goal moving forward is to curate resources that attend to linguistic justice and interrupt the narrative around white mainstream English.

CONCLUSION

The most valuable part of drafting a letter to faculty wasn't the product but the learning that happened for the consultants. We acknowledge that many of our white consultants sat in a lot of discomfort over the last year—discomfort that we purposely created. Through that discomfort, consultants found their grounding for being better accomplices to their Black peers. We are happy to have a public-facing statement primarily written by the student staff on our website, but we are thrilled to have a staff that understands that anti-racist work is central to writing center work.

As other writing centers embark on anti-racist work and faculty letter writing, we have a few lessons and tips to share.

1. Develop a professional development curriculum to ground your initiatives: Our project wouldn't have been successful if we hadn't spent the summer and fall unpacking systemic racism. Our staff knew racism existed, but they didn't have the theoretical language or the lived experiences to understand how racism operated in everyday life. We consistently returned to ideas and authors from our professional development to remind consultants what we were doing and why.
2. Recognize that asking consultants to confront implicit bias and privilege takes time: We knew many white consultants would be doing the deep anti-racist reflection for the first time. We didn't have a good sense of how much time would be needed to do deep reflection that would lead to change. Provide your consultants the time and space to do the work.
3. Have the hard conversations with your staff: There were moments that we wanted to abandon the whole letter-writing activity because it was hard. As white administrators, we had to continually confront our own complicity in the educational system and society at large. As white administrators, we were also afraid that we were focusing too much on giving space to white consultants to process privilege that we were retraumatizing and ignoring the needs of our consultants of color. The only transparent option we could think of at this moment was to have the conversations with our staff and share our own struggles.
4. Cultivate trust, honesty, and transparency with your staff: While the consultants were not always vocal in staff meetings, they were willing to share how they felt in one-on-one settings and in their written reflections. If we had not created an environment where consultants felt free to share their real feelings, we wouldn't have been able to make a pivot toward pro-Blackness actions in the Writing Center. It was important to the consultants that they felt free to share their feelings without judgment from us.
5. Find campus or faculty partners for early buy-in: One of the most successful parts of the letter-writing process was when the faculty members offered peer-reviewed feedback on the draft. It provided consultants a safe group of faculty to "test" their letter on and ease their fears about

releasing the letter. It also provided the Writing Center a chance to build a larger network of faculty who understands writing center work.

REFERENCES

Alexander, Michelle. 2010. *The New Jim Crow: Mass Incarceration in the Age of Color Blindness.* New York: New Press.

Baker-Bell, April, Bonnie Williams-Farrier, Davena Jackson, Lamar Johnson, Carmen Kynard, and Teaira McMurtry. 2020. "This Ain't Another Statement! This is a DEMAND for Black Linguistic Justice!" Last modified July 2020. https://cccc.ncte.org/cccc/demand-for-black-linguistic-justice?fbclid=IwAR3rGMeWiEi4Yk79XVzECyjs6zfgoif4yCsmto8kY2o3CBQxNfZuXIlhsKg.

Baldwin, James. 2021. "If Black English Isn't a Language, Then Tell Me, What Is?" https://archive.nytimes.com/www.nytimes.com/books/98/03/29/specials/baldwin-english.html.

brown, adrienne maree. 2017. *Emergent Strategy: Shaping Change, Changing Worlds.* Chico, CA: AK Press.

Carruthers, Charlene. 2018. *Unapologetic: A Black, Queer, and Feminist Mandate for Radical Movements.* Boston: Beacon Press.

Davis, Angela. 2003. *Are Prisons Obsolete?* New York: Seven Stories Press.

Faison, Wonderful, Talisha Haltiwanger Morrison, Katie Levin, Elijah Simmons, Jasmine Kar Tang, and Keli Tucker. 2009. "Potential for and Barriers to Actionable Antiracism in the Writing Center: Views from IWCA Special Interest Group on Antiracism Activism." *Praxis* 16, no. 2: 4–11. http://www.praxisuwc.com/162-faison-et-al.

Green, Neisha Anne, and Frankie Condon. 2020. "Letters on Moving from Ally to Accomplice: Anti-racism and the Teaching of Writing." In *Diverse Approaches to Teaching, Learning, and Writing Across the Curriculum: IWAC at 25,* edited by Lesley Erin Bartlett, Sandra Tarabochia, Andra R. Olinger, and Margaret J. Marshall, 277–292. Fort Collins, CO: WAC Clearinghouse.

Harden Bradford, Joy. 2020. "Processing our Collective Grief." *Therapy for Black Girls.* July 1. Podcast, 38:56. https://therapyforblackgirls.com/2020/07/01/session-162-processing-our-collective-grief/.

Kendi, Ibram X. 2020. "The Difference between Being 'Not Racist' and 'Antiracist.' " TED. 51:05. https://www.ted.com/talks/ibram_x_kendi_the_difference_between_being_not_racist_and_antiracist.

Lorde, Audre. 1984. *Sister Outsider: Essays and Speeches.* Berkeley, CA: Ten Speed Press.

Love, Barbara. 2018. "Developing a Liberatory Consciousness." In *Readings for Diversity and Social Justice,* edited by Maurianne Adams, Warren Blumenfield, D. Chase J. Catalano, Keri Dejong, Heather Hackman, Larissa Hopkins, Barbara Love, Madeline Peters, Davey Shlasko, and Ximena Zuniga, 610–615. New York: Routledge.

Luu, Chi. 2020. "Black English Matters." *JSTOR Daily.* Last modified February 12. https://daily.jstor.org/black-english-matters/.

Matsuda, Paul Kei, Akua Duku Anokye, Christine Pearson Casanave, Helen Fox, Tony Silva, Guadalupe Valdés, and Bob Weissberg. 2020. "CCCC Statement on Second-Language Writing and Writers." Conference on College Composition and Communication. Last modified May 2020. https://cccc.ncte.org/cccc/resources/positions/secondlangwriting.

McIntosh, Peggy. 1989. "White Privilege: Unpacking the Invisible Knapsack." Accessed February 3. https://psychology.umbc.edu/wp-content/uploads/sites/57/2016/10/White-Privilege_McIntosh-1989.pdf.

Nelson, Libby, and D. Dara Lind. 2015. "The School-to-Prison Pipeline, Explained." Vox. October 27. https://www.vox.com/2015/2/24/8101289/school-discipline-race.

Suhr-Sytsma, Mandy, and Shan Estelle Brown. 2011. "Theory Into/Practice: Addressing the Everyday Language of Oppression in the Writing Center." *Writing Center Journal* 31, no 2: 13–49. http://www.jstor.com/stable/43442366.

Tatum, Beverly. 2017. "The Complexity of Identity: 'Who Am I?' " In *"Why Are All the Black Kids Sitting Together in the Cafeteria?": And Other Conversations about Race.* Retrieved February 3, from https://uucsj.org/wp-content/uploads/2016/05/The-Complexity-of -Identity.pdf.

Wise, Chelsea Higgs, Naomi Isaac, and Kalia Harris. 2019. "Episode #24: Dismantling School to Prison Pipeline." *Race Capitol.* Broadcast from WRIR LP 97.3 FM Richmond Independent Radio. Produced and powered by Black feminists. August 21. Podcast. MP3 audio. 56:19. https://tinyurl.com/55u2z6bd.

Young, Vershawn. 2009. " 'Nah, We Straight': An Argument against Code Switching." *JAC* 29, no. 1/2 (2009): 49–76. https://www.jstor.org/stable/20866886.

11

LEVERAGING FACULTY PEDAGOGICAL DEVELOPMENT TO CENTER RACIAL JUSTICE

A Study in Using Teaching Excellence Forums to Reform Faculty Pedagogy

Deidre Anne Evans Garriott

When I came to the University of South Carolina (UofSC) in the fall of 2019, I was eager to take advantage of the pedagogical support resources available to faculty, especially through the Center for Teaching Excellence (CTE). During both employee and faculty orientations, I found UofSC all the more attractive because of its prominent support of communities of color all over its website. Indeed, as I looked back over my notes from faculty orientation for this chapter, I laughed at 2019-Deidre, who wrote in all caps and underlined, "OMG, the diversity guy is a person of color!" In my whiteness, I thought that a person of color (POC) occupying one of many diversity, equality, and inclusion (DEI) positions on campus signaled an anti-racist educational environment.

Oh, the naiveté of white women!

In September 2019, I attended a CTE workshop where the speaker was going to talk with the participants about allowing students to write in dialect. As I settled into my chair and proudly stamped my name tag sticker on my chest, I looked up to see a white man sitting at the front of the room. "Okay," I thought, "well, I'm white and trying to be anti-racist. It doesn't mean that he doesn't know what he's talking about. And we really need white men advocating for anti-racist work in higher ed. So . . ." Moreover, we know that Black faculty and staff take up too much of a burden to develop and promote DEI content.

The speaker, as well meaning as he was, reinforced racist pedagogies that demand students who speak and write in dialects to code switch into American Standard English (SE). Although the speaker had participants engage in an activity where we learned about and interrogated our

https://doi.org/10.7330/9781646424573.c011

individual biases about language and its use in academia, he still turned back to traditional pedagogies that I had learned were racist and colonial, namely, code switching.[1] The speaker defined dialect as regionally bounded, neglecting the inflections race, gender, and ethnicity have on dialect. In other words, intentionally or not, he erased race and racism from the conversation while we turned our attention to a depoliticized view of language and learning in the university classroom. Finally, the speaker challenged participants to add informal writing assignments that would "allow" students to write in their dialect, but he did not challenge the primacy of what he called "Edited English"; he urged the audience to centralize academic English as the best English to use in formal assignments. Rather than invite instructors to question white linguistic hegemony in their classrooms, he pushed us to create limited opportunities for vernacular writing in low-stakes assignments while still helping students "translate" their work into the "appropriate" modes of academic discourse.

When I watched the YouTube video of this session, I was struck by how my past self so easily fell in step with the speaker by suggesting that participants could at least help students learn by creating opportunities to code switch even as I remarked how important Young's code-meshed call for Conference on College Composition and Communication's (CCCC's) proposals in 2019 was to me personally and to the field. In fact, even though I was praised behind the scenes for pushing back against some of the racial microaggressions that were communicated in the overall discussion, I reflect now that I was not doing enough by not challenging the lesson in code switching.

In the months following this workshop, the CTE asked me to lead its inaugural Masterclass Series in fall 2020 titled "Writing and Critical Thinking." The CTE leaders intended that I provide instructors with strategies to improve students' writing and critical thinking skills (as you can see from the oh-so-creative title), but I saw this series as an opportunity to integrate anti-racist pedagogies into a larger conversation about what we teach, what we expect from student writers, and how to teach *better*. "Better," to me, meant disrupting expectations about student knowledge, "appropriate" (i.e., white) language usage, and implicit racism in classroom lessons. I aimed to use this course to introduce anti-racist, pro-Black pedagogies to the participants, and since that class, I have leveraged every opportunity I have had to collaborate with the CTE to object to white hegemonic language and knowledge, even when

1. See Vershawn Ashanti Young, " 'Nah We Straight': An Argument against Code Switching" (2009).

my presentations do not seem to create opportunities to engage in such anti-racist work.

In this chapter, I argue that one way writing center administrators (WCAs) can and should integrate racial justice into their campus work is by using their platforms to confront pedagogical racism and introduce colleagues to concrete practices informed by racial and social justice theories. Our positions carve out opportunities to dismantle racist pedagogies because we can work closely with other instructors and pedagogical units. To be clear, I am speaking specifically to white WCAs because we should take up the burden of racial justice on campus. Our Black, African American, and other non-Black POC colleagues, especially women of color, already do that work simply by existing as Black (and female) in the academy in the United States. Because our platforms situate us as authorities on writing and the teaching of writing, we occupy unique positions where we can introduce other white faculty to pro-Black/anti-racist pedagogies; moreover, we can draw attention to our missions as racially just sites for pedagogical training when we support colleagues in implementing racial justice in their classrooms. I suggest WCAs partner with existing structures on campus such as teaching excellence centers to promote racial justice pedagogies. By partnering with well-established and often well-funded units, WCAS can extend our anti-racist influences more widely by making the most of such unit's reputations. Our centers also benefit from the added visibility while making the WCA's racial justice missions clear to teachers.

I will briefly summarize the Masterclass Series I facilitated and, especially, the anti-racist pedagogies I integrated into it. Then I will offer suggestions to white WCAs about best practices in challenging traditional teaching practices when speaking to non-writing faculty.

MASTER CLASS SERIES FALL 2020: WRITING AND CRITICAL THINKING

With the help of Xavery Hopkins in the Center of Teaching Excellence, I planned a three-meeting, remote series for faculty at the university entitled "Writing and Critical Thinking." I wrote a brief syllabus that summarized each meeting's theme, activities, and suggested readings. The classes covered "Best Practices of Teaching and Assessing Writing," "Critical Thinking through Critical Reading and Writing," and "How to Engage Students in Writing That Demonstrates Critical Thinking." During each meeting, which we hosted on Blackboard Collaborate Ultra, I offered a brief lecture using PowerPoint to assist me, activities and exercises, and then reflection. Participants would bring learning outcomes and writing assignments for their own current or future courses to workshop in small groups following the brief lecture.

While I did not include anti-racist jargon on the series syllabus, I centered anti-racist practices in each lesson in ways that the predominately white participants may be more inclined to engage with. For example, when I discussed linguistic justice and grading for grammar and mechanics, I asked the group of participants (all faculty, mostly full-time non-tenure-track [NTT] and tenure-track [TT]) where their outcomes demanded Academic Standard English (ASE) and prescriptive correctness. Most of the faculty admitted that their outcomes did not ask for students to use ASE, nor did faculty teach students this specific English. Later, I asked them why they graded English when they did not teach it or include its use on the syllabus. I heard a variety of answers, including that everyone will need to use "correct grammar" in writing in their professions. But when I asked for evidence, no one could offer examples other than professional-writing horror stories as anecdotes—an error on a résumé kept a candidate from receiving a job interview, for example. But none of us had real-world examples of students failing to find a job because of an error. So I asked them to reflect on why they insist on centering an English they didn't teach and, frankly, use themselves only in very specific rhetorical contexts. The answers boiled down to "tradition."

At stake, for me, were students and their educational experiences. Too many students come into writing classrooms with trauma about writing. I hoped to confront the ways that many higher-ed instructors unintentionally elevate practices that are both racist and traumatic by inviting them into a conversation about why we in academia, especially white instructors, continue to enforce particular linguistic traditions. In other words, I sought to invite these colleagues who were committed to the better teaching to the table rather than accuse them of engaging in racist practices. I created opportunities for them to reflect on their practices in relationship with anti-racist writing pedagogies. I also reframed "good writing" by challenging the roles grammar, mechanics, and ASE play in articulating critical thinking and argumentation.

I had realized while attending CTE workshops that the majority of white faculty rarely react well when their practices are accused of being rooted in racism—which, to be clear, most (if not all) traditional academic practices are. And here, I pause to acknowledge problems with my approach, namely, worrying about white people's reactions when they are confronted by the evidence that their actions maybe (are) racist, however unintentionally:

1. I know this paragraph reeks of Robin DiAngelo's concerns in *White Fragility* (2018) and other worlds. In general, DiAngelo argues that white people cannot engage in discourse about racism because they take their race for granted, misunderstand that racism is not a personal failing but an institutionalized system, and center their feelings in these conversations (13–14). While I am hesitant to endorse DiAngelo's book, I agree with her last two premises and would state them more as an enthymeme: "Because white people center their feelings when talking about race and racism, they cannot, will not, or have trouble confronting their own complicity in institutionalized racism."
2. However, in this case, like DiAngelo, I am clearly catering to white fragility rather than confronting it directly. I am not suggesting that my approach is better than others that more explicitly attack racism endemic in higher education. In fact, although I have tried to think up defenses for my decision to be coy with participants of the Masterclass Series about the anti-racist agenda in my pedagogy, I have decided that I don't have a good defense. I wanted white participants to feel comfortable, rather than directly confront the practices that I have learned from the cultural rhetorics and Black writing studies communities are the most racist, I selected a different tactic that had participants use reflective writing and group discussion to interrogate their pedagogical choices within the larger issues in the series.

You may be asking me right now if I would do anything differently, and I would, which I will discuss in the following section; however, I offer this series not as a perfect model for you but rather as an example of how white WCAs may consider partnering with teaching centers on campus with a racial justice agenda.

REALITIES AND SUGGESTIONS

I partnered with the CTE for a variety of reasons that are relevant to my advice in this section. Some of the best anti-racist work happens locally and collaboratively. Moreover, many white academics who are trying to be racial justice accomplices can feel like we're accomplishing nothing in academia. We feel powerless. But when we partner with existing units that promote exciting pedagogies, we can find a community of support and learn from other voices.

We can build on the principles of reciprocity and trust. In these situations, I suggest you attend your university's teaching excellence programming without an agenda other than to learn. While I have not been able to attend as many CTE workshops in the 2021–2022 academic year as I was previously, I appreciate learning more about teaching methodologies, using digital tools in the classroom like augmented reality, and hearing about the other programs on campus. I learn from my science, technology, engineering, and mathematics (STEM), social sciences, and medical sciences colleagues. When I show my willingness to learn in good faith and with goodwill from my colleagues, they are more likely to want to learn from me.

Finally, I have partnered with the CTE for these kinds of workshops because of their reach and credibility on campus. These units often provide a wealth of resources, and support that they offer can make this difficult work feel less isolating. For me, the CTE confers some of its credibility onto me when I lead a session. When we bring anti-racist writing pedagogies into the academic conversation, we should expect some pushback regardless of our partnerships; however, I have found that the challenges I need to address have been more thoughtfully framed because the CTE is known for making space for conversations about teaching that may be new or uncomfortable.

Despite the CTE's reputation and resources, I was not as directly confrontational about racist pedagogies as I may be in other spaces, such as in this collection. I was still relatively new to and unknown on campus; moreover, as of writing this piece, I am full-time, non-tenure-track faculty. My contract is renewed annually each midsummer based on student evaluations and my annual self-assessment, as well as the Writing Center's annual report. I also piloted this series during the fall 2020 semester, during which most of the university had switched to remote modalities because of COVID-19. Moreover, the Republican Party's (GOP's) fearmongering about Critical Race Theory had entered the public discourse around the time of the 2020 general election. Such tactics have entered the South Carolina state legislature; SC Bill 4522, which is still in a committee, could end tenure. Meanwhile SC House Bill 4325 prohibits instruction in Critical Race Theory—which writers of the bill misrepresent. Educators' jobs are tenuous, even in higher ed, in South Carolina. Considering this context and how many TT/tenured faculty enrolled in the series and were white, I felt insecure about the power differential I perceived between the participants and myself.

I share these complex constellations to help you think through your own rhetorical situations as you plan ways to engage faculty in these critical conversations and lessons. To help you do this, I offer some questions to consider as you develop your own faculty outreach plans. I provide questions because I frame all my work through inquiry, so questions are critical to how to design my programming. Feel free to adapt these questions, add to them, or use them (or not) at your discretion:

1. **What is your relationship to the faculty you'll be teaching?** As I shared, I am full-time, NTT faculty at a large, public R1. Because of this, I grounded my work deeply in theory and quantitative research to maximize my credibility and meet the faculty where they are. I relied heavily on position statements from the CCCC as well. Had I been TT, or tenured faculty, I may have relied less heavily on external sources. If I were not faculty at all, I would probably have pulled in even more research and included videos of important rhet-comp scholars speaking on these issues.
2. **What is your primary goal?** While I don't have data on how the participants have used the lessons on anti-racist pedagogies they learned in fall 2020, my own review of my materials tells me that I tried to do too much in a short period of time (three 75-minute sessions). You might create a workshop where you question grading for prescriptive grammar and help faculty develop strategies to talk with students about grammar or, better yet, change their position on the role of SAE. You might lead a workshop just on SAE—what is it? What does current research about its use in the twenty-first-century classroom tell us? What are our options as faculty when it comes to working with language?
3. **What support can you provide following the workshop(s)?** Any white person who has come to racial justice pedagogies should know that anti-racism and just pedagogies are processes, not end goals. Your work will not end when your programming does. What support can you offer faculty as they embark on this journey toward racially just pedagogy?
4. **How will you address pushback, especially as it relates to your writing center's reputation?** In the summer preceding the series, an emeritus faculty member from another department emailed me to attack the recent statements against linguistic justice that many departments of English and writing centers were publishing as a response to the murder of George Floyd and Black Lives Matter demonstrations for racial justice. When I emailed him back supporting such statements, he told me that he would not recommend students in his courses come to the Writing Center I direct. I did not email him back. I tell this story because there will be faculty deeply entrenched in racist assumptions about language and academia. They may try to retaliate, and claiming to defame the center you run is a common tactic. What kind of support system will you need to back you? Are the threats idle or nonmaterial enough not to affect the writing center?
5. **What kind of support will your partnership give you?** Remember that when you partner with a campus unit, you are now both endorsing each other. Are they ready to back you?

In addition to considering these questions as you plan your work, I offer these suggestions:

1. GIVE CREDIT TO THE PEOPLE WHO TAUGHT YOU. Whenever I write a syllabus or offer a workshop, I start by thanking my academic godparents. For example, I say, "I could not have done this work if not

for research and guidance from Malea Powell and Vershawn Ashanti Young." I might describe what they taught me, and then immediately let the audience know that what I am teaching them comes from BIPOC scholars.

2. Foreground BIPOC scholars. The white anti-racist community has embraced DiAngelo, but her work is neither new nor radical. Moreover, when we center white anti-racist scholarship, we center whiteness. If you are building a syllabus for a series, recommending reading, or drawing from research, you must be intentional in building a bibliography of BIPOC writers. If you don't know where to turn, look at DiAngelo's bibliography or use social media to ask for suggestions. Better yet, see the reference sections in this book. While the contributors do cite some white scholars, many of us rely on critical works from BIPOC and Asian-Pacific Islander scholars.
3. Practice how you will answer questions about code switching, code meshing, and grading SAE grammar and mechanics. You might have a variety of answers developed for different kinds of audiences, from hostile to well-meaning.
4. Have frank conversations about your racial justice agenda with the unit you're partnering with. You do not want to surprise them when you begin arguing in support of linguistic justice, changing rubrics, or other pedagogies you suggest. Make sure that they are ready for these conversations too. You may have to move more slowly than you want by having multiple lengthy conversations about your agenda and theirs.
5. Collaborate well with others. You do not want to seem like you're engaging in a hostile takeover of the unit. Work to align your goals, and show that you're committed to collaboration and coalition building with others.
6. Less is more. There are so many different racist and colonial pedagogies we can confront and try to dismantle in the academy. When we try to tackle all of these issues for a workshop, we offer instead many anti-racist platitudes rather than concrete actions faculty can take to change their classrooms. Focus on one issue you want to tackle.
7. Build in time for practice. Come prepared with activities. Consider integrating reflective writing and revision workshops to help participants change their rubrics.
8. Consider building a workshop series delivered over several semesters. Have workshops or lectures you can offer as follow-ups with short notice. While some participants will balk at your message, others will be hungry for more. Be prepared to help them.
9. Admit when you make a mistake. Apologize without defense. Being a white accomplice in racial justice work is fraught with errors and missteps. I made a mistake when I wasn't as directly confrontational about my anti-racist agenda. I explained the reasons why I made those choices, but they are not good reasons. I am sorry for not being bolder. Part of

changing is writing this chapter so I can reflect on the experience, identify what I can do better, and help others benefit from my hindsight.

CONCLUSION

My colleagues in this section tackle other ways that WCAs can impact their local communities. I keep looking at Kamille Bostick's title "Writing Revolution: Reimagining the Role of Writing Centers," chapter 13 in this collection, as I reflect on my struggle to write this chapter. Writing center professionals have obligations to engage in their local communities, and WCAs can serve as examples for tutors by starting and making space for conversations that confront us with our own complicity in racism. While I have focused on what WCAs can do when partnered with university resources for instructors, I appreciate the ways that Bostick and Nicole Emmelhainz and her tutors in chapter 12 look at the impact that student-teacher research can do to highlight ways that writing centers can and should intervene in their communities.

I wrote this chapter not only to discuss what I do and offer my practices to readers to help you think of your own opportunities to reach faculty; I had listened to many BIPOC female scholars who have done this work I am demanding white WCAs do. I heard how triggering, traumatizing, and exhausting this labor—largely unseen—is. White WCAs like me—like some of you reading this collection or chapter—need to take up this work without the expectation of visibility or praise. We should do it to support our BIPOC colleagues who do this work every hour of the day in their lived experiences as Black scholars, instructors, and administrators. And we should not demand thanks.

This work, though, is rewarding, and it answers Bostick's call for writing centers to reimagine themselves. Writing center professionals are already engaging in outreach and special programming. We're already supporting faculty. We're already talking about anti-racist and racially just pedagogies. But we can and should formalize this work so that our racial justice agendas are visible and practiced. We must be bold, and we must not be afraid of angering people on campus, because our students' and colleagues' lives are at stake. So what if our careers are?

REFERENCES

DiAngelo, Robin. 2018. *White Fragility: Why It's So Hard for White People to Talk about Racism.* Boston, Beacon Press.

Young, Vershawn. 2009. " 'Nah, We Straight': An Argument against Code Switching." *JAC* 29, no. 1/2 (2009): 49–76. https://www.jstor.org/stable/20866886.

PART V

Holding Our Professional Organizations Accountable

12

COMMUNITY IS THE CENTER

Social Justice Pedagogy and Practice for More Engaged Writing Consultant Training

Nicole Emmelhainz, Amanda Ballou, and Graciela Greger

INTRODUCTION

A writing center is not a single person, but a small community within a larger community with ties grounded in helping community members develop and express their ideas in writing. Both training for and working in a university writing center during a pandemic brought new meaning to the best practices for writing tutoring, both from the students' and the Director's perspectives. During this time, learning to work in new ways that best support all writers took on new urgency, as did the need for respect, compassion, and flexibility. This chapter presents voices from both students and the Writing Center Director about our experiences during the COVID-19 pandemic and how we explored opportunities to help not only our immediate university community but also the local community outside the campus boundaries.

In the first part, the Writing Center Director at Christopher Newport University (CNU), Dr. Nicole Emmelhainz, will contextualize the revisions she made to the required three-credit-hour, writing-intensive tutor training course, "Tutoring in the Writing Center." She includes a discussion of the course structure, readings, and assignments, specifically the research project option that focused on the viability of a community writing center (CWC) in the nearby communities. This CWC research project provided the first steps to establishing a university-supported but non-university-focused writing center that assists high-school-aged and older citizens of the Newport News / Hampton communities in Southeastern Virginia, diverse communities quite different from that of the university. The research project also established interest and engagement in the CWC from potential writing consultants.

In the chapter's second part, students reflect on the course and the research approach and process. These student coauthors, Amanda

https://doi.org/10.7330/9781646424573.c012

Ballou and Graciela Greger, researched the general topic of the CWC, though each focused on more narrow topics. Amanda focused on how the CWC could benefit local high school students, specifically the ways in which high school students could not only receive help but potentially be a part of the CWC staff. Graciela explored how a CWC needs to meet the needs of the diverse local communities, including implicit bias training and diverse representation on the staff.

Together, we, the students and Writing Center Director, will discuss what we collaboratively learned about how social justice plays a role in both the university writing center and the surrounding community. For example, as Amanda and Graciela explain, one of the potential benefits of providing free writing tutoring is increasing equitable education for a diverse community. In short, researching a community writing center and how such a resource would better support the myriad kinds of writers and writing needs in our local community made the practical and theoretical concepts discussed during the class resonate more powerfully. We all learned to see community as the center of our learning and work as writing center practitioners.

PART 1: A TALE OF TWO SEMESTERS: THE WRITING CENTER DIRECTOR'S EXPERIENCES

Like for many other writing center administrators and educators, the COVID-19 pandemic necessitated changes in my understanding of and approach to both writing center work and instructional pedagogical practices. As I prepared for online classes for the academic year (AY) 2020–2021, I considered many related questions: How can the Writing Center be made more accessible for all students? What practices will need to be changed, and how so? What will current writing consultants need to be trained on that wasn't covered during their semester-long training course? What will students in the upcoming training courses need to be taught as potential writing consultants? How can I, as a faculty member, model more empathy and compassion, so that the students can emulate such attitudes in their writing center work? What will my students, and the students who will use the Writing Center, need to better support them?

Through discussion with other faculty members and students, in particular those who would be working in the Writing Center, the notion of respect became central to planning for an unpredictable academic year. Specifically, Tiffany Rousculp's concept of "rhetoric of respect" became applicable when enacting these new plans. In Rousculp's understanding, respect is different from more patronizing attitudes, including tolerance and acceptance, as a response to difference. Instead, "Respect implies a different type of relationship, one that is grounded in perception of worth, in esteem for another — as well as for the self . . . it entails recognition of multiple views, approaches, abilities, and, importantly, limitations (especially our own). In other words, respect needs flexibility and self awareness" (2014, 24–25). Worth. Esteem for others. Flexibility. All of these characteristics took on added importance during the pandemic but also had the potential for far-reaching needs after the pandemic as well.

Pre-pandemic, our home institution, CNU, had not run online classes. Yet, the accessibility permitted by online classes benefited all students, not just those who needed to stay off campus to protect themselves and their families. The same could be said for the online writing tutoring options the undergraduate staff and I created in response to the initial move to online learning in mid-March 2020. Those options were never previously considered because of the in-person experience the university prided itself on offering. However, as fall 2020 and spring 2021 demonstrated, the online options were popular with all students. Why had I never considered these tutoring possibilities before? What else had I been overlooking (or simply not seeing) with my pedagogy? How else could students be helped through small, easy-to-incorporate changes? In what ways could such changes better practice a rhetoric of respect?

These questions led me to examine related social and racial justice community engagement opportunities as a means of radically revising my approach to both training education and writing center work. However, as Lisa Zimmerelli (2015) explains, "actionable racial justice requires a deeper level of engagement and commitment with what can be challenging concepts and theories, especially for white students and teachers" (63). As a white, middle-class woman, I knew that my experience of the pandemic and racial justice movement was fundamentally not the same as many of my students' experiences. But, as Rasha Diab, Thomas Ferrel, Beth Godbee, and Neil Simpkins explain, I was committed to actionable racial justice through "(1) self-work and (2) work-with-others on both the (3) interpersonal and (4) institutional levels" (qtd. in Zimmerelli 2015, 63). These steps I already participated in as a teacher and an administrator. Given the anecdotal knowledge I had of my students and their participation in social justice initiatives, I believed they would be invested in taking these steps as well. This experience led me to use the move to online learning to drastically redesign the required tutor training course.[1]

Training Course and Research Project Overview

This course serves as required training for CNU students who want to work in the Writing Center. Not all students who take this training course will work in the Writing Center, however. The course also partially fulfills the writing requirement for graduation, which is the most common reason students enroll in it.

Teaching this course is part of my responsibilities as the Writing Center Director. I inherited the course from the previous Director, who taught the class in what I now understand as a more traditional way: focused predominantly on the daily, practical work of the Writing Center while providing some select theoretical readings. Interspersed between the readings from Leigh Ryan and Lisa Zimmerelli's *The Bedford Guide for Writing Tutors* and Ben Rafoth's *A Tutor's Guide: Helping Writers One to One* were grammar quizzes, a midterm exam, and a final exam. One of the main writing assignments was a tutoring observation paper, which the students revised through both professor and peer feedback. I've continually adjusted the readings and assignments each semester since I began teaching this course, most recently and perhaps more drastically during the 2020–2021 academic year.

As Judy Gill (2006) suggests is a frequent pedagogical move by those who teach tutor training, I follow a common formula for structuring the required training course: a mix between practical knowledge and theoretical information. Before the pandemic, in earlier versions of this course as I taught it, the majority of the readings came from Melissa Ianetta and Lauren Fitzgerald's *The Oxford Guide for Writing Tutors*, which has a deliberate focus on contemporary research and research practices in addition to practical matters such as the anatomy of a writing consultation. Readings focused on tutoring practices, authoring practices, tutor and author identities, and tutoring across disciplines. Some theoretical readings about collaboration and motivation were also discussed, though like the inherited version of the class, there wasn't much initially that introduced students to contemporary scholarship. There were no

1. Because the revision of the training course to be discussed is so recent, and the Community Writing Center is still in its early stages, no quantitative data have been collected. Such means of assessing the effectiveness of both the class and the Community Writing Center will begin at a later date, when the university IRB approval has been granted.

readings that directly discussed social or racial justice concerns within writing center work.

Students used weekly reading blogs to practice summarizing and analyzing the readings before discussing them in class. Grammar lessons were regularly reviewed, with students learning not only about how to identify common issues in Standard American English but also how to teach these issues to other students for those students to correct them. In addition to the blogs, students were assigned two major writing assignments: an individually written tutoring observation report (which, as Gill notes, is a very common assignment for tutor training classes) and a collaboratively written research project, which the students undertook with the help of a writing consultant mentor. This collaborative project asked students to design a research project from proposal to final draft but situate it specifically within the context of our university's Writing Center. Overall, the class structure and organization focused specifically on ideas and information needed to run writing consultations, which for many semesters I believed would be the most pressing information potential consultants would want to know.

When the COVID-19 pandemic required the university to move classes online in March 2020, I revised the collaborative research assignment to an individual research assignment, to accommodate students who would have limited internet service and might not be able to connect with their partner. This assignment revision, which asked students to consider what other ways writing centers serve individuals within the campus community or local communities (outside the campus), had students answer this question: How can writing centers assist communities and/or individuals in ways other than just writing? The students' research topics varied greatly, including discussions of racial diversity, gender, multiliterate writers, and writers with learning or physical accommodations needs. Reading their individually produced research, which by the assignment's nature allowed each student to pursue a topic that interested them (rather than negotiate a topic with a partner), gave me better insight into what students may want to learn more about regarding the larger scope and mission of writing center work. For some students, they specifically selected topics about populations they self-identified as belonging to, so there was a potential to open conversations about writing center work that could be deeply personal and engaging for students. This was one opportunity to practice a rhetoric of respect, permitting those "multiple views and approaches" Rousculp believes to be important to this discursive active process.

For the fall 2020 and spring 2021 semesters, which I taught synchronously online, I revised the reading schedule, which included a switch back to the Ryan and Zimmerelli's *Bedford Guide*,[2] and further revised both assignments (see appendices A and B for a condensed course syllabus and the individual research assignment[3]). The first major revision was the readings, to which in addition to the *Bedford Guide* readings, I added theoretical readings that introduced students to social justice issues relevant to writing center work. Specifically, the third week of the semester, we focused on scholarship related to concerns about tutoring to Standard or Academic American English usage. The scholarship discussed for this topic were Laura Greenfield's "The Standard English Fairy Tale," Neisha-Anne Green's "The Re-education of Neisha-Anne S. Green: A Close Look at the Damaging Effects of 'A Standard Approach,'" and Eric Camarillo's "Dismantling Neutrality: Cultivating Antiracist Writing Center Ecologies." Through these readings, the students and I discussed systemic racist and classist teaching practices connected to language use.

These readings allowed us to begin a cursory examination of what Asao Inoue (2016) calls a "white racial habitus" of writing. Though these preferences may be thought of as static, Inoue explains that they are not, and instead the habitus "varies by discipline, class, location, and instructor, hence it is flexible" (n.p.). Because this discussion comes early in the semester, the conversations and ideas developed carried forward into the remaining topics throughout the semester. Topics that initially may have seemed practical and mundane, the everyday work of writing centers, could now be critically analyzed for inherent biases. Students could begin to challenge these practices, such as making statements and asking questions, more deeply and consider ways to make writing center work more equitable.

One of the most prominent topics the students consistently challenged in new ways was the grammar reviews that were still part of the class. For the 2020–2021 AY, I revised how we discussed grammar, and instead of reading and discussing during class reviews about comma usage and incomplete sentences, we read scholarship about the place grammar instruction has in writing tutoring, specifically Bethany Bib's "Bringing Balance to the Table: Comprehensive Writing Instruction

2. The *Bedford Guide* became free to download at the start of the fall semester, which was a major reason for this shift.
3. Included is the spring 2021 syllabus, which was identical to the fall 2020 syllabus. Required COVID-19 policies for in-person teaching have been removed, since both classes were taught online.

in the Tutoring Session" and Li Qi Peh's "Proofreading during a Pandemic." These readings opened up conversations about not just how to work with students on their grammar and other sentence-level concerns, but *why* we may want to do so. However, the earlier foundation of racial justice readings inspired even deeper reflections. Students wanted to know if reaffirming writing rules that were at the very least problematic was in line with the purported mission of most writing centers. There were no easy answers that satisfied everyone, but questions were now being raised by the students about grammar that had not been previously addressed. Such questions led to different perspectives about how we, at our Writing Center, should begin to address the larger systemic issues that scholars like Green, Greenfield, and Camarillo discussed at length in their articles.

These were and will remain valuable discussions to have as a Writing Center staff, as our university context is one that is predominantly white, with nearly 77 percent of the student population identifying as white/Caucasian and only about 12 percent identifying as Black / African American or Hispanic / Latinx ("Diversity"). The makeup in the "Tutoring in the Writing Center" class generally reflected this as well, though there were students who identified as Black / African American, Hispanic/Latinx, Asian, or multiracial in both the fall 2020 and spring 2021 classes. Because the Writing Center is restricted to hiring only students who successfully completed this class, I encourage all students to apply, resulting in diverse representation on our staff. For all consultants, then, they receive training on working with student-writers who use a variety of languages and gain the vocabulary to talk about expectations for academic writing on our campus along with individual student preferences for style. This provides another opportunity to engage in respectful rhetoric.

As Kenneth Bruffee (1978) states in his reflection on what tutor training should do, "any tutor training should try to help tutors develop both socially and academically" (433). Instructors' impetus when creating training classes should be to help students grow in their knowledge of the writing center work as well as how the writing center often serves vital functions within its local community context. Questions and discussions about racial justice issues with language grounded not only the class readings and inquiries into our own Writing Center's mission but also how work of this kind might function outside a university setting. This exploration led to the individual research assignment, for which I revised into two prompts for the 2020–2021 AY: one for writing centers' roles in other capacities and one for community writing centers.

As mentioned earlier, the research assignment for this year was revised from the previous collaborative research project due to students' unique situations during the pandemic. Because the class was taught online both semesters, I couldn't assume students would have the ability to work together consistently outside of class. Thus, the individual research paper still allowed them to complete the required amount of formal writing expected from a writing-intensive class while also giving them the opportunity to explore more about a topic of their choosing. For the spring semester specifically, I added a separate option to research how a community writing center would impact the local community context for the Newport News / Hampton areas, which are the nearby municipalities to our university.

A brief note about each of these cities: The most recent census data detail that Newport News has a population of approximately 179,000 and Hampton has a population of approximately 135,000. Both cities are racially diverse. Newport News has a Black / African American population of 41 percent, with 51 percent of Hampton's population being Black / African American. Citizens who are Hispanic or Latinx make up 9 percent of Newport News' population, with 6 percent making up Hampton's population. Asian Americans make up 3 percent and 2.5 percent of the population in Newport News and Hampton, respectively. Only about a quarter of each city's population has a bachelor's degree or higher, and about 15 percent of each city's population lives at or below the poverty line (United States Census Bureau n.d.).

I provide this information to give a sense of the local community context that grounds the research project for the community writing center. In the assignment, I frontload how researching a CWC makes sense within the context of the class.

> Throughout this course, we will discuss much about the role Writing Centers play in both their unique campus communities as well as with the individual student-writers who use the center to help them develop as writers. We'll also discuss ways in which Writing Centers can participate in larger social-justice initiatives, and for this assignment, I'd like you to research **community writing centers**, what they are, the writers they serve, and how they operate within a non-university setting. Specifically, I'd like you to research the local Newport News / Hampton Roads community to assess and anticipate the needs of the citizens in these communities and how a community writing center could best provide assistance to these citizens. The big question I'd like you to answer is: How could a community writing center best serve the writing (and related communication) needs of the citizens in our community, but not part of the Christopher Newport University community?

The rest of the assignment (see appendix B) asks students to take on many of the research and writing tasks common to a scholarly paper. They write a brief proposal, compile a literature review, and draft and revise multiple times with feedback from myself and their peers.

For those unfamiliar with CWCs, a brief introduction and explanation may be helpful. While adhering to many of the same values and principles university writing centers hold, a community writing center typically serves as a resource for non-university-affiliated individuals. As Tiffany Rousculp reflects on the mission of the Salt Lake Community College (SLCC) CWC, it was founded "to support, motivate, and educate people of all abilities and educational backgrounds who wanted to use writing for practical needs, civic engagement and personal expression" (2014, 6). As a form of community engagement, a CWC may also work with a variety of community partners and organizations to help meet more specific writing needs of certain populations. Rousculp clarifies that unlike community outreach or community engagement learning programs, a CWC "provides a physical space dedicated solely to writing" (2003, 11). Those working for a university-affiliated CWC may include the university's Writing Center administrators, undergraduate and/or graduate consultants, or trained volunteers from either the university or the local community.

As Rousculp overviews, there are numerous community-oriented outreach programs supported by universities across the country,[4] as well as independently run ones (2014, 2–6). One program, sponsored by the Undergraduate Writing Center at the University of Texas at Austin, partners with the local public library system to provide free writing assistance to the community's working-class neighborhoods and citizens. James Jesson (2006) explains that the partnership between the writing center, undergraduate consultants, and the library helps to "satisfy specific community needs . . . solidifies relations between the university and Austin residents [and] furthers undergraduate consultants' professional development" (n.p.). Rousculp explains that the majority of the staff at the SLCC CWC also were either faculty or students from the SLCC or one of their university partners (2014, 15). She, too, believes that the benefit to the students was immense, as they frequently took on roles and responsibilities above and beyond just providing writing assistance (61–63). Both Jesson and Rousculp, as well as Zimmerelli in her description of a writing-oriented service-learning tutor education, discuss the overall

4. In Rousculp's *Rhetoric of Respect*, she highlights fourteen such programs. Unfortunately, as of this writing, it doesn't appear that one can simply conduct an internet search for a comprehensive list of such programs and centers.

positive impact such long-term community engagement programs provide to both the students in the writing consulting roles, as well as the individuals who receive the writing assistance.

It is this long-term scope of such community engagement outreach that creates the potential for meaningful, impactful social justice initiatives to happen. Writing centers are well positioned to achieve this kind of outreach. As Amy McCleese Nichols and Bronwyn T. Williams (2019) explain, though part of larger institutionalized frameworks, writing centers are frequently "grounded in values and practices distinctive from other parts of the university" (88). What's more, rather than approaching community or service-learning opportunities as temporary, writing centers can "offer often unexplored opportunities to be a locus for community engagement within the larger college or university" (88–89). Sustained outreach, then, has the potential to create lasting positive effects on the larger community while engaging members of the university. These reasons, then, make developing and running a CWC with students, already in training for writing center work, ideal actionable ground for applying theoretical and scholarly concepts to practical work.

In the spring 2021 class, eight out of fourteen students completed research projects on this topic. All students discussed the concept of community writing centers, reading Rousculp's article "Into the City We Go" (2003) and researching the local area for existing nonprofits that they could form potential partnerships with. Since this was the last reading of the semester, we discussed generally how a CWC might impact our local community and its citizens. The eight students who selected this focus for their research paper explored more thoroughly elements of the community and specific populations that might be most positively impacted by a CWC. Three students examined the steps needed to establish a CWC and the potential collaboration between the university and community; two explored how the CWC could help high school students; one discussed the ways the CWC could best meet the needs of the Black / African American and Hispanic populations; one researched the ways in which a CWC could help multiliterate individuals; and, finally, one looked at the possibility of the CWC as a resource for unhomed populations.

While the scope of this chapter limits my ability to detail each of these fantastic projects, the class knowledge created by the work of these eight students was immense. Collectively, we learned about the demographic and socioeconomic makeup of the two closest municipalities to the university, whose demographics are not at all like that of the university. As stated above, the university is predominantly white and middle class, while the local communities are largely Black/African American and Hispanic/Latino and at least fifteen of these communities live at or below the poverty line (United States Census Bureau n.d.). Students applied ideas from the established framework of writing center practices to analyze how such a resource could work in our immediate, local context. Two students who completed their research on CWCs, Graciela Greger and Amanda Ballou, next discuss their reflections about their work in the class and specifically what they learned about writing center work in a nonuniversity community.

PART 2: STUDENT REFLECTIONS

Graciela Greger

Prior to completing the course, I had a limited understanding of writing centers. However, I had visited CNU's Writing Center for consultations on multiple occasions, prior to the COVID-19 pandemic, which provided me with an introduction and firsthand experience to refer back to throughout the course. This experience sparked my interest in enrolling in English 339 and ultimately, working toward becoming a writing consultant. Prior to taking this course, my understanding of writing centers was that consultants review written work and provide feedback, but as a teaching opportunity rather than a correcting one, and students visit the center as a result of their own motivation.

This course gave me a much more holistic and in-depth understanding of the purpose and philosophy of writing centers and tutoring. My key takeaways were that writing centers provide a collaborative, individualized opportunity for clients to improve their writing and receive constructive feedback from a trained consultant. Consultants do not serve the purpose of proofreader/editor. Rather, they are there to meet the writer where they are and allow the writer to determine the direction and pace of the appointment. Through this *partnership* between the client and consultant, the emphasis is placed on improving the client's writing ability, so that they come away being able to utilize their newly acquired skills and knowledge moving forward, rather than improving a single piece of written work.

I was also introduced to the work of community writing centers during the course. By exploring this through class discussion and independent research, which culminated into a final research project, I was able to gain a greater appreciation of the role writing centers can have beyond the university setting and the impact they can have throughout the community. For the Community Writing Center research project, I researched the issue of antiracism within the context of CWCs. I chose this topic due to the exigent nature of this issue. During the pandemic, issues of racial inequality were brought to national attention, and further brought to light the need for strong allyship and advocacy; progress cannot be made without intentional, collective efforts. Additionally, I felt that this is a topic that would be invaluable to current and future Writing Consultants and Centers overall. I began my research by referring back to select scholarship we had read for class, and then proceeded to examine additional journal articles and local census data. Due to the diverse needs, backgrounds, and identities of each individual who enters our doors, conducting research specific to the surrounding community allows the CWC staff to better serve their clients and make the space as safe and inclusive as possible.

Through my research, I learned about the important role that writing centers can play in social justice. Antiracist practices are relevant to *all* WCs, not just CWCs, and *all* writing centers and institutions would benefit from further education on this issue and actively working against systems of oppression. Writing centers have the potential to become agents of social change by *actively* working against oppressive language use and acts, prioritizing diversity, equity, and inclusion in all practices, and leading by example. This includes, but is not limited to, providing effective and continued training to all staff on a variety of critical topics, such as multilingualism and implicit bias, and recruiting and hiring a diverse staff. The overarching takeaway from my research is that change starts within the writing center context, but by no means does it end there. The knowledge and experiences gained through the Writing Center extend well beyond the length of the consultation. Writing centers have the potential to encourage progress and make a long-lasting impact.

Amanda Ballou

For my community writing center research project, I focused on a specific sample of the community population: high school students. With this focus, I researched how the community writing center could implement outreach programs into the local schools as well as the benefits of such programs on the students. I chose this topic because I noticed that it was a part of the population that sometimes gets overlooked, even though it is such a formative period in learning critical writing and communication skills.

When I began my research, I found much scholarship on the benefits of writing centers and programming targeted toward high school students as well as specific implementation and case studies of similar programs. I used this research as the basis for brainstorming possible programs for the CWC. I also researched the demographics of the Newport News high schools, which allowed me to get more specific in explaining how the outreach programs could serve the students of this particular community. I found that Newport News County is highly diverse, with a little over half of the students being Black and almost 15 percent Hispanic. Additionally, over half of the students are economically disadvantaged, meaning that they meet any of these criteria including eligible for free/reduced meals, receives temporary assistance for needy families, eligible for Medicaid, is a migrant, or is experiencing homelessness. This demographical data show the importance of providing a writing center that can help people of all backgrounds.

I found that researching the community and assessing its needs were together important for my training as a writing consultant because they helped me to develop important skills for the job. As a writing consultant, it's necessary for me to be able to assess the needs of each individual, so I can better understand and tailor my feedback for them. Additionally, beyond just being a writing consultant, it's important to be able to look at your entire surroundings, rather than just a small portion. The Christopher Newport University community is very different and not representative of the wider Hampton Roads area in terms of its demographics, since CNU is a predominantly white institution. Being able to distinguish this difference is the first step to understanding the community better and beginning to engage within it.

MOVING FORWARD: FROM RESEARCH TO ACTION

In their 2018 keynote address at the International Writing Center Association's Annual Conference, Kendra L. Mitchell and Robert E. Randolph explain that to be successful, social justice initiatives need to include social action. What the CWC research prompt allowed us, both undergraduate writing consultants in training and the Writing Center Director, to see was that establishing a CWC would greatly benefit the local communities. The communities' diverse needs, though, mean that the work to start and run the CWC would too be great. From the students' projects, we know more about the diverse socioeconomic, educational, and racial makeup of the nearby communities. While the research paper was only the first step, student engagement with the project demonstrated that there is an interest in applying knowledge from the course beyond the boundaries of the university campus.

The creation of what will be the Tidewater Community Writing Center (so named as the region between the James River and the Chesapeake Bay is called the Tidewater) will have a direct impact on the "Tutoring in the Writing Center" course. While still in the planning phase, the Tidewater CWC will be housed in a former Episcopal Church school building, which is near two major roads connecting Newport News and Hampton and is a short drive from the university campus. To begin, the CWC will operate one day a week for one-to-one consultations, with appointments encouraged and made on a forthcoming website. Both students in the training course and the Writing Center staff will be encouraged to volunteer, as students at our university can complete volunteer work to earn a graduation distinction. Eventually, the training course may further evolve into a service-learning course, where all students will be expected to complete a set amount of volunteer hours in the CWC. In the future, a training program for non-writing-center personnel will be developed so that other students and staff from the university could volunteer at the CWC as well.

Community partnerships with all local high schools as well as several nonprofits, including Peninsula Reads (a service helping adults with reading literacy), will be our first steps toward building a clientele within the surrounding communities. Based on the first set of research projects, the CWC staff will provide writing assistance for a variety of documents, including professional documents, such as resumes and cover letters and college application essays, and personal and creative writing. With feedback from the CWC clients, more resources may eventually be offered, in order to continually meet the needs of those who visit the CWC and, hopefully, help those who use the CWC to be more confident in their writing communication. Furthermore, volunteer staff who have linguistic proficiencies in addition to English, including Spanish and Korean, will also be trained to help the widest range of potential writers from the community.

It is a goal of all educators that their students not only comprehend ideas but consider them beyond the classroom setting, to find applications, even if in thought, to other contexts. What Graciela's and Amanda's reflections demonstrate is a move to transfer their knowledge making outside the classroom setting. For Amanda and Graciela, who will be working as writing consultants during the 2021–2022 AY, some of that transfer will happen in a university space. But as these reflections also suggest, there are applicable ways to broaden those opportunities for students to apply theoretical, scholarly concepts to real-world settings. Some final thoughts for other writing center directors to consider, if they would like to implement similar pedagogical lessons:

- Have your students research your university (though online searches, interviews, and personal reflections) to create a more holistic understanding of its community members.
- Have students brainstorm other ways writing centers play a role within your unique campus community.
- Research the nearby communities for a clearer understanding of who is a part of them.
- Identify local nonprofits and community resources, and consider how their services align (or don't) with writing center practices. How do they meet the needs of the community? What could writing centers learn by observing these resources in action?
- If you don't already, include diverse scholarly voices within the training program.

As Nichols and Williams explain, writing centers hold a unique position within institutional settings, operating outside of the typical timelines that bind much university work. The community writing center can be the beginning of what will hopefully be the type of engaged, socially oriented community outreach that helps transform theory into action. We see it also as the beginning for more empathetic, respectful connections.

APPENDIX 12.A: TUTORING IN THE WRITING CENTER SPRING 2021 SYLLABUS

ENGL 339: Tutoring in the Writing Center Condensed Syllabus

Course Overview and Learning Objectives: Writing centers are places where writers gather to talk about writing, and this course is designed to enable you to become an active participant in such conversations. During the semester you will

- Expand awareness of your strengths as a writer and a listener
- Increase your understanding of the writing process and the value of revision
- Learn how to facilitate a one-on-one peer consultation
- Review basic grammar and punctuation with an eye toward being able to explain concepts and recognize and correct common errors.

Underpinning these objectives is the broader academic conversation about the theory and practice of writing centers, a conversation that takes place in various academic journals and discussion forums. We will connect with and situate ourselves contextually with the history, development, and roles of writing centers and peer tutoring to better understand how writing centers function both politically and practically within academic settings and the university at large. Additionally, this course will ask you to become more self-reflective and more empathetic toward others and their experiences as writers.

As we'll discuss, the history of writing within the university and larger US educational systems is fraught with anxiety produced from a focus on errors and mistakes. Frequently, writing does not bring pleasure to the student-writer, but the opposite: pain. In order to be a successful writing consultant, you need to learn to be open and accepting of others. Writing is a conversation, and writing tutoring is one way in which this notion becomes clear. As Natalie Goldberg says in *Writing Down the Bones*, "It is good to talk . . . We should learn to talk, not with judgment, greed, or envy, but with compassion, wonder, and amazement" (2005, 77). This course partially fulfills the writing intensive requirement.

Class Engagement and Mindful Learning: Since the goal of this course is to teach you research writing skills, you are expected to attend class and complete assignments which are error-free, properly formatted, typed, and turned in on time. More specifically, your participation in class should demonstrate the following:

- Preparation for class (completing readings, blog posts, blog replies, etc.)
- Engagement in and contribution to class discussions and activities
- Constructive participation in peer review workshops and individual conferences
- Completion of incidental in-class and out-of-class writing assignments
- Visiting the Writing Center at any stage of the writing process for additional support with your writing needs and to help keep you accountable

Part of this course will include mindfulness and empathy practices, because idea creation and writing are fundamentally a personal act, and one that can be stressful and anxiety producing. It's my hope that through incorporation of a variety of optional mindfulness practices, we all will find ways of better approaching both our writing and working with each other. Remember: Everyone in this course, including the instructor, is a human and is learning. Be respectful, be compassionate, be supportive of and to each other. In short, be human in this course.

Reader's Blog: Each student will create their own reader's blog using any blog site they like (Blogger, WordPress, Weebly, etc.). Students will create their blogs in class during week one and email the link to me. Posts should focus on the reading/s assigned for the week, bringing all readings into conversation with one another, if there are multiple readings. Blog posts will have each of the following three components:

- **Summary:** A brief summary of each reading. Remember, summaries should *not* contain every bit of information and detail about a reading but instead focus on the central point or argument of the piece and the major supporting points. Please keep these to about 100 words; brevity is key!
- **Comment:** An observation regarding some aspect of the readings that bring them into conversation with one another. Try to offer an insightful observation that wouldn't be immediately apparent to all readers. Your comment should be around 100 words.
- **Question:** In addition to offering a comment, you should pose a question concerning the readings. This question could inquire about an aspect of the readings that you found confusing, or it could ask your classmates and me to ponder an important implication of a point offered in the readings. Feel free to post more than one question if you'd like.

  Note: Your comment and question can be related or unrelated to one another, but please include both in the same posting.

Your blog posts must be submitted by 9:30 p.m. the evening before the class in which they will be discussed. This allows time for your posts to be read before class begins. We will often use these blogs as a starting point for our class discussion.

Evaluation Criteria: Blogs will be graded for engagement with reading (how much did you read, think about, try to understand, ask questions, etc.) as well as completeness (meaning all components appear in all posts). I will not grade on spelling, grammar, punctuation, etc., but posts should generally be very readable and free from errors.

Grammar Refreshers: To follow all grammar/punctuation lessons are short refreshers (i.e., quizzes) that will help with traditionally common writing concerns. These will be completed on your own time but must be completed **by the end of the semester**. These refreshers will be available as Google Forms in the Classroom.

Writing Tutoring Reflection: You will complete a minimum of **one writing center consultation**, with the option to remotely observe another session as well. You will take notes before and after, reflecting on the experience. Then, you will select **one** aspect of the session and draft and revise a thesis-driven essay of approximately 1,500 words. A more detailed assignment sheet to follow.

Research Paper: Each student will research, propose, draft, and revise a thesis-driven research paper that explores an element of how writing centers may play a role in their communities beyond the helping of writers. Approximately 2,500 words. Components will include a proposal, literature review, draft, and revision. A more detailed assignment sheet to follow.

WEEKLY SCHEDULE

Week 1: Course and people intros; getting tech ready for class; blogs; prompts What is a writing center? What is its role in its campus and surrounding communities?

Week 2: Brief presentation on history of writing centers; North, "The Idea of a Writing Center"; Lunsford, "Collaboration, Control, and the Idea of a Writing Center"

Week 3: Greenfield, "The Standard English Fairy Tale"; Green, "A Close Look at the Damaging Effects of 'A Standard Approach' "; Camarillo, "Dismantling Neutrality: Cultivating Antiracist Writing Center Ecologies"

Week 4: *Bedford Guide (BG)*, Ch. 1, "The Writing Center as a Workplace;" *BG*, Ch. 6, "Tutoring in the Information Age"

Week 5: *BG*, Ch. 2, "Inside the Tutoring Session"; *BF*, Ch. 3, "Tutoring Writers through the Writing Process"

Week 6: Bruffee, "Peer Tutoring and the Conversation of Mankind" and Wingate, "What Line?"

Week 7: Schendel, "We Don't Proofread, So What Do We Do?"; Bib, "Comprehensive Writing Instruction in the Tutoring Session"; Peh, "Proofreading during a Pandemic"

Week 8: *Oxford Guide for Writing Tutors*, "Tutoring Is Conversation / Tutoring is not Just Any Conversation;" *BG*, Ch. 4, "The Writers You Tutor" and *Oxford Guide for Writing Tutors*, "Identity and Tutoring Strategies"

Week 9: *BG*, Ch. 7, "Addressing Various Tutoring Situations"

Week 10: Break

Week 11: *BG*, Ch. 5, "Helping Writers Across the Curriculum"; Bishop, "Is There a Creative Writer in the House?"; Johnson, Clark, and Burton, "Finding Harmony in Disharmony: Engineering and English Studies"

Week 12: How to Write a Lit Review

Week 13: Hiit, "Access for All: The Role of Dis/Ability in Multiliteracy Centers" and O'Leary, "Accommodating Gender in the Writing Conference"; Nan, "Bridging the Gap: Essential Issues to Address in Recurring Writing Center Appointments with Chinese ELL Students"

Week 14: Rousculp, "Into the City We Go"

Week 15: Individual meetings for final research paper

APPENDIX B: INDIVIDUAL RESEARCH PROJECT, COMMUNITY WRITING CENTER TOPIC

Individual Research Paper Option 2: Community Writing Center Proposal

Due Dates	*Points*
Proposal:	25
Literature Review draft:	50
Paper Draft:	100
Paper Revision: Exam period	125

Overview

Throughout this course, we will discuss much about the role writing centers play in both their unique campus communities as well as with the individual student-writers who use the center to help them develop as writers. We'll also discuss ways in which writing centers can participate in larger social-justice initiatives, and for this assignment, I'd like you to research **community writing centers**, what they are, the writers they serve, and how they operate within a non-university setting. Specifically, I'd like you to research the local Newport News / Hampton Roads community to assess and anticipate the needs of the citizens in these communities and how a community writing center could best provide assistance to these citizens. The big question I'd like you to answer is: How could a community writing center best serve the writing (and related communication) needs of the citizens in our community, but not part of the Christopher Newport University community? While the argument of this assignment will be that the Newport News / Hampton Roads community would benefit from having such a community writing center, this assignment may be formatted and organized more like a proposal than a traditional research paper.

Task

There are many areas of research you will need to pursue, through both primary and secondary sources. Here is an incomplete list of some of the research tasks you may need to complete:

- Identifying **who** the community writing center would serve: their education backgrounds, their access to technology, their access to other community resources, etc.
- Researching what kinds of **services or opportunities** the community writing center would need to offer to best meet the needs of the community, such as resume / cover letter assistance; job applications or college application assistance; other business writing help; grant writing assistance; creative writing workshops; etc.
- Identifying **agencies and/or organizations** within the community to potentially partner with, for example, the Four Oaks Day Service Center or the Main Street Library
- Considering what ways to best **promote and advertise** the community writing center so the widest possible audience gets connected to the resource

When you have done enough research to get started, write a **proposal of 100 words** that includes the following:

1. Brief introduction/explanation to approach for proposing a community writing center
2. One or two questions you'd like to answer through research and reflection
3. A "working thesis"—the very early start of the argument that you believe will ground your research paper.

Next, you will compose a **literature review** that provides the secondary-source foundation for your research and proposal. This literature should have a minimum of **three (3)** and a **maximum of five (5)** secondary-resources that come from peer-reviewed journals. We will have a class period dedicated to learning how to write a Lit Review. Here are some additional resources on compiling a literature review: https://writingcenter.unc.edu/tips-and-tools/literature-reviews from the University of North Carolina–Chapel Hill's Writing Center and https://libguides.usc.edu/writingguide/literaturereview from the University of Southern California's libraries.

After your proposal and lit review, you'll be in a great place to start your **draft**. Your draft should include the following:

- Revised thesis (from what was included in Proposal) that incorporates suggestions from Dr. Emmelhainz and your peers

- Incorporation of revised Lit Review (revised with feedback from Dr. E)
- At least **two** body paragraphs that demonstrate further elaboration and support of the revised thesis and present ideas that are supported by the research presented in the Lit Review

Through peer review, conferencing with Dr. E, and visiting consultants in the Writing Center, you will gain feedback to help support you through the writing process of this assignment.

Finally, with your draft feedback, you'll **revise your Research Paper**. This revision should be approximately 2,500 words and adhere to the following criteria:

- Appropriate revision/development of thesis compared to earlier draft/proposal
- Clear introduction and conclusion that situate the thesis within the larger writing center or related scholarly fields
- Appropriate revisions/development of supportive points/paragraphs compared to earlier draft
- Expanded body sections that further support and develop thesis
- Use of MLA style guide for both in-text and Works Cited page

Other Considerations

Like with your Writing Tutoring Reflection, you may use first-person to write this research paper. In fact, you may include personal experience anecdotes to help ground the writing and show your readers why you're interested in writing this paper. I encourage you to visit the Writing Center throughout all stages of your writing: brainstorming, drafting, revising, proofing. Remember, all the consultants have taken and passed ENGL 339, and they are excellent resources for you during your writing!

REFERENCES

Bibb, Bethany. 2012. "Bringing Balance to the Table: Comprehensive Writing Instruction in the Tutoring Session." *Writing Center Journal* 32, no. 1: 92–104. https://www.jstor.org/stable/43442384.

Bruffee, Kenneth. 1978. "Training and Using Peer Tutors." *College English* 40, no. 4: 432–449.

Camarillo, Eric C. 2019. "Dismantling Neutrality: Cultivating Antiracist Writing Center Ecologies." *Praxis: A Writing Center Journal* 16, no. 2. http://www.praxisuwc.com/162-links-page.

Gill, Judy. 2006. "The Professionalization of Tutor Training." *Writing Lab Newsletter* 30 (6): 1–5.

Goldberg, Natalie. 2005. *Writing Down the Bones*. Boston: Shambhala.

Green, Neisha-Anne S. 2016. "The Re-Education of Neisha-Anne S Green: A Close Look at the Damaging Effect of 'A Standard Approach', The Benefits of Codemeshing, and the Role Allies Play in This Work." *Praxis: A Writing Center Journal* 14, no. 1. http://www.praxisuwc.com/green-141.

Greenfield, Laura. 2011. "The 'Standard English' Fairy Tale: A Rhetorical Analysis of Racist Pedagogies and Commonplace Assumptions about Language Diversity." In *Writing Centers and the New Racism: A Call for Sustainable Dialogue and Change*, edited by Laura Greenfield and Karen Rowan, 33–60. Logan: Utah State University Press.

Ianetta, Melissa, and Lauren Fitzgerald. *The Oxford Guide for Writing Tutors: Practice and Research.* Oxford: Oxford University Press, 2016.

Inoue, Asao B. 2016. "Afterword: Narratives That Determine Writers and Social Justice Writing Center Work." *Praxis: A Writing Center Journal* 14, no. 1: n.p.

Jesson, James. 2006. "Professional Development and the Community Writing Center." *Praxis: A Writing Center Journal* 4, no. 1: n.p.

Lunsford, Andrea. 1991, "Collaboration, Control, and the Idea of a Writing Center." *Writing Center Journal* 12, no. 1: 3–10. https://www.jstor.org/stable/43441887.

Mitchell, Kendra L, and Robert E. Randolph. 2019. "A Page from Our Book: Social Justice Lessons from the HBCU Writing Center." *Writing Center Journal* 37, no. 2: 21–40.

Nichols, Amy McCleese, and Bronwyn T. Williams. 2019. "Centering Partnerships: A Case for Writing Centers as Sites of Community Engagement." *Community Literacy Journal* 13, no. 2: 88–106.

North, Stephen M. 1984. "The Idea of a Writing Center." *College English* 46, no. 5: 433–446. http://www.jstor.org/stable/377047.

Peh, Li Qi. 2020. "Proofreading during the Pandemic." *Connecting Writing Centers without Borders: A Blog of WLN: A Journal of Writing Center Scholarship* (blog). August 8. https://www.wlnjournal.org/blog/2020/08/proofreading-during-the-pandemic/.

Rousculp, Tiffany. 2003. "Into the City We Go: Establishing the SLCC Community Writing Center." *Writing Lab Newsletter* 27 (6): 11–13.

Rousculp, Tiffany. 2014. *Rhetoric of Respect: Recognizing Change at a Community Writing Center.* Conference on College Composition and Communication. WAC Clearinghouse, Fort Collins, CO, in association with the University of Colorado in Denver.

Ryan, Leigh, and Lisa Zimmerelli. 2016. *The Bedford Guide for Writing Tutors.* 6th ed. Boston: Bedford/St. Martin's.

United States Census Bureau. n.d."QuickFacts: Hampton City and Newport News, Virginia." Accessed June 15, 2021. https://cnu.edu/diversity/statistics/.

Zimmerelli, Lisa. 2015. "A Place to Begin: Service Learning Tutor Education and Writing Center Social Justice." *Writing Center Journal* 35, no. 1: 57–83.

13
WRITING REVOLUTION
Reimagining the Role of Writing Centers

Kamille Bostick

"I have a HUGE update," the text message read. "Call me ASAP."

It was May 27, 2020. We were well past our virtual session for spring 2020, and Tevel, then a freshman political science major, was not in summer school.

As the Writing Center Director at Livingstone College, a small, historically black liberal arts college in North Carolina, I was used to getting urgent-sounding messages from students.

I was also in the middle of a Zoom meeting in the middle of a pandemic at the very start of the sprawling protests surrounding the murder of George Floyd by a Minneapolis police officer.

Busy, but not overwhelmed, I told Tevel (who was also in my Learning Community and a regular visitor to our campus Writing Center) I would call him as soon as I finished. Seconds later, he replied with a string of emojis bearing tears and teeth—the one I read as "angsty emoji." His written rebuttal followed. A snarky "No rush but hurry up." It was something he had heard me say countless times as I managed the Writing Center to encourage students not to dawdle in starting their drafts or in writing their revisions.

I laughed at my own words staring back at me and went back to the meeting half wondering what the "HUGE" news could be. By the time I was able to contact Tevel, he was gushing, "I'm leading a protest to take down the Confederate statue," he said.

I was caught off guard not by the fact that Tevel would be involved (he has that mix of fearless commitment and conviction that would lead him to be in the center of such demonstrations) but that the protests I had been reading about taking shape across the country were actually igniting my students to action. The momentum was building, and now a student I knew was in the heart of it.

https://doi.org/10.7330/9781646424573.c013

I was proud and tired. I asked Tevel if he was just excited to tell me or if he needed something more urgently. He said he wanted me to look over his speech and a few posts for social media where he was co-organizing a rally to remove the Confederate monument from in front of the courthouse in his hometown. "Peace in the Streets" was already set for June 4, 2020, 4–7 p.m.

Tevel and his co-organizers had the fire of change within them. In cities across the country and the South, a generation of organizers were taking similar steps and urging for symbols of division and the Lost Cause to come down. They blogged, posted, tagged, and tweeted about (in)justice, reform, abolition, dignity, and duty. It was the summer of racial reckoning in America, and I had a choice: tell him that I was only contracted to help with writing associated with academic endeavors or be the resource on writing and effective communication for him at a time when he and the world needed it most.

I chose the latter. A former print journalist, civil rights researcher, museum educator and equity advocate, I was ready and able to meet the moment when the movement made an appointment. In so doing, my view of my role and that of the Writing Center writ large was transformed. The focus could no longer just be essays assigned in Freshman Composition I and II or the upper-level writing intensive courses assessed for MLA or APA citations but creating a space where words, spelling, and punctuation mattered, audience and tone and rhythm mattered because Black lives mattered, and it was time to for students like Tevel to take a stand. At an institution that was created to educate the minds of those whose bodies were once held in bondage, and later was a part of the civic engagement indicative of the student movement during the 1960s, the pendulum had swung back to supporting writers who use their words to change society.

We started that first day with just some basic edits. "Let's make sure to have the commas placed right in the dates on the social media posts," I said. Postings need to be easy to read, and timing needs to be clear. By the day before the planned protest, Tevel and I were talking about citing sources for an infographic and flyer that would be passed out at the rally and the best format for readers. The content that first day (punctuation, attribution) was not new, but the application and context definitely were. Later that night, a text came through.

"Imma need ur help tm to help edit the word choice on my speech," it read. "I want to use emotional language."

I had been working for three years as a Writing Center Director. Maybe only once could I recall when a student asked me whether she was using the appropriate tone or the right sorts of words to create an emotional appeal. It was not because the students did not care about these things but that their assignments never required them to convey true passion or conviction. A small college with limited resources attempting to educate many first-generation college students for careers, writing instruction at my institution was usually very utilitarian. At least the writing/writing assignments that passed through the Writing Center. The unspoken focus was on clarity and execution of discipline-specific genres. Students wrote their share of reader/viewer responses, reflections on internships, lab reports, and research papers that could be used as writing samples for graduate school, but very rarely was writing truly personal or for a widely public audience. Students wrote to show what they had read or learned, or how they responded intellectually to an idea.

Faculty did not maliciously assign writing to be devoid of meaning to the students or beyond the most practical career applications. It was just a matter of capacity (everything couldn't be taught in the confines of the semester) and a reflection on what we prioritized. I cringe to think of how I was guilty myself as an instructor of only assigning one personal essay before telling my students they would need to take themselves "out" of their writing to succeed as scholars. Beyond personal statements and scholarship essays, our Writing Center never held workshops or posted tips about incorporating authentic voice and experience. Given this, it is no shock that even for our most gifted writers, there was a clear distinction between writing as an academic act and writing for life. To look back now, it is also no wonder students seemed to approach the writing of their coursework as practice and not practical. Their lives and dignity were never on the line with an academic argument—just their grade.

Working with Tevel prompted a shift in me. Without fully knowing it, I had internalized an academics-above-all approach to my work. I could cite in my head how employers wanted students who could communicate well in writing ("What Is Career Readiness?" 2021) or how there is a mismatch between college writing expectations and high school preparation (Wahleithner 2020). Those data points had led me away from some of the Writing Center's real-world purposes. Over the summer and well into the fall, my vision cleared. Tevel had to prepare remarks to speak in front of his County Board of Commissioners twice; he had to respond to the hate-filled posts of those who wanted to keep up the statue and keep down the calls for change. He made flyers and gave speeches to supporters and funders, wrote press releases and appeals for news coverage. I was there for almost every draft—urging revision, reminding him to outline, explaining the ins and outs of effective writing and communication, and helping him polish his voice at a time when a chorus was rising.

In a short season, Tevel and I did more work on voice, incorporating outside credible sources, expertly using rhetorical devices, moving between genres such as informative and persuasive, and teasing out the writer's choice or poetic license than we could have ever done within the confines of coursework and the sometimes joy-of-writing-killing assignments students encounter in some classrooms—including a few of mine.

Tevel is a great speaker and proficient writer. His texts reflect the linguistic dexterity of Gen Z, while his academic writing can hold its own among standardized rubrics. Moving him through his edits, then, was a chance to go beyond the basics. We pulled on resources and concepts that rarely get covered with sophomore courses and the undergraduate writing repertoire. It reinvigorated me to be able to have fuller conversations about what "good" writing is. *Think about placement and pace. Consider the power of three. Would a fact be better here? What source would make the most impact? Do you have an ask of your audience? Who is your audience, really? Everyone who reads it will probably not all believe like you do. Don't forget the purpose.*

And, for once, it was not theoretical. When talking about genre, it was so much clearer to the growing writer that the common structure of an essay would not work on a crowd standing in ninety-degree heat or rain ready for change. There had to be something different. A Facebook post that would be read by adults chomping at the keyboard ready to call him an "outside agitator" needed to have precise language to diffuse any "Internet troll" looking to deny the credibility of his claim or white supremacist ready to attack his intellect (see Jackson, Jackson and Tafari's [2019] exploration of cross-boundary discourse and the Rachel Jeanteal / Juror B37 interaction for a deeper discussion of this phenomenon). An address to the county council needed a variety of appeals, and enough credible evidence, and had to stand the test of multiple audiences. Working with Tevel showed the power and utility of the Writing Center. We are not merely on our campuses to copy edit, diagnose weaknesses in a writing assignment, or provide stylebooks and genre resources but to empower students to use their words and the power of language for good. If we are successful, students can feel confident that their writing can be used on any stage or platform to serve not only themselves but their communities.

But are our writing centers able to take this role on? Are our tutors equipped?

Despite what the times and our students might be asking for, too often the foci of our institutions and the classes writing centers like mine most serve are not centered on writing for the real world outside of academia, a boardroom, or some other institution. Most of the curriculum produces writers ready to go further in graduate and postgraduate work. Other than English and communications courses, whose students do not typically appear at the Writing Center door except as tutors, the opportunities appear few and far between to create writing that is meant for public consumption. At my institution, most students using the Writing Center come from the freshman composition courses, writing intensive courses, and senior-level courses to revise papers into graduate school writing samples. In creating programs and workshops that helped meet those ends, I left out chances to nurture writers who had more to say than could fit within the confines of a class assignment. What I had failed to see was what happens when the writing center becomes an extension of the classroom. That extended learning space is not bad, especially when students need additional writing support. It does, however, limit the potential for extended use and further isolates the writing center into being a quasi-independent structure that functions solely for supplemental activities and not a space that could be nurturing future leaders in and users of the craft.

Further, as the way writing is taught in college classrooms continues to be critiqued and to (hopefully) evolve, a writing center that only supplements the instruction of class assignments may prove disconnected from what students want and need. Despite best practice, courses do not always emphasize writing that includes authentic tasks, or what Katalin Wargo (2019) labels "functionally authentic" writing assignments that use skills that will show up in future courses or could be utilized in the real world due to their real audiences, real purposes. This could happen for several reasons including when students, due to various K–12 experiences, do not have the writing prowess of some of their better-resourced peers (Wahleithner 2020). At Livingstone, whenever we encountered weaker or emerging college writers, there was a tendency to overemphasize structure or a particular part of the writing process. The writing center then became a clinic, of sorts, to address those needs. An indirect result of this sort of focus is that students already struggling to find use for class-based writing might also struggle to find meaning for writing altogether and the campus writing centers that do not connect to what they see or need to use in the real world.

Today's college students, the ones who sometimes pass the writing center by, considering it irrelevant beyond coursework, are demanding the world change. On their screens, in their cities, they are starting to "idealize and affirm the physically demonstrative strategies" of contemporary social justice movements (Ligon 2018, 412). In this period of increased civic and personal engagement, students are motivated to lift their voice, to take action, to make headlines, not just read them. At HBCUs like Livingstone, in the wake of a news cycle that constantly bears witness to the race-based aggression and violence (many times at the hands of police) that Black Americans face, "other than just lamenting about those unspeakable losses, young people can be guided in raising their voices—through writing—to effect change" (426).

Writing to speak out about the issues that affect them most might be the most authentic task students can do, yet given the multitude of curricular objectives, the "assignment" may not come from an instructor or be a requirement of a class. When our students are ready to write well, we want them in our writing centers. Before those same students are caught unprepared (i.e., with something to say but no help to say it well), we want them in our writing centers. I did not realize, unfortunately, I was not giving the students at my HBCU a reason nor a signal to seek us out. Alison Ligon (2018, 412) asserts that HBCUs are unique since our campuses house classrooms that can be "primary spaces wherein students are introduced to thought-provoking reading assignments and writing exercises" that move them to recognize themselves and effectively engage in writing that allows social change. With more intentionality, the writing center on any campus can be a space that promotes the skills and creates an environment allied to social justice.

Writing centers that choose to take up the charge to lead workshops on reaching twenty-first-century audiences or speaking truth to power exist. Yet, as Lindsay A. Sabatino reminds us in chapter 6, "Addressing Racial Justice through Re-imagining Practicum to Promote Dialogue on Campus," the pace of total change has been slow. I hope the spirit continues to catch fire and more centers take up anti-racist, liberatory, and social justice practices and approaches. Speaking from experience, it is not always easy or apparent when we have drifted. In my years at Livingstone, time and capacity often prevented me from offering a more robust lineup of workshops. Between needing to help the first-year student referred because of the issues he was having with sentence structure or the social work class that needed a deep dive into APA documentation with a small staff of mostly senior-level tutors with their own capstone papers to execute, there felt like so little time and not much more in budget to make regular offerings about writing for social change or other timely topics. For too long, I felt I was making the preferred trade-off by focusing on the academic needs of my students. The reason they had come to college, after all, was the degree—for many it would be the first college degree in their families. Looking back, I know this was not a fair trade nor one that prioritized all the needs of my students.

By fall 2020, I had started to feel the urgency to learn new strategies to improve students' communication skills in a time when many would prefer to silence them. Centers that are now currently able to provide a balance between the academic or creative needs of students should continue to serve the civic engagement of a student populace not likely to get exposure to or exploration of those writing techniques elsewhere. Just as Nicholas Hengen Fox (2012) worried about the "disconnect between the classroom and the streets" when students left their robust classroom discussions behind, there is something worrisome about writing centers tethered only to the syllabus-based needs on campus (15).

We have seen what can happen for confidence and matriculation when students fully utilize our centers as resources for learning the practices of traditional academia—from documentation and structure, and so on. We have dared to imagine what could happen if they found liberatory practice (tools to sharpen their voice, space to question authority through the written word, skills to communicate their demands, dreams, or disillusion) there as well. Some of us have even been able to turn those practices to everyday action. In discussing what liberatory education can do for public education students, Jefferson, Gutierrez, and Silverstein (2018) explain that the essential tenets of liberatory practice include the centering of cultural and community knowledge, the recognition of the emancipatory nature of education combined with critical consciousness. It is through the empowerment of young people, encouraged not to unthinkingly assimilate but to question and seek justice, that liberatory practice distinguishes itself. A liberatory education gives students—and thus their communities— "the tools, questions, ideas, and collaborative opportunities needed to work towards their own liberation" (Jefferson, Gutierrez, and Silverstein 2018, 744). A writing center that can do much of the same with writing programs and activities could truly aid in the activism and engagement of its students.

Before my summer and fall working with Tevel, I wish I had given myself permission to seek out ways (even with limited time, personnel, and resources) to bring more liberatory practice to the students on my campus. For those worried about the mission of writing enters and wondering if pushing toward a more social justice framework in workshop or instructional offerings might lead away from a focus on core skills or a deep dive into activism, perhaps not. Writing centers have been adapting and transforming, and our students are still growing as writers.

A lot of what is already taught in writing centers is ready to be expanded to assist student activists in the writing outside of the classroom. When I made my pivot, I realized that the same urgency and sense of purpose that I used to plan group writing nights, grammar refreshers, or research strategies can be applied to the work of helping student activists mold their message to serve different media. The same energy that I placed on gathering exemplars of cover letters or cover pages can be expended on helping students streamline their calls to action. As we repackage what can help our student writers and reimagine what else might be needed of our writing centers, I can attest that our practice grows.

Ligon (2018, 426) contends that since injustice and inequality have not gone away, we have not seen the last of students who will "pick up the mantle of engaged writing and creative expression. Still, they must be guided, encouraged and affirmed."

Since that first urgent text in the summer of 2020, I have seen Tevel grabbing that mantle. In the tradition of those before him, he has extended his activism to advocate for saving a neighborhood school and to speak at community commemorations. There have been more rallies, more letters, and more speeches. He has had to perfect Chicago/Turabian style for a term paper and do his first case study. For each, he made an appointment at the Writing Center to plan, draft, revise, consult, or celebrate a job well done. The resources were there regardless of the assignment, and so was the support. While the Confederate statue remains in front of the courthouse in Palatka, the struggle also continues, and Tevel still visits the Writing Center to craft his responses to injustice as well as get feedback on the case studies that will prepare him for law school. For the many Tevels on our campuses, those students who need the skills, practice, and expertise to do the work of trying to change the world, writing centers are the perfect spaces to perfect their craft or build their toolkit as they embark toward writing revolution.

Ultimately, urging a reimagination of how writing centers operate widens opportunities for students and facilitates to change on a local or national level. It is not easy work but necessary work. The year following Tevel's entry into activism was also a year of hybrid learning and in-person COVID-19 protocols for me. Meeting our remote students' needs was an added challenge but also a sobering one. In the face of so much disparity, there was still the necessity to serve students where they were—and many of them were ready to say something to powers that be.

My task has been to ask myself what I could give them in service of that readiness. I had to ask myself a lot of tough questions and shift my own practice. Perhaps other writing centers may be stronger for the same set of questions for their students:

- What are we able to do as a Writing Center that connects students to the writing help or practice they need to effect social change?
- What skills, talents, resources, and lenses do we as Writing Center staff possess that could benefit student activists in their writing? What parts of ourselves are we not bringing because of fear or just lack of awareness?
- Are the tips and strategies offered to students transferable to liberatory practices? (i.e., Are we encouraging voice? Are we strategizing about audiences and ways to reach those within our communities or those without? Are we equipping students with multimedia skills?)
- Are we ready as practitioners to meet the moment?

REFERENCES

Fox, Nicholas Hengen. 2012. "Teaching (is not) Activism." *Radical Teacher* 94: 14–23. https://www.muse.jhu.edu/article/485090.

Jackson, Karen Keaton, Hope Jackson, and Dawn Tafari. 2019. "We Belong in the Discussion: Including HBCUs in Conversations about Race and Writing." *CCC* 71, no. 2.

Jefferson, Antwan, Cindy Gutierrez, and Lisa Silverstein. 2018. "Liberatory Public Education: A Framework for Centering Community and Democracy in Public Education." *Urban Review* 50, no. 5: 735–756. https://doi.org/10.1007/s11256-018-0467-8.

Ligon, Alison D. 2018. "Mediating Modern Written Expressions of Black Masculinity: When Coloring inside Collegiate Lines Is Enuf." *Midwest Quarterly* 59, no. 4: 411–428.

Wahleithner, Juliet M. 2020. "The High School–College Disconnect: Examining First-Generation College Students' Perceptions of Their Literacy Preparation." *Journal of Adolescent and Adult Literacy* 64, no. 1: 19–26. https://doi.org/10.1002/jaal.1057.

Wargo, Katalin. 2019. "A Conceptual Framework for Authentic Writing Assignments: Academic and Everyday Meet." *Journal of Adolescent and Adult Literacy* 63, no. 5: 539–547. https://doi.org/10.1002/jaal.1022.

"What Is Career Readiness?" 2020. National Association of Colleges and Employers. https://www.naceweb.org/career-readiness/competencies/career-readiness-defined/.

14

PRACTICING WHAT WE PREACH

Anti-racist Approaches in SWCA

LaKela Atkinson

In their 2018 IWCA keynote address, Kendra Mitchell and Robert Randolph Jr. questioned the progress in Writing Studies by interrogating the conference theme, "The Citizen Center," asking, "Haven't we done this before? What have we done about it?" (Mitchell and Randolph 2019, 23). As two African American speakers, they represented marginalized groups. Through their embodiment and experiences, they were negating that racism in the field had been addressed. The conversations were plenty, but they did not move the field to real change. The conversations may temporarily create excitement and engagement about the ways the organization may change. But who gets to determine how Writing Studies changes, and who traditionally holds power? In other words, their questioning is about longtime change and ways that it can be replicated in the work that we say we are doing.

When my involvement in the Southeastern Writing Center Association (SWCA) organization began in 2008 at the insistence of my Writing Center Director (WCD), Dr. Karen Keaton Jackson, I was naïve about what writing conferences entailed. Having worked in a writing center for less than a year as a graduate writing consultant, I felt neither confident nor experienced enough to share concerns about serving my fellow peers. How could I inform scholars who had been in the field much longer than me? Why would my experience matter to them? However, my experience was beneficial and offered practical strategies—the type that was foundational in SWCA. The common goal was to discuss issues that were in our Writing Center and learn how we might address them while gaining presentation skills and networking with others. What I soon learned is that each writing center's identity puts it in a position of unique and different experiences. The presence of each writing center professional matters in aiding another writing center with an issue regarding writing, personnel, or accommodations.

https://doi.org/10.7330/9781646424573.c014

When Keaton Jackson informed the Writing Center staff about attending our first conference, she also prepared the graduate consultants at North Carolina Central University (NCCU) by sharing context about the environment and helping us create presentations for the conferences. She ensured that we represented ourselves and the institution well as students at a historically black college and university (HBCU), from appearance to the level of preparedness we showed when presenting. Her guidance was particularly helpful, as I learned that SWCA was predominantly white. I must admit that because my K–12 experience was predominantly with Black students and I had attended an HBCU for my bachelor's and master's degrees, I felt intimidated and a bit out of my league. However, my supervisor's approach to her role as also an informal mentor was particularly important in helping me navigate these spaces.

My involvement in SWCA has evolved over time. I presented at conferences as both a graduate student and later as a professional writing consultant working in my HBCU from 2008 to 2015. During this time, my Writing Center Director was elected to the SWCA board for North Carolina in the mid-2000s, and I recognized a turn in the diversity and representation of HBCUs in the organization. I was elected as HBCU representative for the SWCA in 2019. To provide a little context about the HBCU rep position, I share the history behind the position. Then, I discuss how efforts of HBCU representatives helped address racism in the SWCA community. I use a Critical Race Theory lens to discuss ways that I have used my position to encourage greater representation among marginalized groups within the SWCA. The position description for the HBCU representative can be found in the appendix to this chapter.

FRAMEWORK

Through Critical Race Theory (CRT), I discuss ways that I have used my position to encourage greater representation among marginalized groups within the organization. This theory analyzes the inherent racism in the legal system and its promotion of power for dominant groups and simultaneous denial of power to other groups, in and beyond the legal context. While race refers to a social construct that identifies one's ethnicity, Critical Race scholars assume that racism is embedded in American society as a result of historical issues around race (Ladson-Billings and Tate 1995). In other words, CRT emphasizes that being targeted for discrimination is connected to one's racial identity. By shedding light on the inequities in education and opportunities among people of color, the theory also challenges the dominant belief that access is the same for all groups. Further, CRT also emphasizes its focus on ensuring that people of color can live without harm while valuing people's embodied experiences. In addition, this approach highlights lived experiences of individuals by promoting the use of firsthand narratives (Ladson-Billings and Tate 1995). Last, an interdisciplinary perspective helps critical theorists better understand the experiences that people of color face (Solórzano and Yosso 2002). For this chapter, I focus primarily on the themes of intersectionality between race and racism, challenge to dominant ideology, and centrality of experiential knowledge.

HBCU REPRESENTATIVE BACKGROUND

Dr. Hope Jackson (2021, personal communication), former North Carolina A&T State University Writing Center Director, recalls that she and Keaton Jackson were fairly new Writing Center Directors representing two North Carolina HBCUs when they met at an SWCA Conference in 2004. It was at this conference, Jackson says, that the writing center directors observed the lack of diversity in the organization. Thus, they discussed hosting a conference at an HBCU. At the insistence of Dr. Keaton Jackson, Jackson agreed to host the SWCA conference at North Carolina A&T University in Greensboro five years later. Jackson recalls how her staff sent personalized invitations to HBCUs via mail and called these institutions to make sure director information was accurate and that they personally invited the directors to the conference. Not only did they make direct connection with the institutions, but they understood some of the complexities that exist at HBCUs. For instance, Jackson mentioned how common it is for some HBCU writing centers to lack a phone or other key office supplies that may be more readily available at predominantly white institutions (PWIs). With this cultural knowledge, she successfully encouraged many HBCUs to participate in the 2009 SWCA conference, leading to the most diverse group of HBCUs represented thus far, and she attributes the high attendance of HBCUs to the institution's personalized efforts in reaching out to the HBCUs. An acknowledgment of and willingness to address the inequities that exist in marginalized institutions are what aided Jackson and Keaton Jackson's efforts to encourage more representation and interest in a primarily white organization.

Keaton Jackson (2021, personal communication) recalls proposing the HBCU position idea at a SWCA Conference board meeting in Florida around 2013. Dr. Christine Cozzens gave a passionate speech of support about the position. Yet, the board did not immediately approve the idea. In 2014, a local conference at East Carolina University (ECU) was focused on diversity, where Dr. Vershawn Young was the keynote speaker. Specifically, the theme was "Our Language, Ourselves: Rethinking Our Writing Center Communities" (SWCA 2021). Jackson saw this as yet another opportunity to raise the conversation regarding the position and the benefit it would have for the HBCUs in the organization. During the closing SWCA board meeting, another board member formally proposed the HBCU position, which was approved in 2014. While her efforts were initially ignored, Keaton Jackson's consistency in advocating for HBCUs led to the establishment of the position. In 2015, Dr. Robert Randolph, another former North Carolina A&T State University Writing Center Director, became the first HBCU representative elected (Randolph 2021, personal communication). Since that time, there have been two other representatives: Joel Williams from Edward Waters College in Jacksonville, Florida (SWCA 2021), from 2018 to 2019, and myself, from 2019 to 2021.

MY STORY

After a range of involvement in SWCA, Keaton Jackson approached me about the possibility of serving as the HBCU representative in 2018. Her faith in me and guidance led me to start with a grassroots approach. Because she had been heavily involved and had built a network, I pulled on her wisdom about approaching this position. Based on the position description, one of the responsibilities of the representative is "creating a network of SWCA HBCU members so that the organization can focus on meeting the needs of these institutions." Academic, personal, and social networks are valuable for educators of color for advancement, as they offer varied support and allow individuals to overcome others' presumptions of their incompetence (Castaneda, Flores, and Niemann 2020; Clark 2020; Deo 2020; Atkinson 2021).

Before I established a connection with the HBCUs in the network, I familiarized myself with the HBCUs in the organization. Although I was a product of an HBCU, I also knew that there was much to learn about other HBCUs. Having connected with local and national HBCUs, I know that there is no monolithic experience across institutions. At the advising of my mentor, I conducted outreach with the HBCU within the SWCA region to (1) request updated contact information on writing center administrators (WCAs) (2) inform these organizations about my goals in the position.

Initially, I emailed listed contacts on institution websites from spring to summer 2019 to establish a directory of current writing center administrators. I placed phone calls to these writing centers or closely connected offices when I could not reach a director or coordinator. I also contacted state representatives for additional information, as they were more familiar with the institutions because of their locations. These personal efforts closely resembled Jackson's efforts in organizing the 2009 Southeastern Writing Center Association (SWCA) Conference. I did not realize it then, but Jackson and I both engaged in personal approaches that were needed because of our knowledge of our audiences. Additionally, I informed the network of my goals for this position. This allowed me to practice transparency and hold myself (as well as allow others to) accountable for my goals for this position. What I found in this grassroots approach was that many writing center directors were rather new in their positions and also new to the SWCA organization. This meant that many were still learning about their institutions and positions. In doing so, many found that basic necessities, like funding for staff, were unavailable.

By utilizing available digital platforms, like Zoom, I connected with the institutions in an intimate setting without concern for travel costs. Zoom provided a layout where people could share knowledge and experiences for seasoned and new writing center staff. In this way, I worked to value experiential knowledge, as emphasized by CRT. The participants' work serving students at their individual institutions guided my understanding into the needs that separated these institutions from others and helped me gear discussion topics to the institutions. In addition, I shared more about the organization for newcomers as well as opportunities to be a part of the organization and suggest ways that the HBCU network might be beneficial to the institutions. When learning about their needs, I considered efficiency and secure methods of providing feedback. I was interested in learning about directors' preferences for discussion topics. While I had prepared options, respondents had an opportunity to include additional options that they wanted to discuss. Google surveys yielded responses, though few participants were consistently engaged in providing this feedback.

Over the last two years, topics ranged from tutoring practices to writing center staffing issues. I advocated for a Zoom account paid for by SWCA for the HBCUs, which I was able to get. This way, there was a consistent meeting platform for the HBCUs that did not require individual members to use their own accounts, nor be relegated to platforms that were specific to certain organizations. Although I generally received minimal feedback, the feedback I received was consistently from members who were interested in participating and learning more about how they could grow by being involved in the organization. Although the account was not specific to the HBCUs, the importance of access was seen and honored. While I had been unable to get large engagement for the organization itself and consistent SWCA conference attendance, I was better positioned to have people attend a Zoom meeting for an hour or so at the convenience of their schedules.

In 2019, I had attempted to plan a collaboration between the HBCU Consortium held in Atlanta. Because I valued the input of the HBCUs, I inquired about their desire to participate in a collaboration with the organizing institution if already attending. While there was interest, this event never happened because I was unable to solidify plans in ample time. However, I believe that this would have been a great opportunity to connect with other HBCUs beyond the organization and network in ways that may be beneficial beyond the network and region. When I presented this as a funding request to the SWCA board in July 2019, they were supportive. I later rescinded this request because it was not something that was feasible. Then, the pandemic hit in 2020, and physical meetings were put on hold or cancelled. Not only did many writing centers have to make the transition to online tutoring, but funding requests looked much different, as it was difficult to justify the need for spending.

In 2020, I requested funding for HBCUs to have supplies related to funding and COVID. Again, I inquired about the network's needs for funding, as its input was important. Again, I consulted with my mentor because, not only did she have experience working with the position, but she had a clearer understanding of WCAs' needs, given her writing center background and work on HBCUs. I received support among the Board for this request, and other Board representatives saw the importance of supporting centers whose remote resources were limited for supplies, while continuing in-person support, or who now were newly or totally reliant on online support. This advocacy was an indication that resources are not accessible across the board. They are and have been inequitable for HBCUs for quite some time and continue to be so.

Even as I write this article, the turnover at some of these HBCUs has increased. New or interim directors have been hired in these spaces, and I am creating a plan to increase outreach efforts. I think about the grassroots efforts and the impact they had for Jackson over ten years ago and the initial success I had with reestablishing a network in 2019. Building a network is important, especially for HBCUs because, as Jackson said, there is a certain amount of cultural sensitivity fellow HBCUs have that is not understood outside of these spaces. I do not claim to know all there is about HBCUs and anti-racism. At times, I find myself unconsciously reinforcing racist actions and having to reflect on my choices because of the "result of my exposure to one set of acceptable societal standards" (Atkinson 2021, 31) even prior to higher education. As I consider my positionality, I think about how CRT allows me to consider the role of race in the organization.

During the summer of 2020, during heightened racial tensions across America, many institutions and organizations established anti-racist statements in response. Southeastern Writing Center Association was one of those organizations. While the intention was positive, my concern was that a primarily white organization did not reach out to the HBCU organizations to get input on this statement. After seeing the statement, I questioned the Board's decision to compose a statement without the input of those most greatly impacted by racism. Board members responded well with the intention to be more inclusive in the future. My intention with reaching out to the Board was to inform them that as a primarily white board, they represent traditional power structures. Historically, these power structures are rooted in racism. And while individuals may not identify as racist, carrying out practices and processes that exclude people of color can unquestionably be considered as such. As a follow-up on the desire to be more inclusive, the Board discussed ways that we may include the input of marginalized voices and asked me to communicate with the HBCU network. While input was limited within the HBCU network, I discussed an idea from my mentor that allowed students' voices to be amplified, particularly those of color. Keaton Jackson and I brainstormed a way to focus on students. In particular, she suggested a student panel in lieu of a keynote panel at the annual SWCA Conference. The conference was virtual due to the pandemic, which allowed for more diverse groups to attend and engage in ways that may not have been possible otherwise.

After presenting the idea of a student panel, I and three other co-organizers—Dr. Janine Morris, Dr. Deidre Anne Evans Garriott, and Mr. Duane Theobold—worked to create a Call for Papers (CFP), email blurb, nomination form, and proposal rubric. The purpose of this student panel was to support the theme of "Transformation in the Era of Change" in a way that debunked traditional authority structures. By allowing students, specifically African American students, to discuss their experiences, students' voices were centered. They told their own stories about what it meant to be both a student of color and a consultant of color in a college writing center. The panel promoted the use of counterstory (Martinez 2019) when it allowed the students of color the opportunity to change a narrative that centered white voices, opting for one to center voices of color instead.

Not only did the conference center the experiences of people of color, but it centered the experiences of students of color. Since students are usually the recipients of knowledge, the conference helped to debunk the idea that knowledge is a one-way process but rather transactional or mutual. Critical Race Theory argues against privileging one way of knowing (Martinez 2019, 405). Thus, students are also holders of knowledge about their needs and concerns, as they experience these. As an African American woman, I also learned from the students as well. For instance, their experiences and critique of the CFP were a reminder that not all experiences are similar and perceived the same among people of color. Because the conference was virtual and allowed for input via a Zoom chat feature, people were able to share their thoughts, agreement, and displeasure regarding the panel and other sessions. Sometimes our efforts are not always successful, and giving others a platform to openly be critical can be part of anti-racist work. Most important, it was an opportunity for students who were often marginalized, overshadowed, or ignored to be put in the forefront. While the conference focused on Writing Studies, some students shared about experiences in their classrooms or their institutions overall, where they focused on the trauma of being an African American student, particularly at PWIs.

As I consider the changes over the last ten to twelve years of my involvement with SWCA, I believe that the organization has grown in its willingness to learn about how it can be more inclusive. When I was involved in 2008, I remember seeing few Black and Brown bodies in the organization. Although the organization is open to all southeastern institutions, it is still overwhelmingly white in representation. The organization is growing in its ability to meet the specific needs of HBCUs. In many ways, HBCUs are catching up with the opportunities that were more readily available to their white sister institutions. Having attended the 2009 SWCA Conference, I recognize that despite increased engagement efforts from the organization, participation among HBCUs has dissipated over the past ten years. While there are many reasons that this can be explained (funding, turnover, distrust), research also points to key reasons for limited engagement within primarily white organizations.

Having grown in my involvement and position, I recognize the importance of having marginalized groups in positions where they can share their concerns and be heard. Consistent efforts to involve people of color, students, and writing center professionals will be key. I expect to work at centering the experiences of marginalized groups in a recurring and purposeful manner. This may be through events, meetings, or conferences. In order to do that, I will utilize my HBCU network and marginalized groups beyond the network to help me identify my biases and approaches. I also value the help of allies, as there are groups and individuals that sometimes work on our behalf to plant seeds for the work that we must do.

CONCLUSION

Overall, the SWCA HBCU position has given me insight into the anti-racist work that has been done as well as the work needed on behalf of marginalized institutions and populations. With the history of the SWCA position in mind, I believe that well-established professional organizations, like the IWCA, should acknowledge and respond effectively to the concerns of its members, especially those with limited representation within the organization. While it is important to establish inclusive positions, professional organizations should ensure that their practices align with their philosophies. This means working with the people who are not fairly represented in order to understand how to better serve them. As instances of social injustice continue to be heightened, I caution boards from establishing positions hastily but rather in ways that address the systemic issues regarding racial inequities. In this role, I have found the Board to be supportive of suggestions and activities I and other board members have raised regarding HBCU engagement. Beyond the Board, informal mentoring guided me through this new position. For any effective representative, especially those in newer board positions, listening and offering resources (e.g., mentoring, funding, and collaboration) will be necessary in other organizations, like IWCA.

As I have encountered, there may be challenges for a newer role like mine that urges the organization to engage in action. Utilizing networks—formal and informal—can guide someone in a position like mine. Collaborating across institutions can also increase the opportunity for anti-racist work because of greater exposure of various issues and needs. I continue to learn from those around me who do and do not represent marginalized populations. Thus, this is a position that will benefit from collective support with multiple perspectives. As I learned in expressing my concern to the SWCA Executive Board, our actions can be so rooted in racism that we are unaware of them. As a result, the outcome can have a negative impact. However, the willingness of the Board to become more inclusive because of the impact indicated a willingness to collaborate and best support its members. At times, the representative will need support, which may not appear in the same way as more established positions. For me, mentorship allowed me to learn from those in similar positions and build upon their success. For this reason, boards must be adaptable and innovative with positions if they desire to increase reach when normal meetings and engagement are not possible. This is also an example of anti-racist work. As I continue to learn and grow in the anti-racist work I do, I believe that the HBCU position has provided a solid foundation of models for other marginalized institutions, like Hispanic-Serving Institutions (HSIs) and Tribal Colleges.

APPENDIX A: HBCU REPRESENTATIVE POSITION DESCRIPTION

HBCU representative (Term: 2 years—maximum two consecutive terms, voting)

The HBCU representative will focus on creating a network of SWCA HBCU members so that the organization can focus on meeting the needs of these institutions. The HBCU representative should work closely with at-large members, respective state representatives, and the Outreach Coordinator to organize events and meetings and should maintain and develop a database of their member and event information in the SWCA Dropbox. Service on a SWCA committee is also required. (Required attendance at the Annual Conference and all Board meetings.)

REFERENCES

Atkinson, LaKela. 2021. "Racial Minorities: An Exploration of Perceptions among Educators Color." PhD diss., East Carolina University, Greenville, NC.

Castaneda, Donna, Yvette. G. Flores, and Yolanda Flores Niemann. 2020. "Senior Chicana Feminist Scholars: Some Notes on Survival in Hostile Contexts." In *Presumed Innocent II: Race, Class, Power, and Resistance of Women in Academia,* edited by Yolanda Flores Niemann, Gabriella Gutiérrez y Muhs, and Carmen, G. González, 83–94. Logan: Utah State University Press.

Clark, Meredith D. 2020. "Hashtag." In *Presumed innocent II: Race, Class, Power, and Resistance of Women in Academia,* edited by Yolanda Flores Niemann, Gabriella Gutiérrez y Muhs, and Carmen G. González, 269–279. Logan: Utah State University Press.

Deo, Meera E. 2020. "Securing Support in an Unequal Profession." In *Presumed Innocent II: Race, Class, Power, and Resistance of Women in Academia,* edited by Yolanda Flores Niemann, Gabriella Gutiérrez y Muhs, and Carmen, G. González, 300–312. Logan: Utah State University Press.

Ladson-Billings, Gloria, and William F. Tate IV. 1995. "Toward a Critical Race Theory of Education." *Teachers College Record* 9, no. 7: 47–68.

Martinez, Aja Y. 2019. "Core-Coursing Counterstory: On Master Narrative Histories of Rhetorical Studies Curricula." *Rhetoric Review* 38, no. 4: 402–416. https://doi.org/10.1080/07350198.2019.1655305.

Mitchell, K., and R. Randolph. 2018. "The Citizen Center." Keynote address, International Writing Centers Association (IWCA) Conference, Sheraton, Atlanta Hotel, Atlanta, October 11.

Solórzano, Daniel G., and Tara J. Yosso. 2002. "Critical Race Methodology: Counter-storytelling as an Analytical Framework for Education Research." *Qualitative Inquiry* 8, no. 1: 23–44.

Southeastern Writing Center Association (SWCA). 2021. "SWCA Conference Archives." https://southeasternwritingcenter.wildapricot.org/conference-archives.

15

REMAKING IWCA

A Call for Sustained Anti-racist Change

Genie Nicole Giaimo, Nicole I. Caswell,
Marilee Brooks-Gillies, Elise Dixon, and Wonderful Faison

We acknowledge the work of the most recent social justice task force: Trixie Smith, Elise Dixon, Karen Moroski-Rigney, Stacia Moroski-Rigney, Marilee Brooks-Gillies, Nicole I. Caswell, Wonderful Faison, Katie Levin, Jasmine Kar Tang, Floyd Pouncil, Scott Chiu, Rachel Azima, and Genie Nicole Giamo. And we acknowledge the work of those who have come before us (including current task force members who have worked with International Writing Centers Association [IWCA] on other anti-racist initiatives): Moira Ozias, Beth Godbee, Frankie Condon, Bobbi Olson, Talisha Haltiwanger Morrison, Elijah Simmons, Keli Tucker, Rasha Diab, Thomas Ferrel, and Neil Simpkins. We also recognize the work done by IWCA affiliates, such as SWCA, and colleagues in HBCUs, specifically, Dr. Hope Jackson, Dr. Karen Keaton Jackson, Dr. Robert Randolph, Mr. Joel Williams, and Dr. LaKela Atkinson. We want to honor everyone named here but also the many others who gave their time, their knowledge, and their expertise to the project of making our field more inclusive, anti-racist, and progressive.

INTRODUCTION

Anti-racist work often gets pushed to the margins when organizations and programs don't intentionally build anti-racist work into their core. Even worse, as organizations engage anti-racist work, the work typically happens in silos, which leads to the work becoming isolated and lost. Rather than acting as a collective with work building on each other to address a collective goal, organizations that push anti-racist work to the margins don't make meaningful change. For writing centers, we see this happening in our professional organization, International Writing Centers Association (IWCA). In July 2020, writing centers in the United

https://doi.org/10.7330/9781646424573.c015

States were navigating travel bans on international students, Black Lives Matter protests, and an uncontrolled COVID-19 pandemic. Our professional organization was silent. As writing center professionals, we have been actively involved in the organization for several years (up to a decade and a half!); therefore, we knew that our colleagues have focused on anti-racism in special interest groups, conference themes, and special issues of our academic journals. However, we didn't know where to locate these resources or why they weren't being used to address the ongoing crises facing writing centers. So, in an open letter (Smith et al. 2020) shared with the membership, we asked IWCA to engage in anti-racist work and make a set of changes to its organizational structure and goals.

Our experience is a teachable moment in how organizations do not always evolve with their membership. In a field like Writing Center Studies/Administration, certain changes occur at an accelerated pace because of the high turnover in our field, as well as the large numbers of us laboring precariously (without tenure, on contract, or part-time). The localized nature of our work also allows for relatively quick changes in specific writing centers, if not the larger culture of the institution. Yet systemic change comes slowly. Our professional organization, then, seems to be organized for a far less complex—and much whiter, abled, and privileged—set of members. Its organizational structure is labyrinthine and opaque. Social justice and explicitly anti-racist work, then, does not seem welcome or, at best, is pushed onto the members who request support and guidance.

How, then, do we engage in the complex work of changing organizational structure and priorities collectively? Initially, we thought that we could simply request our organization to take anti-racist stances in its mission, position statements, and goals. What we did not necessarily anticipate is the natural reticence of organizations to take stances—controversial or not—and the fact that there simply is not enough bandwidth to attend to these issues among its leaders. The board selects priorities and carries out goals related to those priorities, yet if racial justice is not a priority, what then can we say about the work that we do collectively to make our profession inclusive, intentionally anti-racist, and protective of our workers? Issues of racism simply do not disappear because organizations fail to take a stance; in fact, the non-stance of organizations exacerbates inequity.

We separate out the people serving on the IWCA board from IWCA as an organization. If we were to focus on the people, we'd be crafting feelings of hurt where whiteness would be recentered: "Personalizing institutional racism creates a space for whiteness to be reasserted" (Ahmed 2012, 147). Rather, we critique IWCA as an institution—an organization reproducing whiteness. International Writing Center Association isn't unique in that it's an organization built on institutional whiteness. Institutional whiteness infiltrates our daily lives, in and outside the academy, from the programs we run, to the departments and colleges we work in, to the national organizations we belong to, to the spaces we traverse. As much as we work to resist institutional whiteness, we too, as a group of writing center administrators, fall victim to whiteness. Sara Ahmed in *On Being Included* writes that "diversity becomes about changing perceptions of whiteness rather than changing the whiteness of organizations" (2012, 34). As members of the IWCA Social Justice Task Force (ISJ TF), we wanted to address the institutional whiteness of our organization and our individual centers. We wanted the work of the ISJ TF to be a change agent; however, what we intended to do and what IWCA intended for us to do ran into conflict.

This chapter details our collective approach to anti-racism work and stories our experiences attempting to initiate change in the IWCA. Drawing from organizational research on anti-racist activist work, we examine how the fatigue of being a diversity worker in higher education leads to inaction and frustration (Ahmed 2012). While we engage in anti-racist work individually in our centers, the lack of a collective response continues to push anti-racist work to the margins. We conclude with suggestions for how academic organizations like IWCA might address issues of racial inequity and social justice in such a way that supports its membership and situates anti-racist work at the center of our work.

BUT FIRST, SOME BRIEF BACKGROUND

Since writing our open letter in summer 2020, the authors of this chapter, alongside several other colleagues, have been involved in social justice and inclusion work for IWCA. Our charge has expanded to encompass several tasks including knowledge collection, assessment, restorative listening sessions, and organizational document revision.[1] Subgroups from the task force have run listening sessions, have created

1. Our change reads as "I am formally asking you to chair a task force and your co-authors to serve on that task force. In that role, you not only could develop a statement, (which must be put up for a membership vote after going through committee per our constitution, which is part of the reason we didn't pen one and distribute it on our own) but also an anti-racist tool kit, a series of resources and steps that our members can operationalize in their centers to demonstrate their lived commitment to Black Lives Matter."

a survey on how members of our field engage in social justice work, and are rewriting IWCA's mission statement. Like colleagues in other rhetoric and composition organizations, we do this work because we were asked to do it and because we believe that we need to make profound changes to our whitely organizations and our values.

The creation of the IWCA Social Justice Task Force was a move for the organization to appear as though it was committed to diversity work. As Ahmed reminds us, "Diversity becomes a matter of rearranging things, so that an organization can appear in the best way" (2012, 107). Our initial call to IWCA took the form of a letter. In our letter, signed by 169 writing center professions, we called on IWCA to take a stand against racism and create materials that would support members in furthering anti-racist work. International Writing Center Organization responded to our letter by asking the initial drafters to form a task force. When the letter went public, IWCA had to respond in a way that demonstrated to the members it had "listened"—the creation of the task force was a public-facing move to demonstrate commitment. Yet the move was not public facing at all. The organization emailed membership and the WCenter LISTSERV with an announcement about the creation of the task force but did not include who was on the task force. Much of the work of the task force has happened behind closed doors. There were a few public listening sessions in the fall during an online conference event that lasted for a few hours, but otherwise the work has happened away from the public. There's also no mention of the task force or its members as an IWCA initiative on the website. The public-facing move in the summer allowed IWCA to appear as though it was taking the claims of the open letter seriously and acting immediately; however, after the public-facing move, the organization created barriers to the task force actually doing the work.

Like our colleagues in other professional organizations (like CWPA [Inoue 2021]), we have been sidelined, stonewalled, and gaslit throughout this process. At the same time, we know that we are not the first people to do this work or have such experiences; members of our organization have been engaging in anti-racist work for over a decade and a half. So, when we were asked to provide anti-racism resources to IWCA members, could we not help but wonder where all the years of collective work on this and other social justice initiatives has gone? In chapter 14 of this collection, LaKela Atkinson documents a similar kind of recuperative approach that includes tracing HBCU involvement and inclusion in the IWCA affiliate SWCA over nearly two decades. Specifically, as the HBCU representative for SWCA, Atkinson documents the need to reach back out to colleagues through "personal efforts" over a decade after predecessor and mentor Dr. Keaton Jackson engaged in grassroots organizing of HBCU writing center practitioners. From these efforts—which seem to tread similar but necessary ground in terms of reaching out organically and consciously to HBCUs—Atkinson identified several labor-focused issues that HBCU writing centers currently face, including rapid turnover, little to no funding, and other pandemic-related issues. Atkinson identifies how well-meaning but predominately white organizations frequently fail to include the very voices they claim to uplift in their statements and initiatives. We also have seen these kinds of fault lines in the anti-racist initiatives of organizations in our field.

So, in addition to all the official tasks that we were given by IWCA leadership, we developed a task of our own, which was to investigate what had come before us. We turned to official and unofficial histories of the development of the anti-racism special interest group (SIG). We reviewed parallel experiences of social justice task forces in other professional associations in our field. And we thought about what would need to happen, organizationally, for IWCA to "walk the walk" of social justice and inclusion work, not just "talk the talk." The rest of this chapter articulates this journey and concludes with recommendations we hope IWCA and other whitely organizations adopt.

INSTITUTIONAL AMNESIA

While the digital age makes archiving (and finding) information for organizations far easier than the previous pen-and-paper approach to marking history, when we were asked to do the social justice work—including anti-racist work—that we asked IWCA to do, we found years' worth of anti-racism resources created by the anti-racism SIG that were not featured by IWCA. We found bibliographies on personal websites, Word Press accounts (Ozias, Godbee, and Condon 2010), a white paper (Godbee and Olson 2014), and bits and pieces of the SIG's history in publications (Ozias and Godbee 2011). Nowhere did we find the collective products of a decade and a half of work featured on IWCA's official website. This was distressing because the work of our colleagues—especially colleagues of color—seemed to have disappeared into the various bureaucratic mechanisms that accompany website moves and board turnover.

To remedy what we saw as our organization's amnesia, we conducted some restorative history work. Through reviewing archived conference programs, we found that the first time that the SIG was mentioned was at the 2007 conference (Stuehrk Scharold 2007), where it was called the "anti-racist activism" SIG. From this information—as well as shared memories of the authors—we developed a list of colleagues who were instrumental in founding the anti-racism SIG. We contacted our colleagues and asked them to share their memories of establishing the SIG. Some never responded. Some referred us to a previously published (though hard-to-find) history of the SIG. One colleague talked about how the process for creating the anti-racism SIG was bureaucratic and time consuming; ultimately, the colleague found that the process revealed how, organizationally, IWCA maintains the status quo. We then analyzed the published white paper and previously unpublished records that were housed on one of the affiliate organization's Google Folder.

In their 2014 white paper, Beth Godbee and Bobbi Olson share the goals of the IWCA SIG on anti-racism activism, which overlap with our own. These include

- Identify and share practical strategies for disrupting systemic racism in our institutions and writing centers.
- Collect and supply speaking notes, presentation materials, workshop ideas, and other documents that can help educate and raise awareness in our local centers.
- Help writing center scholar-practitioners network with others who are interested in learning more about, participating in, or extending current efforts at anti-racism.
- Support efforts of the IWCA Diversity Initiative.
- Share stories as well as artifacts (including photographs, comics, news clippings, television programs, or narrative responses) that help anchor conversations about white privilege and racism in its multiple forms in our writing centers. (Godbee and Olson 2014, 7).

To this end, SIG members were engaged in a number of activities to make anti-racism work more visible and impactful. In particular, the white paper provides an overview of their "large-scale, long-term annotations project" (Godbee and Olson 2014, 1) to provide "a model for linking scholarship with collective organizing; for publishing as a 'Collective'; and for finding *praxis* within ongoing learning, research, and professional service" (2). The white paper shares more than seventy annotations of scholarly works "focused on race/racism, anti-racism, and racial justice" (2) that provide a productive foundation for writing center administrators and tutors to learn from. Godbee and Olson indicate that they see the published annotations as a small part of a larger, ongoing annotations project that could be updated each year and hosted on the IWCA website (2).

Yet, in reviewing the majority of these suggested goals, we cannot help but feel like—several years on—many of these have either not been accomplished or, if they have, WCA has not highlighted them. While we found resources in various places on the internet, we did not find a repository easily accessible and updated on the IWCA website. While some movement has been made to offer support to practitioners in minority serving institutions, representation on the Board as well as at conferences remains low. And, finally, little movement has been made on the "storying" of white privilege and racism goal, as well as on the strategy sharing goal for disrupting institutional and other racism. We are left wondering why the work of the anti-racism SIG wasn't supported, or, if it was, why wasn't it promoted and highlighted by our organization? Such goals remain as important today as they were in 2014, or in 2007, yet our organization seems content with a "set it and forget it" approach to the work of the anti-racism SIG. This is, of course, unacceptable.

While part of our work started with consulting old IWCA conference programs and the multiyear work of the anti-racism SIG, we did this through Google, not through consulting the organization's website. This is part of the challenge of doing social justice work—if an organization does not intentionally feature this work, and the products of this work on its website, it appears that they are not doing this work. So, while many individuals in our organization have given their time, their emotional labor, and their intellectual work over the years, the organization seems silent by omission. To combat institutional amnesia, we need a better record-keeping system that provides a historical record but, also, remains up-to-date with its members' work.

HOW VALUELESS MISSION STATEMENTS SIGNAL NON-INCLUSIVITY

In conducting a rhetorical reading of the current mission statement—which our task force has also been charged with revising, pending approval by vote—we note the apolitical, valueless qualities of the statement. In the mission statement, the coded text that is **bolded** aims to situate the organization within the broader professional field of Composition by linking it to the National Council of Teachers of English (NCTE) and identifying its founding date. The coded text that is in *italics* focuses on the professionalization of the field and its members. The coded text that is <u>underlined</u> situates the organization within a broader international context but leaves specific concerns of our field unarticulated.

Current IWCA Mission Statement

> The International Writing Centers Association, a **National Council of Teachers of English affiliate founded in 1983**, fosters the *development of writing center directors, tutors, and staff* by *sponsoring meetings, publications,* and *other professional activities*; by *encouraging scholarship connected to writing center-related fields*; and by providing an international forum for writing center concerns.

A mission statement that does not articulate values signals the kinds of values that the organization had at its founding and, perhaps, continues to have. In this instance, the organization appears largely apolitical, concerned with professional standing and with connections to a broader professional and scholarly discipline. And while in the early 1980s, this might have been a more sufficient mission statement for IWCA, in the 2020s this mission statement ignores the ways in which writing centers have become regular—if still precarious—fixtures in higher education, especially in the United States. It also ignores the ways in which higher education and our profession have changed in the past four decades.

A subgroup within the ISJ TF has drafted a new mission statement for IWCA, which the executive board is currently reviewing. In it, we advocate for broad definitions of writing and writing centers and acknowledge that writing centers are situated in dynamic, broad, and diverse social, cultural, and institutional contexts. We emphasize a commitment to supporting social justice, prioritizing transformative pedagogy, facilitating dialogue and collaboration, and listening to and engaging with members. In particular, we ask that the organization affirm a mission that promotes scholarship and pedagogies that give underrepresented tutors, directors, and institutions equal voice and opportunities in the decisions that affect the community.

While there might be discomfort with revising a mission statement to be more intentionally political and anti-racist—people might get offended, people might not renew their membership, and so on—we ought to delineate between peoples' comfort and their safety. As Sara Ahmed (2012) shares, "if diversity and equality work is less valued by organizations, then to become responsible for this work can mean to inhabit institutional spaces that are also less valued" (4). One's comfort with the organization's values and goals shouldn't take precedence over publicly committing to welcoming and protecting its members of color. These protections should be informed by those it intends to protect. However, we must be careful not to fall into habits that cause us to infantilize or fetishize members of color, their problems, or the systemic issues within writing centers that cause those problems.

WE CANNOT IGNORE THE COLLECTIVE NATURE OF THE WORK WE DO

The choice to make an organization, a community, a department, a center, or a discipline is rhetorically complex. Activists engage in making in both tangible and intangible ways: in the tangible act of making signs, art, and protests, all that lead to the development and creation of activist organizations and movements themselves. All academic communities—this one included—have much to learn from the rhetorical "acts of making" engaged by activists.

Members of a community like IWCA (re)shape that community with everything they make: every action they take, task force, conference, mission statement, journal, or subgroup they develop. In addition, when these makings (like the collective, historical anti-racist work done over the years) are then invisibilized through exclusion, this is *also* a part of the shaping of that community. Indeed, from a cultural rhetorics perspective, "cultures are made up of practices that accumulate over time and in relationship to specific places. Practices that accumulate in those specific places transform those physical geographies into spaces in which common belief systems can be made, re-made, negotiated, transmitted, learned and imagined" (Powell et al. 2014). A community of practice is built through layered storying and actions of the members of that community, for better or worse. This layering means that organizations are made and remade every moment and completely relies on the varying levels of participation from all its members, including peripheral ones. We want to stress that the work we have done as a task force to uncover previous iterations of anti-racist work in writing centers, as well as the current work we have been tasked with, are part of a layered practice of the IWCA organization actively sidelining anti-racist actions.

For a professional organization like IWCA, all our interactions contribute to the overall making and ethos of the organization as a whole. We might also work to acknowledge that sometimes, what is made will not be made tangible or visible. We may not always have tangible evidence of what we create, but the creations are world-(un)making nonetheless. In this case, IWCA's consistent decision to sidestep anti-racism and other issues of social justice and equity may contribute to the organization's unmaking, at worst, or, at least, loss of membership.

To that end, engaging in and having the responsibility to engage inaction mean acknowledging that one has the agency to necessitate action. And having agency means needing to act. This cyclical relationship is complex and can be emotionally difficult for members of an organization who have experienced marginalization like the writing center administrators in IWCA. Understanding the cyclical nature of action, responsibility, and power/agency means understanding the emotional complexity of this cycle and one's place within it. In essence, taking action is not simply about doing something—it's also about acknowledging that one has the power and responsibility to do something. Making that acknowledgment can be difficult for a person or an organization; seeing someone stall in their actions can be confusing for an organization's leader, as well.

The bigger takeaway is that we cannot wait for the institution to make changes. We need to make the changes on the ground. In which case, we need to ground our work in the community rather than simply in the organization or its members.

TAKEAWAYS: ACTIVIST LESSONS FOR ACADEMIC ORGANIZATIONS

We know that the status quo cannot be separated from white supremacy. Indeed, according to Mark Latta (chapter 2 in this collection), writing center professionals contend more conscientiously to the degree to which white supremacy and settler colonialism have shaped our writing centers and the institutions in which these centers are situated. The status quo regulates all kinds of damaging attitudes and behaviors, and, by virtue of it being the status quo, it also normalizes these issues while erasing differences. As Ahmed notes, "When history accumulates, certain ways of doing things seem natural. An institution takes shape as an effect of what has become automatic. Institutional talk is often about 'how we do things here,' when the very claim of 'how' does not need to be claimed" (2012, 25). We cannot accept the status quo because it is so very damaging to people of color and others who are marginalized by our institutions and our profession. To that end, in the text that follows we offer takeaways from doing activist work for our organization that we hope can be instituted by IWCA and other professional organizations in our broader field.

We offer these recommendations not as a checklist of definitive solutions but as part of the ongoing work necessary to remake IWCA as a more inclusive and equitable organization.

- **Revise institutional bylaws:** Bylaws are crafted to maintain institutional whiteness and status quo. Bylaws can be used as roadblocks and excuses for why certain kinds of work can or cannot be done. Bylaws serve as "the sedimentation of history into a barrier that is solid and tangible in the present, a barrier to change as well as to the mobility of some, a barrier that remains invisible to those who can flow into the spaces created by institutions" (Ahmed 2012, 175). For example, in IWCA the executive board assignments/descriptions privilege running the organization and organizing conferences over anything else. The bylaws don't allow for anti-racist work outside of supporting the conference. They need to be revised.

- **Eliminate SIGS and centralize their work:** Another outcome from our work is to reconsider the special interest group moniker for political, bodily, and material concerns that affect our profession. We need to move beyond anti-racism as an add-on or a special interest topic. By separating diversity out of the main mission of the organization, we only reinforce "the whiteness of what is already in place" (Ahmed 2012, 33). Anti-racism work should be woven into the fabric of our organization from governance structures and board makeup and a memorandum of understanding (MOU) structures down to how conferences, events, and other projects are run. Inclusion, we argue, shouldn't be a special interest concern but a main goal of the organization.
- **Make diversity a central, public-facing commitment:** Already, service work expectations are high in our field, and the work can be thankless and recursive (many times, it seems like we are re-creating work that has already been done rather than building upon its foundations). To work more smartly, then, and to feature and honor the work of those who gave their time and intellectual effort, we need a better system in place for cataloguing, maintaining, and featuring social justice work. Create a public archive where the long history of anti-racist work is documented, centered, and maintained.
- **Create a culture of continuity:** As we discovered, our charge to create an anti-racism toolkit was one that others in our field had already done. We ask our organization to honor, highlight, and keep track of the work of those who have come before. This work involves a better record-keeping system, as well as better promotion and housing of materials. It also includes better-organized mentorship work that helps volunteers transition from one year to the next.
- **Invest in members:** In addition to valuing members' work and advocating for members' rights, consider compensation for extensive service work. Social justice works calls on us to be change agents, but we cannot do the work for free. The changing landscape of higher education has created a culture where service work does not serve the economy of the academy. One way to invest in your membership that is not just monetary is through becoming a think tank / policy center for writing center work and the field and providing advocacy and data support to members.
- **Engage in structural redesign of IWCA:** The Council of Writing Program Administrators (CWPA) has decided to cancel their conference and close their journal submission portal, and has promised to dedicate money, time, and engagement to social justice work. This

includes fundamentally redesigning their organization from top to bottom, not just in a piecemeal way. We ask IWCA to do the same and to connect with CWPA—and other organizations—to learn more about how this work is being done.

- **Follow and respond to political conversations:** Address and take a stand on the current push from various state legislatures to ban Critical Race Theory (CRT) at university and K–12 levels. We need a statement from IWCA on its stance on diversity in writing centers, and we need more data on this topic too.
- **"Work with the people who are not fairly represented" in the organization:** We echo Atkinson's call in chapter 14 in this collection for organizations like IWCA to refrain from hastily created anti-racist initiatives. To establish meaningful and inclusive initiatives, it is also critical to engage in intentional and thoughtful outreach to people of color and other marginalized people "to understand how to better serve them."

CONCLUSION

While we find these takeaways to be key steps in (re)building an organization that makes appreciable progress toward anti-racism, we want to stress that no matter what the IWCA board chooses to (not) do, the work toward social justice and equity isn't going to stop for those of us working day-to-day in our writing centers and beyond. We suggest that this organization—as well as others in and out of our discipline—pay attention to the anti-racist and social-justice-oriented work that has already been done before planning what to do next. Much of our frustration stems not just from being asked to do the work we asked the board to do in the first place but from the fact that so much good work has already been done, and subsequently been invisibilized through bureaucratic sidelining and the choice to not highlight that work.

Organizations need clear missions to anchor their work and to be responsive to current events, so members have updated resources to turn to in times of crisis and in other times of need. Writing center administrators can't always wait a year for position statements to feel protected or supported in the equity work they may be engaging in; faster information is needed in order for an organization's constituents to feel supported. For example, universities across the country are struggling to find ways to support students of color when CRT has been nationally recognized as divisive and legislation has been implemented to end it as well as gender education in schools. Statements from our professional organizations—accompanied with a foundation of values that seek to take appreciable steps toward addressing racial injustice—help those of us support our arguments for creating equitable spaces in our own institutions. We need timely, structural change so that we can address the events and issues happening in the moment that affect our safety, our work, and our lives.

Changing the whiteness of organizations, however, needs to be an intentional, collaborative effort. Most of the IWCA affiliate organizations populate their boards every two years with unpaid volunteers. The constant turnover of leadership doesn't foster an environment of change—rather, our organizational structures foster environments of complicity, stability, and reproduction. In environments of complicity, change won't happen until it's called out and demanded. If your local organization isn't doing this work, speak up and let them know your needs and desires. One option is to reach out to writing center administrators in your region and collectively work together to advocate for change. Together you might brainstorm: What's missing from your organizations? Who is missing? Who is being silenced? What opportunities do you see for intervention? While we've been advocating for an overhauling of organizations, sometimes when just starting out, change needs to feel more manageable. Maybe it's bringing a diversity position to the leadership board or creating a new grant/scholarship that supports scholars of color. Once you've created a network of support and brainstormed ideas, reach out to your leadership board asking for change and offer to begin to do that work with leadership buy-in.

We recommend organizations create task forces with the charge to overhaul the bylaws and intervene in the whiteness reproduction loop. We also think that partnering with other organizations engaged in such work can yield new ideas, initiatives, and other possibilities; even as IWCA has grappled with becoming a more anti-racist organization, parallel organizations like CWPA have also engaged in decentering whiteness and white supremacy in its organization. As this work transcends any one organization, a collaborative and wider-ranging approach signals a lot about our values, and our intentions, and, hopefully, positively impacts outcomes from such work.

More specifically, we can also learn from other organizations outside of our field already engaged in this work. The Library Publishing Coalition Diversity and Inclusion Task Force created a six-month road map that organizations could use as a starting point. But, for a task force to be successful, it needs to have buy-in from the membership, transparent communication, and collaboration from the current leadership board. To that end, we suggest

- At least one leadership board member on the task force to serve as a liaison between the task force and leadership board. Someone on the task force needs the institutional power to make the recommended changes the task force suggests.
- A digital presence (Twitter, Facebook, website), with consistent updates on the workings of the task force.
- An opportunity for membership to share stories, experiences, and feedback with the task force.
- An intentional task force membership with a range of experiences, diverse backgrounds, and understanding of how deep whiteness runs in our everyday practices.
- A post-task-force action plan. Once the initial work of the task force is complete, who will follow up for revisions? How will the work continue to develop?

Smaller organizations may be able to do this work more quicky because of fewer bureaucratic bylaws, smaller memberships, smaller leadership boards, and more flexibility. This is an opportunity for smaller organizations to provide examples on how to do this work for IWCA and other large organizations.

Of course, if you are constantly hitting roadblocks and being gaslit, that organization is not worth your time: walk away. You can use your efforts to create grassroot communities of support that have anti-racist principles built in from the beginning (such as NextGen or Institute of Race, Rhetoric, and Literacy). Bring together those who are having the conversations on Twitter, Facebook, and LISTSERVS, and support each other.

REFERENCES

Ahmed, Sara. 2012. On Being Included: Racism and Diversity in Institutional Life. Durham, NC: Duke University Press.

Godbee, Beth, and Bobbi Olson. 2014. "Readings for Racial Justice: A Project of the IWCA SIG on Antiracism Activism." Marquette University E-Publications.

Inoue, Asao. 2021. "Why I Left the CWPA (Council of Writing Program Administrators)." Asao B. Inoue's Infrequent Words. Blogspot. http://asaobinoue.blogspot.com/2021/04/why-i-left-cwpa-council-of-writing.html.

Ozias, Moira, and Beth Godbee. 2011. "Organizing for Antiracism in Writing Centers: Principles for Enacting Social Change." In Writing Centers and the New Racism: A Call for Sustainable Dialogue and Change, edited by Laura Greenfield and Karen Rowan, 150–174. Logan: Utah State University Press.

Ozias, Moira, Beth Godbee, and Frankie Condon. 2010. "Seeking Your Input on the IWCA SIG on Antiracist Activism." Anti-Racist Writing Centers. Blogspot. http://antiracistwritingcenters.blogspot.com/2010/10/seeking-your-input-on-iwca-sig-on.html.

Powell, Malea, Daisy Levy, Andrea Riley-Mukavetz, Marilee Brooks-Gillies, Maria Novotny, and Jennifer Fisch-Ferguson. 2014. "Our Story Begins Here: Constellating Cultural

Rhetorics." Enculturation: A Journal of Rhetoric, Writing, and Culture 25. https://www.enculturation.net/our-story-begins-here.

Smith, Trixie, Elise Dixon, Karen Moroski-Rigney, Marilee Brooks-Gillies, Nicole I. Caswell, Wonderful Faison, Katie Levin, Floyd Pouncil, Scott Chiu, and Genie Nicole Giamo. 2020. "Open Letter to IWCA Executive Board." Google Docs. https://docs.google.com/document/d/1Z7Z1UlkckRJrTyv8UKyE63Tq6HqxWF9vUDOoYbQw7vE/edit.

Stuehrk Scharold, Dagmar, ed. 2007. "IWCA: A Space for Writing: Writing Centers and Place." Houston, April 12–14.

AFTERWORD

Kendra L. Mitchell

I learned about this book project while advocating for peer writing tutors. Talisha and I were discussing a peer tutor's keynote panel for the upcoming National Conference on Peer Tutoring in Writing (NCPTW) conference. We were in our respective workspaces on Zoom—she in her campus office—and I in my makeshift home office. The conversation shifted from our outlining the wording for the panel nomination to something along the lines of "would you mind writing the foreword to our book?" She told me that had used parts of Robert's and my 2018 IWCA co–keynote address. She and Deidre gleaned these pointed, rhetorical questions—"Haven't we done this before? What have we done about it?"—and responded with a collection of essays that do more than just talk about social justice in Writing Center Studies. To be clear, the keynote was not targeted toward the organizers. Elsewhere, Robert and I praise the organizers for their advocacy. No, our questions were targeted toward the systems of oppression that hinder forward movement toward social justice for all.

It is refreshing to know the editors and the authors heard us clearly, as each essay boldly names a thing a thing. For example, in "Another White Voice in the Room," chapter 2, Mark Latta argues that the predominately white administrators and professionals must "contend more conscientiously to the degree to which white supremacy and settler colonialism have shaped our writing centers and the institutions in which these centers are situated and those in writing center leadership positions who are predominantly white yet also living in various degrees of precarity—must grapple with how some of us reap unearned privileges as well as the degree to which we have internalized the system of injustice we claim to want to disrupt and dismantle." This piece sets the tone for the willingness for our non-BIPOC colleagues to do the personal and academic work to actualize writing centers as intentional sites for social justice in predominantly white institutions (PWIs).

https://doi.org/10.7330/9781646424573.c016

The turnover rate of Black writing center scholars in historically black colleges and universities (HBCUs) and minority serving institutions (MSIs) is high—LaKela Atkinson discusses this in "Practicing What We Preach," chapter 14, regarding her advocacy work as the HBCU representative for Southeastern Writing Center Association (SWCA). Perhaps the answer is to pursue cross-institutional relationships as I stated in our original call to action (2018) and, as Atkinson points out, along with her call for innovative outreach and support from the SWCA board for historically marginalized institutions. If we take those points into consideration, we must incorporate Giaimo et al.'s call in "Remaking IWCA," chapter 15, for sustainable changes such as compensation for service on these boards, among other recommendations.

Robert and I wrote our 2018 keynote with Tribal Colleges and HSIs in mind, so I was relieved to read about Tribal Colleges' writing centers from "Tutoring and Practice at a Tribal College," chapter 1, Jennifer Martin. Her chapter embodies and invokes anti-racist practices we could not address in our keynote because her scholarship occurs on her/their terms. I appreciated the interior look into a Tribal College's approach to something as "simple" as the select capitalization of english (the lowercased *e* is intentional). There is something to be learned from this practice just like there is much we have learned from hooks's intentional lowercased name and disregard for parenthetical references in her text. I immediately downloaded Younging (2018) to learn more about his style guide.

Brianna Johnson, Rebecca Johnson, and Nicole I. Caswell's "From Anti-Blackness Professional Development to Pro-Blackness Actions," chapter 10, pushes the collection and the field beyond what we do not agree with (racism) and toward an affirmative statement for pro-Blackness. The directors model what sound anti-racist leadership looks like. They became students of Black English grammatical structures and disseminated this information campus-wide.

Rachel Herzl-Betz, in "Why Do White Tutors 'Love' Writing?," chapter 3, uses empirical data to look for correlations between race and affinity to work in writing centers. She admonishes that this critical assessment must be done on an ongoing basis to maintain the anti-racist work. Jamie P. Bondar, Kristina Aikens, and Devon Deery, in "Toward Anti-racist Writing Center Hiring and Retention Practices," chapter 4, echo similar motivations as Herzl-Betz, but their pre-work focuses on retaining BIPOC staff by creating safer work environments. The authors make explicit their hiring and retention practices to set up an ongoing anti-racist critique of those practices in a much-needed approach to resist the pervasiveness of racist practices.

In chapter 7, "Working toward Racial Justice in the Writing Center," Rachael Shapiro and Celeste Del Russo tackle both the staff and university administrative cuts across institutional type and echo sentiments of other contributors of stating the obvious-but-often-forgotten fact: Imagining writing centers' roles as social justice spaces is a move that directly confronts our past narratives, challenging the idea of writing centers as 'neutral' on any front. To situate language diversity and anti-racist pedagogy at the center of tutor education, rather than a special topic or special interest group, means centering language diversity in tutoring strategies and practices.

Though tutor advocacy was one of the many drivers for our keynote, this collection thoroughly describes Robert's and my vision of what an anti-racist tutor education could be. These authors embraced the driving questions of this call as they relate to empowering the tutors. Zandra L. Jordan's "Beyond the Tutor Training Seminar," chapter 5, and Lindsay A. Sabatino's "Addressing Racial Justice through Re-imagining Practicum to Promote Dialogue on Campus," chapter 6, reinforce the benefit of anti-racist pedagogy that challenges existing structures that allow racial justice initiatives to become the status quo. Jordan carefully charts out the need for and the benefit of a womanist approach to racial justice work in ongoing tutor education. She carefully provides an exigence with key definitions and examples of her practice that could easily be adapted and expanded in diverse writing center spaces. You can't say it any plainer than Jordan's essay. Our entire writing center theoretical framework needs this boost if we are to take anti-racism efforts seriously. Talisha Haltiwanger Morrison, in chapter 9, "Tutors Matter, Too," amplifies the need for tutor advocacy in anti-racist work: "A racial justice approach to writing center administration acknowledges and values our tutors of color. Through it, administrators offer flexibility and allow for our conceptions of the writing center, especially those in primarily or historically white spaces, to be disrupted." Nicole Emmelhainz and colleagues, in "Community Is the Center," chapter 12, use a similar approach to inspire her students to research and develop a community writing center, and two of her peer student-tutors reflect on the impact of that experience. Lisa Eastmond Bell speaks in chapter 8 to systemic oppression in WCs predetermined roles in "Disrupting Systems." Bell challenges the field to reconsider how it recenters whiteness by the types of sessions administrators normalize.

The theory, practice, reflection, and sustainable recommendations have been amply supplied by our capable colleagues. This edited collection responds aptly to the steady call for structural change in our organizations, tutor practices, and tutor education. The ball is the reader's court. Will you labor against anti-racism where you are, or will you wait for another keynote?

INDEX

Locators followed by "*f*" indicate a figure. Locators followed by "*t*" indicate a table.

ABOUT THE AUTHORS

EDITORS

Talisha Haltiwanger Morrison (she/her) is Director of the OU Writing Center and the Expository Writing Program and an Assistant Professor of Writing at the University of Oklahoma. Her interests include racial justice and Black Feminist perspectives on writing center administration and community-engaged writing. Haltiwanger Morrison's work has appeared in journals such as the *Writing Center Journal* and the *Journal of Multimodal Rhetorics* and in the edited collection *Out in the Center* (Denny et al. 2019).

Deidre Anne Evans Garriott (she/her/hers) is the Director of the University Writing Center and Instructor in the Department of English Language and Literature at the University of South Carolina. Her interests include public memory and identity and social justice Writing Center pedagogies and administration. Evans Garriott's work has appeared in *ePortfolios@edu, What We Know, What We Don't Know, and Everything in Between* (2021), and *Interpreting and Experiencing Disney: Mediating the Mouse* (2022).

CONTRIBUTORS

Kristina Aikens has directed the Tufts University Writing Center since 2010. She has presented and published on topics of anti-racist writing tutor education, peer mentorship and leadership, and linguistic diversity and creativity in academic writing.

LaKela Atkinson holds a PhD from East Carolina University, and both an MA and BA from North Carolina Central University. Atkinson is a visiting Assistant English Professor at Wake Forest University and served as the 2019–2021 HBCU Representative for the Southeastern Writing Center Association (SWCA).

Amanda Ballou is a Junior at Christopher Newport University studying English with a concentration in writing and minor in Psychology. She worked as a Ferguson Fellow for Social Entrepreneurship to help build and support the Tidewater Community Writing Center. She is also a Writing Consultant at the Alice F. Randall Writing Center.

Lisa Eastmond Bell is the Coordinator of the Utah Valley University Writing Center. She is President of the Rocky Mountain Writing Centers Association and has served on the board of the International Writing Centers Association. Her research and scholarship focus on online learning, support for multilingual writers, and tutor education.

Jamie P. Bondar is the Director of Tutoring and Peer-to-Peer Success Services in the Center for Learning and Academic Success at Suffolk University in Boston, where he also serves as a Senior Lecturer in English and a WK Kellogg Foundation Truth, Racial Healing, and Transformation facilitator.

Kamille Bostick is Director of Programming at the Center for Racial Equity in Education (CREED) and a doctoral student at the University of North Carolina–Charlotte, where she focuses on literacy and writing practice. A former newspaper reporter, high school English teacher, and college composition instructor, she centers her work on educational equity, access, and empowerment. Kamille is the former Writing Center Director at Livingstone College in Salisbury, NC.

Marilee Brooks-Gillies is Associate Professor of English and Writing Center Director at IUPUI. Her recent scholarship has been published in *Praxis, The Peer Review*, the *Journal of Multimodal Rhetorics*, and the edited collections *Emotions and Affect in Writing Centers, Linguistic Justice on Campus*, and *Graduate Writing Across the Disciplines.*

Nicole I. Caswell (she/her) is an Associate Professor of English and Director of the University Writing Center at East Carolina University. Her research aims to forward social justice issues in the areas of emotions, writing assessment, and writing centers.

Devon Deery has directed the Writing Center at Stonehill College since 2011. She teaches a variety of writing courses and has published poetry, fiction, and a children's book. She earned her BFA and MFA degrees in creative writing from the University of Maine system.

Celeste Del Russo is Associate Professor of Writing Arts and Director of the Rowan Writing Center. Her research interests include writing center pedagogy and writing for social justice. Her publications have appeared in *WLN, Praxis*, and *The Peer Review*, as well as in collections including *Linguistic Justice on Campus: Pedagogy and Advocacy for Multilingual Students.*

Elise Dixon is Assistant Professor of English and Writing Center Director at the University of North Carolina at Pembroke. Drawing from cultural and queer rhetorics, she focuses her research on how writers compose together as a world-building practice. Her scholarship has appeared in the *Peer Review Journal, Writing Lab Newsletter*, and many book chapters.

Nicole Emmelhainz is Associate Professor of English and the Writing Center Director/ Writing Program Administrator at Christopher Newport University. She is the Co-Founder and Co-Director of the Tidewater Community Writing Center, an open-access educational resource that serves communities in the coastal Virginia area.

Wonderful Faison (Dr. Wonderful) is the Director of the Richard Wright Center for Writing, Rhetoric, and Research at Jackson State University. Her works include the edited collection *Counterstories from the Writing Center* and articles "Full Disclosure: Black Rhetoric and Writing Assessment" and "Race, Retention, Language, and Literacy: The Hidden Curriculum of the Writing Center."

Genie Nicole Giaimo (They/She) is Assistant Professor and Director of the Writing Center at Middlebury College. Their current research utilizes quantitative and qualitative models to answer a range of questions about behaviors and practices in and around writing centers, including tutor attitudes toward wellness and self-care practices. Their books include the edited collection *Wellness and Care in Writing Center Work*, an open-access digital project, and *Unwell Writing Centers: Searching for Wellness in Neoliberal Educational Institutions and Beyond* (Utah State University Press).

Graciela Greger is a Junior Communication Studies major and Writing and Political Science double minor at Christopher Newport University. She is a Writing Consultant at the Alice F. Randall Writing Center at the university.

Rachel Herzl-Betz (she/her) is the Writing Center Director and Assistant Professor of English at Nevada State College. Her research focuses on intersections between disability, Writing Center Studies, and educational access. Most recently, she has pursued projects centered on equity in writing center recruitment and the impact of "access negotiation moments" for disabled writing instructors.

Brianna Johnson is a writer living in Havelock, North Carolina, with her husband and daughter. Brianna graduated from East Carolina University with a master's in English and Creative Writing. During her time of study, she worked alongside The Writing Center on campus and worked toward social justice by sharing her testimony.

Rebecca Johnson, PhD, is Assistant Director of the East Carolina University Writing Center. She received her PhD in Media, Art, and Text from Virginia Commonwealth University. For over a decade, she has worked in different areas of education, including writing centers, libraries, and composition classes.

Zandra L. Jordan directs the Hume Center for Writing and Speaking at Stanford University. She is a rhetorician and ordained Baptist Minister, and her scholarship explores womanism, racial justice, and writing center administration. Her work is featured in *WPA*, *The Peer Review*, and *Teaching Theology* and *Religion*, among other journals and edited collections.

Mark Latta, PhD is the Director of Community Engaged Learning and an Assistant Professor of English at Marian University in Indianapolis. He also directs the Flanner Community Writing Center. His work intersects urbanism, critical community literacy, and posthuman decolonizing practices.

Jennifer Martin is a Citizen of the Cherokee (Aniyunwiya) Nation. She received her BS in Native Environmental Science at Northwest Indian College, where she was also a writing tutor for five years in the NWIC Math and Writing Center. In 2020, she completed her MA in Culture and Colonialism at the University of Ireland Galway and currently works as the Healing Spirits Gardener at the Lummi Tribal Health Clinic through the Diabetes Prevention Program.

Kendra L. Mitchell, PhD, is Assistant Professor of English and Modern Languages at Florida A&M University, where she teaches composition and historical linguistics. Mitchell's specialties include Writing Center Studies and Black Language Studies. Her publications can be found in the *Writing Center Journal*, *Praxis Journal*, and several book collections.

Lindsay A. Sabatino is Associate Professor of English and Director of the Writing Center at Wagner College. Her research explores purposeful tutor education, multimodal and digital composing, Game Studies, faculty development, and writing studio spaces. With Dr. Brian Fallon, she coedited *Multimodal Composing: Strategies for Twenty-First-Century Writing Consultations.*

Rachael Shapiro is Associate Professor of Writing Arts and the Provost's Fellow for Diversity, Equity, and Inclusion at Rowan University. She has taught developmental, freshman, critical research, professional, and digital writing classes, in addition to years of writing center work. Her research focuses on literacy and social justice.

COVER ARTIST

Maria Echave Sierra is a multilingual international Senior at the University of Oklahoma studying Psychology with a minor in Human Relations. She has an associate's degree in English Literature from Tulsa Community College. She is also an Undergraduate Writing Consultant at the University of Oklahoma Writing Center.